Collecting
New Jersey
Antiques

Collecting
New Jersey
Antiques

A comprehensive collection of the major articles on
antiques of New Jersey, written by the
foremost authorities.

BOOKS ABOUT NEW JERSEY

Union City, New Jersey

Books About New Jersey
published by
Wm. H. Wise & Co., Inc.
Union City, New Jersey

Manufactured in the United States of America

Library of Congress # 78-52530

ISBN 0-8349-7536-X

1 2 3 4 5 6 7 8 9 10

Acknowledgments

THE publishers wish to express their heartfelt thanks and appreciation to the individuals and institutions who, by their constant and open-handed assistance, have made *Collecting New Jersey Antiques* a book for not only the serious collector, but one for the weekend enthusiast as well.

In particular, the publishers wish to thank *The Magazine ANTIQUES* for permission to reprint "The Ware Chairs of South Jersey" from vol. IX, no. 5; "Wistarberg and South Jersey Glass" from vol. X, no. 4, copyrighted by George S. McKearin; "Sidelights on the Wistars and Their Glass-House" from vol. X, no. 4; "Three Generations of Cabinetmakers, Part I" from vol. XIV, no. 3, copyrighted in 1928 by W. M. Hornor, Jr.; "Three Generations of Cabinetmakers, Part II" from vol. XIV, no. 5, copyrighted in 1928 by W. M. Hornor, Jr.; "Trenton Clockmakers" from vol. XXIII, no. 5; "Henderson of Jersey City and His Pitchers" from vol. L, no. 6; "Furniture of Monmouth County" from vol. LIV, no. 1; "For the casual collector: *Antiques in New Jersey*" from vol. LXII, no. 3; and "Some notes on South Jersey glass" from vol. LXII, no. 3.

Contents

Collecting
New Jersey
Antiques

An Introduction

Antiques
in New Jersey

IN 1698, Gabriel Thomas, in his account of Philadelphia
and West Jersey, wrote that "while Philadelphia was developing much more extensively," the Jersey towns, "especially Salem and Burlington, had many of the same advantages of
climate, situation, and produce, and that they were engaging in
trade almost as actively, even though on a smaller scale, than
Philadelphia."

They may have been "engaging in trade," but it does not
appear that local manufactures gained much momentum until
after the Revolution. The New Jersey colonists seem to have
imported most of their household furnishings either from abroad
or from the nearby craft centers of New York and Philadelphia.
This very fact, however, has resulted in a tendency to overlook
the work that actually was done in the region.

One of the outstanding "collectors' items" is South Jersey
glass, which is described in Mr. McKearin's article. These
delightfully decorative pieces, revealing the ingenuity of individual craftsmen, have been called American folk art in glass.

In the field of ceramics, the earliest reference is a 1688
document stating that Daniel Coxe, who later became gov-

ernor, "hath...at Burlington two houses and kill with all necessary materialls and implements with divers servants who have made a greate progresse in a Pottery of White and China ware." We have no information as to the kind of ware that Coxe made, and, needless to say, no example of it.

"The clays of northern New Jersey, from Staten Island to Gloucester County," says John Ramsay in *American Potters and Pottery,* "are admirably suited to the manufacture of stoneware...New Jersey stoneware has a fine, dense body, light gray or cream in color, with a smooth glaze." Van Wickle's stoneware pottery was in operation at Old Bridge at the beginning of the nineteenth century. Other potteries were located at Sayreville, at South Amboy, and on Cheesequake Creek in Madison, where three successive factories were in operation from the late eighteenth to the mid-nineteenth centuries.

Redware was not as important as stoneware, but a fair amount of it was produced in New Jersey. In fact, as John Spargo pointed out in *Early American Pottery and China,* some of the slip-decorated redware formerly attributed to Pennsylvania was actually made in New Jersey. John McCulley of Trenton, among others, was turning out redware plates and jars from 1779 to 1852, and the Prudens of Elizabeth made a good deal of slipware and some sgraffito from 1818 to 1879.

One of the most important New Jersey potteries was that of Jersey City. After an ambitious project for making porcelain there had petered out, the works were taken over in the late 1820's by the Hendersons, who successfully pioneered in mass-produced molded ceramic wares. The first Henderson product was a kind of stone pottery called flint stoneware. As Lura Woodside Watkins puts it, "Henderson turned the course of potting in America...as did Wedgwood in England, away from the primitive traditional wares fashioned by individual craftsmen to ceramic forms that were created by designers and carried to completion by professional workmen."

One of these designers, Daniel Greatbach, who was later to achieve renown at Bennington, worked for the Hendersons, and created "almost all the designs of an ornamental nature which were made at these works between the years 1838 and 1848." It was here that he first produced his famous hound-handled pitchers.

The story of silver, like that of ceramics, begins with references to silversmiths of whose work no trace remains. (In this field we are particularly grateful to Carl Williams, from whose *Silversmiths of New Jersey* most of our information is derived.) Isaac Pearson was established in Burlington by 1710. David Lyell, who worked in New York until 1717, moved that year to Middletown Point in Monmouth County. But that is most of what we know of them.

In the 1740's James Bruff came to Elizabeth. "He did a bit of private coining," Williams says, which was not appreciated by the authorities, and they inconsiderately put him in jail. His son, Charles Oliver Bruff, became a successful New York silversmith.

Some of the New Jersey silversmiths had contacts in high circles. Elias Boudinot, father of the more famous Elias who was President of the Continental Congress, made a tankard for Benjamin Franklin before leaving Philadelphia for Princeton about 1753. Cary Dunn, who announced in the *New Jersey Journal* of November 19, 1782, that he had moved from Morristown to Newark, made a handsome coffeepot for Chief Justice John Hay.

After the Revolution, the number of silversmiths in New Jersey increased considerably. Williams says that "during the decade 1790-1800, there was scarcely a town of any size which did not support a silversmith and clockmaker, and the more populous centers usually had three or four." Samuel Stout of Princeton took an active part in town affairs, and was among those who organized the first fire company in 1788. Abner Reeder, working in Trenton from the end of the eighteenth century to 1830, produced some distinguished pieces in the classic style, like the cream pitcher and sugar bowl shown here.

Many craftsmen who are identified chiefly with New York and Philadelphia spent some time working in New Jersey. The New York silversmith, Daniel Van Voorhis, advertised in 1783 that he had headquarters in Princeton, where he remained for over a year. The New York pewterer, Francis Bassett, advertised in the *New Jersey Journal* for May 31, 1780, that he was prepared to make and mend all "sorts of pewter, such as plates, basons, tankards, quart pots, etc." at his shop in Horse Neck near Elizabeth.

The craftsmen with the most colorful career was John Fitch, a Trenton silversmith in the 1770's, an example of whose work appears here. His history, recounted by Carl Williams in his volume on New Jersey silversmiths, reads like a movie scenario. We begin dramatically with his abandoned wife, carrying one infant and expecting another, following him "half a mile along the road" (one wonders whence this statistic was derived), pleading vainly for his return. In Trenton, Fitch eventually took over the silversmithing business of his employer, who had drunk himself into ruin, and became prosperous enough between 1773 and 1776 to hire nine journeymen. Only 2 cream pots, 7 tablespoons, 2 teaspoons, and a pair of sugar tongs, Williams says, are known to have survived of the sizable output made by Fitch "not only for Trenton customers but for those living as far as thirty miles away." Ten years later, Fitch was busy with his steamboat invention, which antedated Fulton's *Clermont* by some twenty years. His 1790 steamboat plied along the Delaware and the Schuylkill for a time, but business was so poor that the schedule was given up. In disgust at this failure, Fitch went off to Kentucky.

One of the most neglected fields has been that of New Jersey furniture. Only a few cabinetmakers have been known by name, and for the rest we have been inclined to assign pieces found in New Jersey to some other place of origin, usually Pennsylvania or New York. The Egertons of New Brunswick are

From left to right, a cream pitcher and sugar bowl made for Joshua Wright, mayor of Trenton in 1806, by Abner Reeder who worked in Trenton from 1798 to 1830. The remaining cream pitcher shown is by John Fitch who worked in Trenton from 1769 to 1776.

A beaker by Henry Lupp who worked in New Brunswick from 1780 to 1800 "N. Brunswick Dutch Church."

discussed by Hornor (see FURNITURE section), where he notes that "Matthew Egerton *(1739-1802)* was employed over a period of years creating, fabricating, and selling an inestimable amount of handsome, well-constructed furniture." His son, Matthew Jr., followed the same trade, and "was a man of property and a prominent member of the community." Their work was so similar that it is sometimes hard to tell it apart.

John Jelliff of Newark advertised in Newark's *City Directory* in 1855-1856: "Wholesale and Retail Fancy and Common Chairs, Keeping Constantly on hand at his Ware Rooms, Rocking, Fancy, Cand Bottom, and Common Sitting Chairs." Ten years later he was advertising "Rosewood, Mahogany, and Walnut Chamber Furniture of every Description and Price."

In her article on Monmouth County furniture Elizabeth Wyman writes: "Monmouth County is primarily agrarian, and most of the early houses were farmsteads, the furnishings necessarily of the simpler sorts. Probably no cabinetmakers of the stamp of Benjamin Randolph or Duncan Phyfe worked here, though a general statement that every cabinetmaker capable of fine work gravitated to the nearby cities of Philadelphia or New York would not be true."

Contrary to the old belief that there were no New Jersey cabinetmakers, more and more pieces are turning up that seem to have been made there. Gradually distinctive New Jersey characteristics are emerging from the researches, and pieces formerly credited to the Philadelphia school are being re-evaluated in the light of cabinetmakers known to have lived and worked in New Jersey, particularly in Monmouth County.

—JANE BOICOURT

Advice to the Beginning Collector

COLLECTING antiques...some call it a disease, others label it an addiction. Symptoms range from mild, occasional urges to go out and find something interesting to full-time wanderlust, complete with raging hunger for the best, the unique, the most valuable. The afflicted come from all walks of life, every income bracket, and any age group. Their whims have been known to unsettle decorating schemes, undo the best laid vacation plans, change the course of careers, to make and break marriages and fortunes. No one knows whether it is an ailment you have to inherit or catch, but there is every indication that no one is completely immune and that serious cases are on the upswing.

How you have become what the oldtimers call a "beginning collector" will undoubtedly affect your course through the next phase. If you have arrived with a family tradition of old and beautiful things, you may already have found a specialty of your own and be off and buying. If, like many more, you've only recently realized that mass production and planned obsolescence leave our surroundings impersonal and barren, you may just be starting to search out the furnishings or memorabilia that help transform lifeless environs into something more individual. In any case, you're feeling the stirrings of taste, creativity and curiosity that are the root of it all.

Just about the time you find yourself caught up in a new and challenging field that feels like an art form, one with reverence for history and timeless beauty, you bump into the awkward fact that it is also a business. It seems that appreciation is not enough. You need information, instant wisdom, and, you fear, a magical seventh sense that will protect you from making poor investments. The need to know more is sometimes overwhelming, and the amount to be learned can seem intimidating.

If you are the cautious or scholarly type, you may begin at the library. For you, a stack of books on American Federal furniture or World War I mementos is just what you need to get over the initial case of nerves. And you will be sure to pick up facts that will help. While you are there, take a look at bibliographies, noting other titles you would like to check out, and especially any that appear over and over again in any one field. That recurring author or title may put you on to your first "bible" for the journeys ahead.

If you are allergic to that kind of research, cannot find what interests you, or are just one of the many who prefers to get out in the field, do not despair. You are not destined to be bamboozled by tricky experts or doomed to silly purchases you will regret. There are mailorder houses, classified ads in antiques and collectors' publications, and neighborhood garage sales to keep the timid close to home. However, you probably have at least a germ of the collector's need to get around, shop the market, and talk to fellow addicts. The next stop for scholars is the first for you—meeting the merchandise and its devotees on their own turf. Tuck a note pad into your pocket and get going!

Your first contacts are likely to be dealers in their shops. You will find them around the corner, through local newspapers, in the Yellow Pages and regional association directories, and along every roadside. The names over their doors will give you a hint about the wares and the personalities of the proprietors, and they may be your first introduction to a few terms that antiques dealers hold dear.

According to U.S. Customs law, an antique is 100 years old or more. Most dealers agree with this definition, but some will accept the term only for those things that were made before 1850 or even 1830. These older items are the rarest and most expensive. So unavailable are they at reasonable prices, in fact, that there is now general acceptance that there are no longer any bargains among true antiques. Therefore, many reputable dealers now carry reproductions, clearly identified as such. They also carry younger merchandise, defined as heirlooms (at least 50 years old) and collectibles (anything people will pay for, including last year's Woolworth special).

A tour of local shops, either in your own town or any of our established suburban communities, will turn up a cross-section you will find useful when you are ready to wander farther afield. Visit several shops, more than one if possible to firm up your instincts. If that sign over the door says "Antiques" and the owner's name and if it marks a spot that has enjoyed local business for many years, then there had better be some real antiques inside. If the title suggests cute, "boutique-y," or merely nostalgic contents, there's no guarantee you'll find any-thing truly old, much less a storekeeper who knows anything about antiques. The emphasis here is upon appeal, and the stock may well be exactly what you find appealing. But it offers no assurance of lasting investment value, and no guidance beyond the development of your own taste.

Used or secondhand dealers offer pretty straightforward items, while the possibility of a real find is usually remote. The main thing to identify here is the common junk that may not appear as such in fancier surroundings.

Generally speaking, you will learn more and find trust-worthy values in the "better" shop (where the dealer shows signs of knowing the field, some reasonable willingness to share it, and readiness to admit what he may not be sure of). He will ask less than top dollar for the less perfect or less than perfectly pedigreed. He will point out reproductions and flaws. You may spot some readily available reference books and journals for the trade, such as *Antiques, Antique Monthly, The Antiques Dealer, Hobbies,* and some proof of acceptance in a professional association. The honest dealer with a genuine love of antiques is not as rare as you may have heard. Taking care to develop a relationship with one may be the wisest thing you can do, and will certainly give you a standard to go by when your collecting sends you out into unfamiliar territory.

A word about tourist traps: resorts and developing historical sites attract both antiques businesses and visitors with vacation dollars in their pockets. Although reputable dealers may run seasonal businesses—at the N.J. Shore in summer and Florida in winter—they often rely upon high traffic and high prices in these locations for profits and buying capital. Even good year-round businessmen will price higher in season to finance their purchases of authentic, lower-margin-of profit pieces. They may display less valuable goods for the tourists they find are more interested in souveniers than in serious collecting. So, try to shop these places out of season to avoid the highest prices. Go just before or after the heaviest tourist period. Let the dealer know by asking pertinent questions, that you are a collector. The reward may be good information from a bored and grateful fellow collector, and you might just end up touring the back room or living quarters where the real treasures are hiding out, away from the traffic.

When your goal is still to gather information, steer clear of the obviously unfriendly or overworked shopkeeper. Where you find no prices displayed, keep your questions to a minimum and move on to warmer climes. When prices are marked, you can assume that the dealer may have included the 10 to 20% discount he will offer to other dealers. If you find that you are seriously interested in buying, you will learn to open the subject of price reduction with as courteous and honest a comment as possible. Let the proprietor know that, lovely as the piece is, it is out of range of your budget. Never, never try to haggle your way through all of his stock, and always accept a negative reply to the suggestion of reduction with good grace.

One good way to save gasoline and to contact a number of dealers is to seek out a good antiques show. Like the business itself these one-day, to one week long exhibit/sales have proliferated in recent years. Before you drive half-way across the state to attend one, try to check ahead. If you are after genuine antiques or nervous about authenticity, aim for one of the "veteran" shows. These shows are usually charity affairs and command a high admission fee. They are controlled by a committee of experts who screen exhibitors for reputation and quality of merchandise. You will see authentic wares at high prices, but you will also find dealers who may be good to visit later when you are looking for something special. Some of the larger shows in Manhattan—the Eastside Settlement House, Madison Square Garden, and 7th Regiment Armory, among others—are well worth a visit. Also, there is usually at least one big one in Morristown each year.

Far more common are the local shows where real antiques may be less abundant, even nonexistent. The annual church and charity shows are easier to find out about, better publicized, and are interested in maintaining a good reputation among collectors and other dealers. When you spot an announcement for one, try to contact the chairman or the office of the professional show director or manager. Again, take notes. Professional managers tend to attract the same dealers and type of merchandise to many shows in a season. Your notes and a season's schedule will help you spot the ones you would either hate or love to encounter again. For maximum personal contact with dealers at a show, try to attend during early hours or off days. For a possible bargain, be around at the end of the last day. Some dealers would rather shave prices than pack up a heavy piece for the trip home.

The large one-day shows, shopping mall and parking lot

"peddlers' days", and so-called flea markets are another matter. They are designed to appeal to the general public looking for diversion or recreation. Merchandise will be varied, usually of the collectible sort. It is seldom a shop owner's best, and is often made up of the small, impulse-buying type. Many of these exhibitors are collectors with no permanent place of business. They may be honest devotees who sell in order to buy more themselves. If you are alert you may see some dealer-to-dealer trading right on the floor. But the less carefully run markets will admit any exhibitor who buys a booth, and you may come across an opportunist with a year's stock of garage sale pickings who will be happy to sell at a profit. No one can force you to buy, and if you are looking for inexpensive additions to a budding collection, these extravaganzas can yield results. If you are seriously on the trail of heirlooms or nostalgic peices, if you have companions along who may be less than enthralled with your specialty, or if you are just eager to know what's selling at what prices, they can be great fun.

Two similarly difficult sources you should consider are the auction and the garage sale. The art of buying at auction is something special, not easily explained in brief. And garage sales are as unpredictable as people who hold them. If you know what you want, have good control over your spending impulses, and lots of time and patience, you may be lucky enough to find the right sale or the right little gem buried among the worn tires and battered, plastic toys. The best way to improve your odds is to read the local classifieds religiouly, learning to distinguish genuine homegrown clean-outs from the repeaters, those dealers-in-the making who empty out poor, dear grandma's attic too often to be believed. Their prices will include the profit they want to make, although their merchandise may be more intriguing than someone else's throwaways.

As for the unconventional avenues for collectors, if you have a little extra energy to devote to your search, do not overlook thrift shops. Professional pickers have always known about

A side chair attributed to John Laning of Cumberland County, under whom Maskell Ware was an apprentice.

them, since they hold the promise of yielding the unexpected. But charity-run shops can offer some bargains in the "antiques of the future" class, certainly at lower prices than you would be charged at a flea market. The genuine estate sale is a rare and special opportunity. Every once in a while you will find an odd garden piece, or even an entire set of kitchen chairs you would be happy to pay more for through a dealer. Contractors and wrecking companies, especially those working in inner-city and urban renewal areas sometimes pass along beautiful architectural pieces at good prices. And if you are truly brave, do not discount curbside trash. There are still some miracles to uncover here, but you have to know local regulations and schedules to beat professional scavengers and to avoid scrapes with the law. Some towns will sell you a license to scrounge for a modest payment, and you're respectable overnight.

Finally, a word about money. Investing in old things involves some risk. The genuine antique holds its value, for its appeal rests in craftsmanship and ageless beauty. When you decide to invest in younger things, be sure that your investment is at least partly a matter of taste. When you cannot be sure of a return of your investment, much less an improvement, be sure you love what you buy. If you find yourself drawn to things that are in high demand, your chances of selling for at least even money are greater. You may sell, as dealers do, to buy a better piece. You will not be the first of the afflicted to take the next step—maybe a garage sale, maybe a buying trip outside the state, then a booth at next fall's flea market. Perhaps, then, you will start thinking seriously about looking at that place in the country—the one with the little outbuilding, just the right size for showing a few small things.   —Barbara French

SECTION TWO
Metalware

The Blacksmith's Magic

S OME of us can recall how as children we stood in the door- way of a blacksmith's shop to watch in fascination while a horse was shod. There was the glow of a red-hot fire and of sparks flying from an anvil, the smell of hot metal and of leather—in short, there was a sense of other-worldness to a young child's mind. There is magic wrought by a blacksmith, which few, if any, of us have opportunity to see, as he converts a bar of iron into an object of utility and beauty. Because the implements and utensils made by the old-time blacksmith were functional in character, we have regarded them as worthless and thrown them out, failing to appreciate the skill and niceties of craftsmanship that went into their making.

From the time the first settlers arrived in Jamestown, Virginia, or Plymouth, Massachusetts, the blacksmith was an essential member of the community, without whose help little work could have been done in a pioneer settlement. It was he who made the blade of a felling axe used to clear ground when erecting a home, and who provided the heavier broad axe with which trees were trimmed for use as beams and rafters. There was also the drawknife, with blade of iron or steel, with which the beams were smoothed and their edges beveleld, and the frow, an indispensable tool for riving house shingles, clapboards, and fence palings. Some of these old tools are no longer needed and are finding their way into museums collections to be regarded as curiosities.

In the development of early America the blacksmith worked closely with carpenter and shipwright, providing all the hardware needed. Lumber for building was plentiful in our wilderness but where did the iron come from? In the 1630's the Reverend Francis Higginson of Salem, Massachusetts, wrote back to England, "Before you come be careful to be strongly instructed what things are fittest to bring with you for your more comfortable passage at sea, as also for your husbandry occasions when you come to the land. For when you are once parted with England you shall meete neither markets nor fayres to buy what you want. Therefore be sure to furnish yourselves with things fitting to be had before you come: as all manner of carpenters tools, and a great deale of iron and steel to make nails, and locks for houses, and furniture for plows." The pastor also listed such essentials as iron cooking pots, kettles, gridirons and skillets. Note that the smith was to bring with him on the voyage "a great deale of iron and steel." At first he was largely dependent on bar iron imported from Europe, that from Sweden or Spain being considered the best. By 1632 bog or pond ore, a soft iron ore found in marshes and river beds, had been located in New England. Ten years later the first successful ironworks in the Colonies was established at Saugus Center, Massachusetts. In 1648 Governor John Winthrop of Massachusetts Bay wrote of the Saugus works, "The furnace runs eight tons per week, and their bar iron is as good as Spanish."

A large proportion of rocks on the surface of the earth contain iron to some degree and are, therefore, potential iron ores. Such rock ore was commonly known as "iron stones." When either bog ore or "iron stones" was subjected to intense heat in a blast furnace, the iron melted and separated from other mineral matter. The early blast furnace was a crude affair requiring vast quantities of timber to maintain heat sufficient for smelting. During the process of smelting the partially melted ore formed into a stringy, spongy mass called a "bloom." This was broken into pieces small enough to handle, reheated to refine it, and then worked on an anvil under a hammer—in which case it was termed wrought iron—or else completely melted and poured into molds to form objects of cast iron. Until an iron mine was opened at Salisbury, Connecticut, in 1732, this primitive method was a blacksmith's only means of obtaining the ore locally. It is interesting to note that iron ore of excellent quality was found along the shores of the Delaware and Trenton, New Jersey, became the center to which the ore was sent by wagon or boat for shipment to Philadelphia.

Iron was one of the earliest and most important of our American industries, which, during the latter part of the 18th century, reached its zenith in New Jersey and Pennsylvania. The quantity of iron being shipped back from the Colonies by the mid-18th century was sufficient to alarm the British manufacturers who, of course, wished to hold the monopoly. They had reason to be aroused for it was this same iron industry that supplied our revolutionary armies and made our independence possible.

In making objects of wrought iron the anvil served as the blacksmith's workbench. In his shop was a forge or open hearth, and a large pair of bellows—usually operated by a helper—which supplied the stream of air needed to keep the fire hot. Until modern times, the size of a piece of iron to be forged was limited, not so much by its weight as by the amount of heat that the smith, who must work close by, could bear. A piece of metal had to glow red-white before the smith could manipulate it, for every article of wrought iron was shaped on the anvil and hammered out by hand whether it was a nail or a weathervane for the barn.

Holding the piece of white-hot iron on the anvil with his tongs,

Above: A wrought-iron grille from Charleston or possibly Southwest, intended for a lunette or window grille.
Below: Types of hinges, both Swiss and American from the seventeenth and eighteenth century.

the smith would turn it from side to side, his blows weaving and twisting as the iron gradually took shape under the hammer. All wrought iron is malleable, or capable of being easily bent, but before a piece assumed its final form the smith might need to reheat it several times in the forge. Many objects of wrought iron show surface irregularities caused by hammer blows.

As its name implies, cast iron was shaped in a mold of sand or wood and the maker of such pieces was known as a "molder." Credit is given to Joseph Jenks of Lynn, Massachusetts, for making the first models and castings, in 1646, for the cast iron pots, skillets, and tools produced at the Saugus foundry. Because of its carbon content cast iron is brittle, easily broken, and when subjected to wear and exposure has a granular surface.

Whether he worked on an anvil or cast his metal in molds, the Colonial ironworker was indispensable to his community for it was to him that men turned whatever their needs might be. Among the blacksmith's tasks was the making of nails, hinges, latches and locks, bull rings, pitchforks and other farm implements, horse and ox shoes, or the runners for a sleigh. Sometimes the blacksmith even made sleighs and wagons. For the fireplace he turned out cranes, andirons, ash peels, a rotary broiler or a Dutch oven, pots and skillets, ladles and cake turners. In certain areas, such as Charleston, South Carolina, the blacksmith created beautiful and intricate designs for the railing of a balcony or stairway.

The blacksmith was versatile, creative, and frequently showed great discrimination. It is quite fascinating to study the various designs he used in making so simple an item as an iron rest—no two are ever alike for each expresses the maker's whim of the moment. Or take the handles in a group of ladles, forks and spatulas, the heart-shaped motif punched in one declaring its Pennsylvania origin, while others show different methods of twisting the handle end to form a loop for suspension. There is an amazing variety of designs to be found in old hand-wrought latches and hinges: tulip and other flower forms, ball-and-spear, arrow head, swordfish, or the gracefully curved side hinges that derived from the English "cockshead." One might think so utilitarian an article as a chopping knife offered little opportunity for variation, yet of the dozen examples studied no two showed the same form. One studied was made by Cyrus Hadden of Newark for his mother in 1837. Cyrus may have been a smith's apprentice at the time for he did the work, at the age of 17, in a blacksmith's shop on Springfield Avenue near Smith Street.

Part of the wrought iron in the Newark Museum's Collection was assembled by Albert H. Sonn, the artist, who had a keen appreciation for the blacksmith's skill. To Mr. Sonn a hand-wrought piece was not just a useful object, but was in a unique sense an expression of the craftsman. For the smith hammer and anvil were but extensions of himself, they were his means of self expression and achievement, they filled his desire to please a friend or to do a more perfect job.

The present machine age has given us much to admire in the way of fine metalwork, but let us also respect the crude charm and beauty of form to be found in these hand-wrought objects of iron.   —MARGARET E. WHITE

Highlights on Newark Ironware

NO seventeenth-century Newark ironware has come down to us, and as far as is known it did not get into contemporary records. We can only assume what it was like from the ironware in other settlements at the time.

We can be pretty sure that the first permanent Newark houses had in them and on them only the ironware that was absolutely necessary and that it was severely plain—probably "bean" latches, strap and perhaps H and HL hinges, and the simplest kind of bolts, cooking utensils, and fireplace equipment. Life in the young settlement was so hard for the first two generations that there was not time or energy or means for any extras or frills, and the sternly religious character of the people would have been against them anyway.

For some time even the handmade iron nails with the familiar irregular tops and the sharp points that could be clinched at need were so scarce that they must have been sparingly used. So probably few, if any, of the early batten doors were nail-studded.

What we call hardware today was known as ironmongery then and until well into the 1800's. It was hand-wrought, of course, and much of it came from England. Cast-iron articles were classed as hollow ware.

For the eighteenth century the story is a little better. We do have some ironware of that period, but it is late; the first fifty years are a blank on that score. The two choicest examples are the handsome weather vane on "Old First" Presbyterian Church on Broad Street and the attractive though less elaborate one on the old stone schoolhouse in the Museum garden. The tulip motif scrolls below the arrow on the school vane of 1784 are exactly like those on the fine vane of 1791 that still points the wind on the spire of the old Springfield Church. The same smith must have fashioned both. Was he of German extraction, or did he come from the German section of Pennsylvania? The tulip motif, and the heart in the Springfield vane, were characteristic of decorations in both places. But, of course, he may just have copied them.

There is said to have been a vane pierced with an early 1700 date on the spire of the second structure of "Old First." Unfortunately, nobody cared enough to preserve it when that building was razed about 1808 or 1809.

The appealingly simple vane on Trinity Cathedral spire seems to be of copper; but there are two choice relics of ironware, of what appear to be eighteenth-century date, on the inner front doors of this building, and the outline of a third.

What was once a Housatonic (Connecticut)-type Suffolk thumblatch similar to the eighteenth-century ones on Plates 59 and 61, Volume 1 of A. H. Sonn's *Early American Wrought Iron,* is now serving as a handle on one of these doors. Its original use was so far forgotten that it was mounted with the opening for the thumbpress on the bottom instead of the top.

The upper hinges on the two inside center front doors of Trinity, with wrapped joints and a fine curved sweep, are of eighteenth-century design too. (Compare with a very similar one, Plate 131, Volume 2, Sonn, *op. cit.)* They may date from the early nineteenth century, perhaps when the second structure of Trinity was built in 1809 or at a later remodeling. The pattern, at least, is old.

Below the handle on the left door of this center pair is the outline of either a bolt or a latch-lock escutcheon of colonial pattern. (For examples in Pennsylvania dating from about the 1740's see Plate 98, Volume 1, and Plates 118 and 121, Volume 2, Sonn, *op. cit.*).

Less important perhaps but also interesting are the two worn and ruggedly plain footscrapers at the entrance to "Old First" (1787-1791), and the five different old shutter fasteners of eighteenth-century pattern on the rectory of the House of Prayer (the old Plume house) and the one or two still left on the old Sydenham (Sidman) house on De Graw Avenue.

At another eighteenth-century house in what was once Newark township but is now East Orange—the old Elihu Pierson house on North Arlington Avenue—there are two old ironware trasures. Though no longer in use, a fine wrought-iron knocker latch with heart-shaped escutcheon is still cherished. So are the quaint ox-shoe hinges on a cellar door. The main section of this house was built in 1764, the former kitchen wing probably earlier.

Even in the later 1600's when Newark was settled, some of the ironware—the pots, pans, kettles, and some of the fire-dogs—were cast iron. More and more cast iron came into use during the 1700's, things like chimney backs and jamb plates and the first Frankin stoves, often called fireplaces because they really were small-scale iron fireplaces extending into the rooms.

In 1768, Newarkers could have bought cast-iron firebacks, hearth and jamb plates, firedogs, iron sash weights that were "two pence the pound cheaper than those of lead," as well as cooking utensils and other cast-iron ware at what was con-sidered the town's first foundry—the Vesuvius Air Furnace. It was established by three of the Newark Ogdens—Gabriel, Lewis and Moses—in partnership with Edward Laight of New York. The ore for the foundry came mostly from Morris and

Sussex County mines, in some of which the Ogden family had interests from time to time.

This furnace was on Washington Street at James, about where the Second Presbyterian Church stands. Moses Ogden managed it, and his home was just a little north of it on Washington Street. By the 1790's it was best known for its stoves, and it continued in operation until shortly before 1810 when it made way for the first structure of the church. There is no record of its continuance anywhere else.

In the nineteenth century, cast iron really took over almost completely. The old hand-wrought hardware gave way to cast iron, often following the earlier hand-wrought patterns. Door-knobs came in and with them the cast-iron box locks and later cast-iron keyholes protected by covers that matched the knobs. Instead of door knockers there were bell pulls on the front door jambs. The iron founders of the 1830's and 40's were also bell hangers. These pull bells were followed by bell twists usually above or below the letter slots on the front doors of the 1870's, 80's and 90's.

Stoves for home heating and cooking began to come into general use in the 1820's and 30's. Some of the parlor ones were almost incredibly fantastic in design. Newark foundries were turning them out, but the merchants also handled out-of-town makes.

Toward the end of the 1850's, Newark stores began to put on iron fronts. This was followed in the 1880's and 90's by a vogue for ornamental sheet-iron cornices and bays.

The nineteenth-century iron porch railings, balconies, basement window grilles, and lacy iron porches in Newark sometimes combined wrought iron and cast iron with excellent effect and pleasing lightness; but many of the later examples were heavy and ugly. The only lacy iron porch I know of in the old Newark area is a very fine one on the old building of the Bloomfield Seminary. A few porch railings of the late 1840's are still in use on the brick row in Fulton Street built by the Van

Seiburt Hall of the Bloomfield College and Seminary demonstrates the delicate effects arrived out when wrought iron and cast iron are combined.

Rensselaers. There are some later railings and newels, basement window grilles, and even a balcony or two, still in place; but it won't be for long. Almost overnight they disappear.

From about the 1840's on, the footscrapers were built into the porch railings close to the newels. By all odds the most unusual ones I have yet seen anywhere were two solitary examples on the sidewalk close to the porch steps at 48 and 50 New Street. The one shown was twenty-seven inches high and twelve inches wide, and its neighbor was a little bigger. The houses they served dated from the 1850's or early 60's and were near the old Connison and Helm Foundry.

Much of the cast iron cresting that graced every available inch of the roofs and window lintels of the mansards of the 1860's and later, was of fine design and is still to be seen, though it is fast disappearing.

There was even a vogue for cast iron gravestones in the 1870's, though that was really not a new idea. Some eighteenth-century iron worker had had the same inspiration, for not long ago a cast iron gravestone marked "N.I.–1717" was unearthed at Exton Farm, High Point, New Jersey, near the ruins of an old forge.

Newarkers could get most of this ironware locally, for Newark foundries were producing it as early as the 1830's. Smith and Wilcox at 11 Bank Street, and Cyphers and Duvall on Canal Street near Cherry, were advertising iron stoop railings "plain and ornamental" in the late 1830's and were also doing bell-hanging.

Another noted Newark foundry was Ward's Globe Ironworks on Market and Congress streets opposite the Gas Works. This was ready for business in June of 1850. I found one store on New Street with iron columns stamped with the Ward name, and this foundry also made the ironwork for the new city hall in 1864.

Masters in this field were Cyrus Edwards and Matthew Ely, who were in business from the 1840's and supplied quantities of ironwork on Newark houses and buildings for many years. The finest example of nineteenth-century cast-iron ware still functioning in Newark is the handsome gateway at Mt. Pleasant Cemetery. Mr. William Webb, secretary of the Mt. Pleasant Cemetery Company, who very kindly looked up the records for me, says these gates were made by Cyrus Edwards in 1877 and cost $594.

There are still many good examples of later nineteenth-century ironware in Newark that are well worth collecting and preserving, but every day more of it is discarded and lost. If the ironware itself cannot be kept, at least the best examples could and should be photographed as a record. So much of it was locally made, and the iron industry has been so important for so long in Newark, that future generations ought to be able both to see and study examples. It is really an essential part of Newark's history and cultural heritage.   —IONE M. SONN

Silver

ARLY workers in gold and silver, commonly known as goldsmiths, were held in high esteem. In Europe the goldsmith's craft was the choice of men who, being of noble birth, were above working at a trade. In the American colonies the silversmith had of necessity to be a man of integrity. On his honor alone depended the fineness of the silver he was commissioned to make from coins or outmoded silver vessels that first had to pass through his melting pot.

Our colonial silversmith was well trained. To learn the craft, a youth had to serve an apprenticeship of about seven years with some reputable silversmith. During this term, usually between the ages of fourteen and twenty-one, a pupil lived with his master. Only upon satisfactory completion of his training was the young man admitted as "freeman," with permission to practice his trade. We have reason, therefore, to respect the craftsman and his works, and to be proud of any examples of silver that we own.

Not only were our silversmiths skilled in their craft, but they were respected members of their communities, often taking an active part in civic affairs. Such a man was David Lyell, an early silversmith of New Jersey. Born in 1670, Lyell came to New York in 1699 from London, where he had been a goldsmith. Until 1717 he engaged in the latter business in New York, dividing his time between that city and Perth Amboy, then capital of the province of East New Jersey. In both places Lyell was prominent in social and political life. He was appointed to the Council of the province of East New Jersey, which office he held until 1723.

No silver by David Lyell has been located, but he has been represented in a Newark Museum exhibition by a portrait miniature done in plumbago and wash on parchment by John Watson. Since Watson came to Perth Amboy from Scotland in 1715 and Lyell died ten years later, the miniature presents the subject in his maturity and, presumably, in a semi-official capacity. The minature of Lyell is from the Lelia A. and John Hill Morgan Collection, and was lent by Yale University Art Gallery.

For the same exhibition, the New Jersey Historical Society lent a teapot made by Elias Boudinot for John and Abigail (Phillips) Stockton of Princeton. Also by Boudinot is a covered sugar dish, evidently made during his Philadelphia period, 1740-53. Originally the bowl belonged to Mrs. Ann Henry Durkin, who came to Philadelphia from Ireland in 1765. From her it passed to her granddaughter Ann, born in 1793. Her initials and date are engraved. Since then, the bowl has been handed from mother to daughter in unbroken succession. Exhibited with the sugar bowl was a miniature of Mrs. Ann Durkin by an unknown artist.

A sugar urn and cream jug made by Henry Lupp of New Brunswick for Rynier Veghte and his wife, Catharine, of Somerville, New Jersey, were also included. The Veghte family came to this country from Holland in 1660. During the Revolution, Rynier served as lieutenant and later as captain of the Second Battalion, Somerset Militia.

Also by Lupp is the tea set that belonged to General Anthony

The tea set *(above)* was made by Henry Lupp (working 1783-1800 at New Brunswick) for General Anthony Walton White. *Below:* Sugar basin made by Elias Boudinot in Philadelphia or Princeton, *circa* 1750-60, originally owned by Mrs. Robert Durkin.

W. White. This three-piece set with matching teaspoons was used by General White in his New Brunswick home "Buccleuch," which had been built in 1739. His father Anthony White married Elizabeth, daughter of Lewis Morris, who was governor of the province of New Jersey. A miniature of General White in uniform is owned by the Rutgers University Library.

Henry Lupp's father, Peter, was represented by teaspoons once used by Abraham Van Doren and his wife Ann Van Dyke. The latter were of Griggstown, New Jersey.

When Matthias Halsted's daughter, Susan Blanchard Halsted, was married to John Low about 1800 she was presented with a sugar bowl and cream jug made by her uncle, Benjamin. At that period Benjamin Halsted was working in New York, but he began his career as silversmith in Elizabethtown with his brother Matthias as partner. The young married couple also had a ladle by Benjamin with bright-cut decoration on the handle. These pieces have remained in the Matthias family ever since.

One of the outstanding American pieces to have been exhibited is a coffee pot by Cary Dunn, presented to Sarah Van Brugh Livingston and John Jay at the time of their marriage in 1775. It was lent by the Museum of the City of New York. The wedding took place at "Liberty Hall" in Elizabethtown, the home of Governor William Livingston. Sarah was named for her great-grandmother, the wife of Captain Peter Van Brugh of Albany. These names are of interest in connection with a pair of silver candlesticks by Myer Myers of New York, having been shown in the Newark Museum and Brooklyn Museum exhibition of Myers' work.

These candlesticks are inscribed "The gift of Peter and Sarah Van Brugh to Cathae. Livingston." Was Catharine the granddaughter of Peter and Sarah Van Brugh and the sister of Governor Livingstone? She was born in 1733 and later married a Mr. Lawrence. However, there is an interesting hitch in these facts, for Mrs. Sarah Van Brugh died in 1742, three years before Myer Myers began working as a silversmith. Those who own family silver inscribed in some manner might find it worth their while to check names and dates. Rightly documented silver by American craftsmen brings higher prices, and is far more desirable to museums and collectors than pieces of obscure origin.

Two silver tankards owned in New Jersey are especially valuable for the family records associated with them. One of these tankards was made about 1725 by Peter Van Dyck, one of the foremost craftsmen of early New York. It belonged to Mrs. Sarah Cornell and is marked with her initials. When she married Henry Wisner in 1769 she took the tankard to her new home and it has remained in the Wisner-Thorne family ever since.

The other tankard was by Andrew Tyler, a contemporary of Van Dyck who worked in Boston. It belonged to the Rev. Samuel Moseley, who graduated from Harvard College in 1729 and married Bethia Otis, daughter of John Otis. On the handle are the combined initials *M* over *S B*. In 1735 Samuel Moseley was made chaplain to Governor Jonathan Belcher of Massachusetts. The tankard has remained in the Moseley family.

Of considerable interest historically is the mug of Sheffield plate given to one of the pallbearers at George Washington's funeral. Each of the six or eight pallbearers received a similar gift from Martha Washington, as was the custom of the day. The mug is lent by the Cornwallis Headquarters of the New Jersey Federation of Women's Clubs.

Quite unusual is the group of silver wine labels selected from her collection of several hundred by Mrs. Philip H. Hartung, American representative of the British Wine Label Circle. Some of these labels bear names of vintages unfamiliar today and belonging to an era when fifteen or more wines were set forth in labeled decanters from which a guest might choose.

The diversity of form, use, and historic interest, to be found in objects of silver adds greatly to its appeal. This diversity may be noted in the pieces often on view at various county Historical

Associations. The Monmouth County Historical Association has shown a pipkin, or brandy-warmer, with handle of turned wood; an example of the cleft or trifid handle used for spoons and forks during the second half of the seventeenth century; a fine trencher salt made by Koenraet Ten Eyck who was admitted 1716 as "freeman" in New York.

In the churches of our state are preserved many beautiful pieces of silver of which we may all be justly proud. Some of this communion silver is of English or European origin, some pieces are by colonial silversmiths who worked in the Dutch tradition. Among the finest examples are the beakers and chalices made by the Bergen Reformed Church, Jersey City; Saint Peter's Church, Perth Amboy; Saint Mary's Church, Burlington. Excellent illustrations of them are to be found in *The Old Silver of American Churches* by E. A. Jones, first printed for the National Society of Colonial Dames of America in 1913.

The only way we can know about interesting pieces made or owned in New Jersey is with the co-operation of their owners. If you have old family silver, do find out when and by whom it was made, whose initials (if any) are engraved on the pieces. Then, if your pieces seem to warrant it, tell your museum about them. However, be sure that the dates of the silversmith and of the original owner correspond. Sometimes a bit of genealogical work is needed.

The style in which a piece of silver is made may give its approximate date. For instance, a cream jug of inverted-pear shape cannot date much before 1750. The graceful urn shape based on classic models belongs to the late eighteenth century. There is a tendency to attribute a piece of silver to a fixed date or craftsman without due consideration for the style in which it is made. With all antiques there seems to be a tendency to fix an earlier date than is justified, even though this date does not necessarily add to their interest or value.

—MARGARET E. WHITE

SECTION THREE
Furniture

Three Generations of Cabinetmakers

MATTHEW EGERTON, 1739-1802

A GOOD deal of speculation has arisen as to the author-ship of a number of fine pieces of late eighteenth-century furniture which have been found in New York, New Jersey, and Pennsylvania, and which, in their design and workmanship, seem all to bear the mark of the same hand, working with veneers and inlays after the manner of Hepplewhite and Sheraton. There is, indeed, little doubt that one maker, perhaps with employees and apprentices, was busily engaged during a considerable period of years in fabricating much of this fine work; but who this craftsman was, or where his shop may have been, no one had dared surmise until, quite recently, the finding of several labeled pieces permitted comparisons enabling us to ascribe the work as a whole to a family of Egertons, who lived in New Brunswick during the latter half of the eighteenth century and the first third of the nineteenth.

For three generations, this family made innumerable ex-quisite secretaries, clock cases, bureaus, chests, bedsteads, tables, and other articles of household use and adornment. But there is no evidence to prove that they ever constructed chairs: no bills, inventories, or accounts mention such articles of furniture; nor have any chairs been located bearing an Egerton advertisement. There were regular chairmakers sufficient to supply any demand in this field. From a search of early twentieth century sources, it appears that the flourishing town of New Brunswick had several such men. Campbell Dunham, for example, limited himself to Windsor chairs alone, while Richard Jacques was a "Spinning-wheel and Windsor Chairmaker." John Ryckman, however, "lately removed from New York," in 1793, was termed a "Cabinet and Chair-Maker." At all events, the allied trades prospered well in the busy community, and Willet Warne notified the local artisans that he had a variety of trade supplies for sale.

The historic associations of New Brunswick have never been fully discussed, although many celebrated Colonial and Revolutionary names are closely identified with the development of the town. Commencing with Thomas Lawrence, who received a deed in 1678, and Cornelius van Langevelt, to whom other land was conveyed in 1681, the population of New Brunswick has been divided between folk of English and of Dutch descent.

Of the former, probably, were the Egertons, though concerning the origins of this family little is known. Matthew Egerton, born about 1739, was a warden of Christ Church until 1785. Again, in 1790, his name appears on the vestry records, where it remained until his death. His wife, however, joined the Dutch house of worship, June 28, 1782. She was Catelyna (Catherine) Voorhees, born February 18, 1742, the daughter of Lucas (Luke) Voorhees or Van Voorhees, and Altje Ryder. Matthew Egerton died May 3, 1802, leaving a widow, five children, and twelve grandchildren. He is described as having been a wealthy cabinetmaker on Burnet Street, near Schureman.

Not much has been recorded of this artisan's public or private life, although General William S. Stryker, in his *Official Register of the Officers and Men of New Jersey in the Revolu-*

tionary War, lists him as a private from Middlesex County, in the State Militia. Undoubtedly he was an educated man, for he possessed a small collection of books at the time of his death, and his son Luke, born 1768, matriculated at Queen's College, now Rutgers, and received his A.M. degree in 1794. Luke became a teacher, and seems never to have been interested in the family trade.

Matthew owned valuable property, and, on May 20, 1793, he sold to his son "Matthew Egerton Jun." a lot on Burnet Street, forty feet in width and one-hundred and fifty-six feet in depth, for one hundred and twenty pounds currency. This parcel adjoined his own house and cabinet shop in Burnet Street, near the Raritan River.

Upon the senior's death in 1802, Catherine Egerton, his widow and executrix, with Abraham Schuyler and Staats Van Deusen, his executors, advertised:

> For sale at public vendue, on Monday the 7th September next, at ten o'clock in the forenoon, at the house late the dwelling of Matthew Egerton, dec., complete set of cabinetmaker's tools of every description, and a large stock of excellent seasoned stuff, consisting of mahogany, cherry, black walnut, and bilsted boards and also some articles of valuable household furniture.... Also at 4 o'clock in the afternoon, six acres of land, lying in the vicinity of the city, and a valuable building lot adjoining the river, at the lower end of Burnet street, late the property of Matthew Egerton, dec.

The "articles of valuable household furniture" mentioned in the advertisement consisted of his "Book-case Desk containing a small collection of Books," valued at forty-five dollars; "Maple dining table," four dollars; "Cherry Breakfast table," worth the same amount; "Bilsted Breakfast table," at two dollars; "looking glass," at three dollars and fifty cents; "large white pine chest," four dollars; "Gin case with 4 square bottles," fifty cents; Coffee Mill; six silver teaspoons; "1 feather bed, bedstead and beding," worth twenty-seven dollars; and a "cat-tailed bed, bedstead and beding." The tools included

Egerton secretary of the late eighteenth century with what appears an upper drawer, actually constitutes the drop front of the desk.

thirty-five molding planes, a tool chest "4 shop benches with all the tools in (the) shop," and a grindstone, totaling fifty-seven dollars and a half. A cherry desk and a bilsted chest were among the unfinished articles in the workroom. The stock of woods was valued at one hundred dollars, excluding fourteen posts and a small pile of chestnut rails.

A typical labeled example of Matthew Egerton's cabinet-making is illustrated here. Its interior shows the degree of perfection which Egerton achieved in the use of both veneers and inlays. Within the cabinet of this piece the maker pasted his label, an oval medallion on which the inscription is printed.

Nearly identical specimens of this fine secretary are to be found in and around Princeton, Freehold, Trenton, Philadelphia, and elsewhere. The tapering French feet, the oval inlay on the drawers, the stained inlaid eagle on the centre of the desk door, the advantageous use of deep mahogany grain, are all features encountered on other articles, which, though mostly unmarked, seem, almost certainly, to be the work of the same designer and manufacturer.

Matthew Egerton was employed over a period of years, creating, fabricating, and selling an inestimable amount of handsome, well constructed furniture, which, though it may have been originally labeled, is now to be identified only by its similarity to known Egerton pieces.

Despite the fact that all attributions are, at best, but the result of comparison and judgment, it seems reasonable to offer the exceedingly fine mahogany clothespress, as an example of Egerton's work. This impressive piece has descended to Howard Townsend, of New York City, from the family of Colonel John Bayard, whose singular services rendered during the War of Independence are familiar to most readers. After being deprived of his estate in Cecil County, Maryland, because of his attachment to the patriotic cause, Colonel Bayard removed to New Brunswick, where, in 1787, he married, as his third wife, Johannah, sister of General Anthony Walton White,

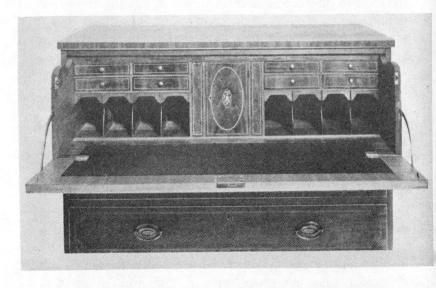

Above: Interior view of the secretary. *Below:* Matthew Egerton's label found on the secretary pictured.

aide-de-camp to General Washington. There he built a hand-some mansion which offered hospitality to many distinguished guests, including Alexander Hamilton and Judge John Patter-son. In 1790, the Colonel was elected Mayor of the city, and, a few years later, was appointed President Judge of the Court of Common Pleas of Somerset County. Colonel Bayard died in New Brunswick, January 7, 1807.

For his fine home on Albany Street, now a part of the Lincoln Highway, he not improbably purchased some furniture from the Egertons. At all events, many details in the construction of the press here pictured suggest the art of Matthew Egerton at its best. The inlaid bands follow the general contour of the bracket feet, the lower drawers, and the doors. The usual oval decora-tion is also present, but, to create further contrast, there are double lines of satinwood. All the woods used have been chosen with characteristic care. The Gothic cornice which crowns the piece is, however, of a type never before noted on a marked Egerton piece.

It is quite evident that Matthew Egerton expended much time and thought on the exteriors of sideboards, clocks, chests, and the like; but, doubtless, only where the remuneration warranted it, were interiors as well finished. Blocks appear to have been used invariably to strengthen essential joints.

MATTHEW EGERTON, JR., AND HIS SONS

IN 1802, when Matthew Egerton died, the family name was perpetuated by his three sons, Matthew, Luke, and Abraham Schuyler Egerton. Of the last, no facts remain; Luke was a graduate of Queen's, now Rutgers, College, and chose teaching as a profession; while Matthew, long before his parent's decease, had decided to follow his father's trade and art. Thus, perhaps as early as 1785, Matthew Egerton, Junior, was the proprietor of a shop, fabricating his own fine furniture for the citizens of New Brunswick and adjacent places. He married Maria (1772-1856), the daughter of John and Aeltie Bergan, by whom he had three sons, John Bergan, baptized May 13, 1791; William, baptized December 1, 1793; and Evert, baptized August 30, 1795. Two of these children were later associated with their father, and, likewise, in the third generation of the family, were cabinetmakers.

But, to return to the second generation, it is ascertained that, although he was working alone a few years previously, "Matthew Egerton Jun.," on May 20, 1793, purchased from his parents, for one hundred and twenty pounds, current money, the lot, forty by one hundred fifty-six feet, adjoining the property of his father in Burnet Street where he erected a dwelling and, perhaps, a shop. Like his father, Matthew, Junior, was a man of property and a prominent member of the community. Among other real estate, he held three hundred and ninety-four acres in Warren County, New York; seventy-five acres on the outskirts of New Brunswick; a house and lot on New Street, afterward conveyed to Bishop Croes; several valuable properties on Schureman Street; and his dwelling and two-story cabinet shop, each on its own lot situated in Burnet Street, in front of his meadow land.

From the *Guardian or New Brunswick Advertiser* for Tuesday, October 18, 1796, is quoted the following advertisement:

> To be sold at Private Sale and immediate Possession Given. A Valuable house and lot in Albany Street, opposite the printing office, New-Brunswick; the lot is 25 feet front and rear, and 150 deep, binding on an alley in the rear, the house has a brick front and is 22 feet by 30 feet with 4 fire places, a celler under the whole, and a convenient partaule and kitchen adjoining; the lot is in board fence, and has a stable on the rear, the house is new, and is advantageously situated for business. For terms apply to Messrs. Gifford and Scotland, No. 25 John Street, New-York, or the subscriber who will show the premises. Matthew Egerton, junr. New-Brunswick, September 5, 1796. N.B. An indisputable title will be given.

Clothespress of the late eighteenth century attributed to Egerton.

The *Fredonian,* during March, 1822, gave a long account of the launching of the New Jersey Bank for Savings, wherein the one hundred and twenty-eight Articles of Association were quoted, followed by the names of the associators, including that of Matthew Egerton, who, after the death of his father, in 1802, had dropped the use of "Junior." At the same time he was chosen second vice-president of the organization, which opened its office in the counting room of John N. Simpson, Burnet Street, March 23, 1822, "from six to nine in the evening and every succeeding Saturday."

Another glimpse of the private life of this craftsman may be gained from the accounts of the New Brunswick Library, which charge Egerton with one yearly share in the corporation, at the rate of one dollar, August 1, 1825. He was likewise affiliated with the Dutch Reformed Church, where he owned a pew. On June 19, 1835, a terrific tornado visited the town, and contemporary records disclose that "the dwelling and cabinet warehouse of Matthew Egerton, in Burnet Street," as well as other properties owned by him, were "much damaged."

The earliest marked example of the work of Matthew Egerton, Junior, which has come to light, is an extremely tall, chiming, grandfather clock, with the maker's label on the inside of the door. Two varieties of this label have been found: one, possibly the more ancient, is octagonal; the other has a scalloped edge. In spite of its great height, the carefully inlaid mahogany case of this timepiece maintains true proportions. Like similar Egerton clock cases, it has French feet, fans, and circular satinwood inlay on the base and long door, insets of rich mahogany, and the effective use of feathered edges at advantageous places. Made to special order for Colonel Morgan of Marlboro, New Jersey, it combines several uncommon features, notably the open fretwork on the hood, permitting full volume of the five ditties rendered by the concealed chimes. The mechanism was made by Leslie and Williams of New Brunswick. The above-named Leslie may have been William Leslie, fellow warden of

Christ Church with the elder Egerton; while Williams is probably the clockmaker found in Trenton at the beginning of the nineteenth century.

Many clock and watchmakers were busy about this time in New Brunswick, for, besides Leslie & Williams, may be listed Charles Wheeler, Isaac Reed, Silas W. Howell, and Henry Lupp (Leupp). Then too, communication was frequent with Bound Brook, the home of Hurtin & Burgi—in partnership as early as 1766—and with Flemington, where Joakim Hill worked. Since several clock cases with Hill movements resemble the Egerton piece just described, it is more than likely that some connection will be found to have existed between Hill and Egerton. Mrs. H. E. Pickersgill of Perth Amboy, New Jersey, owns a labeled clock without any inscription on the face.

Even were the maker's label not pasted within the Hepplewhite cellarette only slight persuasion would be necessary to convince collectors that this little gem was made in the Egerton shop. Here, well-proportioned form and grace of line are enhanced by inlaid bands, dainty drops, and fans. A single drawer extends across the front of the swell top, while a double cupboard occupies the centre of the recessed lower section. Four slightly tapering legs are shortened in effect by substantial bands of satinwood. As in all the foregoing Egerton examples, the greatest care has been taken to select the most beautifully grained woods and to display them to the best advantage.

From the marked similarity between the output of Matthew Egerton the elder (1739-1802) and that of his son of the same name, we may safely assume that the younger man learned his trade from his father. In some instances, the work of the two is so analogous as to make it extremely difficult to differentiate between their productions. When an example does not bear a label, it would seem only natural to consider its age: and to attribute Matthew, Senior, all pieces made before 1802, and to his son, those of a later date. However, a study of authenticated specimens shows the fallacy of such a procedure. The marked

Above: A cellarette made and labeled by Matthew Egerton, Jr. *Below:* An unlabeled sideboard reasonably attributed to the Egerton shop, somewhat complementary to the buffet above.

secretary discussed earlier, it should be noted, was probably made some years later than the inlaid grandfather clock that carries the advertisement of Matthew, Junior. In point of time, it might even be said that father and son were contemporaries; although the latter lived and worked for thirty-five years after the death of the former.

To continue with the New Brunswick family of cabinet-makers: it will be seen that not only did Matthew Egerton, Junior, follow the craft of Matthew, Senior, but that two of the grandsons, John Bergan and Evert, in turn, doubtless served apprenticeships under their father.

The younger son, Evert, formed a partnership with his parent under the firm name of Matthew Egerton (Jr.) & Son. He bought, May 1, 1830, a lot in Burnet Street, where he erected a home, but his work may have all been done in the old family shop.

The inventory of John Bergan Egerton's estate would suggest that this elder son conducted an independent business at a different location. Yet, on the interesting combination map and directory of 1829 he is not listed as either a landholder or proprietor.

On his furniture labels the elder Matthew called himself a "cabinetmaker"; his son styled his occupation that of "Joiner and Cabinetmaker"; and, although no marked pieces by the third generation have been found, it is known that these latest members of the family were seriously engaged in that calling. Nevertheless, at the same time they found employment in papering walls—as is ascertained, for instance, by the minutes of Rutgers College, under date of Tuesday, July 14, 1829: "M. Egerton & Son for papering rooms $10.75." Again, Ferdinand S. Van Arsdalen was presented a bill, May 10, 1831, "To putting on 24 pieces of Paper & Do. Borders @ 2/$6-50."

Another phase of the work of this establishment, and, in all probability, no small part, was the making of funeral equipment. One of the most interesting of the old bills for this labor is one which records an indebtedness of the estate of Abraham V. Arsdalen to the amount of $13.73, including ten dollars for a walnut coffin, "rais'd & lined." The receipt is made out and signed by the senior member of the firm of Matthew Egerton & Son.

Just what kinds of cabinet work this shop produced during the last two decades of its existence, is easily determined from contemporary autograph records and by a study of local furniture; but where to turn for positive examples presents a far more difficult problem. A marked Matthew Egerton, Junior, cellarette is illustrated in this article, but no authenticated sideboard, of the type required exactly to supplement this piece, has so far been discovered. The wood, finish, and treatment of the later and more ornate sideboard, stamp the piece unquestionably as a product of the Egerton shop. In fact the centre part of this sideboard really duplicates the cellarette.

Interesting new points appear with the old: four colored urns decorate the spaces flanking the upper drawers; diamond-shaped insets protect the wood about the keyholes; original forms supplant the more familiar drops; continuous diamonds introduce a novel style of banding; and small knobs have taken the place of the oval brasses. Two half-moon dining tables, in the same collection as this handsome sideboard, are certainly parts of the one suite. The conventional shape, the carefully selected woods, and the identical inlay, are noticeable features of these tables.

Now, bearing in mind the known work of both Matthew Egertons, and with the assistance of documentary evidence, we may reasonably assert that the firm made such pieces as that of the cherry "Bookcase Desk" or '1 Desk & bookcase," mentioned in the acounts. The workmanship, lumber, and finish are, assuredly, those of the Egertons. Nor do the elements of the design greatly differ from those seen in labeled examples of a few years previous. For instance, the types of knobs and keyhole guards employed, the careful choice of wood, and the

Above: The maker's label for the late eighteenth century grandfather's clock case by Matthew Egerton, Jr., *right.*
Below: Detail of the hood and dial of this clock whose works were done by Leslie & Williams.

management of the inlay, are all associated with Egerton work; while the stained decorations, though new in pattern, betray the earlier style of workmanship. The former feathering of the grain is omitted, and a certain decline in general quality is evident. The reasons for this do not necessarily reflect upon the ability of the surviving members of the Egerton family, but may properly be charged to the rapid degeneration of Classic taste, and to the advent of ingenious machinery for the mass production of such legs as those which support this desk.

In the absence of further labeled specimens, it may be instructive to study such contemporary evidence of the firms activities as is preserved at New Brunswick and elsewhere. In a list of furniture made by Matthew Egerton & Son, it may be learned that the firm constructed mahogany bureaus at $20, $25, and $35; a bookcase at $50; a pair of end tables at $25; a work stand at $13; pine dressing tables at $3 and $10; and a cherry bureau at $10. Evert, the surviving member of the old firm, after the death of his father, also made such pieces, as well as a side table costing $35, square stands, wash stands, and bedsteads of several varieties.

A memorandum, dated December 7, 1838, of the property and credits of "Matthew Egerton, late of the City of New Brunswick in the County of Middlesex and state of New Jersey, deceased, which were left unadministered upon by John B. Egerton decd. the original administrator," lists the following:

Map of New Jersey	$2.00
Beetle wedge and wheel Barrow	4.00
Gold Watch	25.00
two guns	5.00
New Cabinet furniture in possession of Eliza Egerton administratrix of Evert Egerton decd.—remains of the firm of Matthew Egerton and Sons	108.00
Ten Shares of New Brunswick fire insurance Stock	125.00
Abraham Buckelew note & interest	21.38
Evert Egerton due Bill and interest	131.00
Do Do due for benches & tools	150.30
Do Do· Do for Cabinet Materials	131.74

Evert Egerton balance on settlement the cash account
of the late firm 335.95
Pew in Dutch Church 130.00
½ Sign Board over the shop door 4.00

Cabinet Materials in the Store House

Stock of Mahogany Boards & Plank 12.00
Six sets high Bed Posts $10.50—4 Sets French do $2.25 .... 12.75
Three Do. Field Do. $2.00—4 Sets Stump Posts $1.50 ...... 3.56
35 feet Curled Maple joist @ 3 cts $1.05—Lot Cot joist $3 ... 4.05
Lot of Bilsted Coffin Stuff $5—2 Lot Bed tops $4 .... 9.00
Lot of Bilsted Coffin Stuff $5—Lot 2 in poplar plank $10 .... 15.00
Lot of Cherry Boards $2.50—Lot inch Bilsted $2.50 ..... 5.00
Entire Lot of Walnut Coffin Stuff 15.00
Lot of inch Walnut $3.50 Lot Maple Boards $3.00 ...... 6.50
Lot of White Pine in the Garret of Store House 35.00
Remaining lumber in the Store house 1.00

Barn Lumber

Entire stock of ½ Poplar on the Barn Stairs 18.00
Lot of Cherry joist $3.50—Lot of Swingle $1 .... 4.50
A Lot of Prime Cherry in the Barn 85.00

Stock of Furniture Ready Made in The Ware Room

Three Cherry Breakfast tables with drawers 13.50
Four do. Dining tables @ $5.50 .... 22.00
two do.   do.   @ $6.00 .... 12.00
One Cherry Bureau 10.00
Three Mahogany Breakfast tables @ $11 .... 33.00
one do. Dining table 12.00
Scroll Block Side table 25.00
Four Lyre Front Bureaus @ $25 .... 100.00
Dressing Bureau Marble top 40.00
  do   Mahogany top 30.00
  do   do 25.00
Two pier tables @ $40 .... 80.00
Two Sofas @ $60 .... 120.00
One Wash Stand or Closet—Marble top 18.00
Cherry Cradle $4—two Book Shelves @ $2 .... 8.00
One painted Wash Stand 3.00
One Childs Cribb (Painted) 5.00

```
Seven field Bedsteds @ 4$ 75 cts ..................... 33.25
Five high Post Bedsteds @ 5$ 50 cts ................. 27.50
One French do $4 One do $5 One Stump do $2.50 ..... 11.50
Two single Cotts @ 3 Dolls 6$ one double do 4$ ...... 10.00
Two Painted Wash Stands @ $20/—$5
   two Candle do @ 8/ ............................. 7.00
```

Further than this, little is known of the business and its output; but when the second Matthew's estate was settled, there was mentioned a "Claw Table" and for the next twenty years it seems to have been a treasured family piece, so that it ís possible that he may have fabricated carved articles in addition to inlaid work.

As already remarked, no labeled or otherwide proved example of the work of John Bergan Egerton has yet been located. But, very fortunately, among the papers of a renowned New Brunswick lawyer, recently presented to Rutgers College, occurs an inventory of John B. Egerton's "goods, & chattels, rights and credits & personal property," appraised at $5,612.31, on May 4, 1838.

Mention of a number of bonds, notes, twenty-five shares of stock of the New Brunswick Fire Insurance Company, and a Silver Patent lever watch, valued at thirty dollars, precedes the statement of more important items connected with the business. This list seems so valuable for reference that it is here quoted. The lumber mentioned shows that mahogany, curled maple, cherry, poplar, walnut, and white pine were used by this member of the Egerton family of cabinetmakers, in addition to the bilsted and walnut coffin materials. The items of furniture, including tables, bureaus, sofas, candlestands, bedsteads, and wardrobe, are self-explanatory, and will served as a schedule of work done by John Bergan Egerton, prior to May 4, 1838. The tools are those customarily found, even today, in cabinet shops. "A Box With Carving tools, gauges, &c." would indicate that the "Lyre Front Bureaus" and other pieces received this treatment. The "Hard Ware" included glass and brass knobs, castors, drawer locks, and table hinges.

A secretary-bookcase probably made by Matthew Egerton and Son, almost certainly by some member of the family.

Early in 1837, Matthew Egerton, Junior, departed this life. Two of his sons, John Bergan and Evert, died in the following year, from what cause, it is not known. The three generations of New Brunswick cabinetmakers had all passed away, and by July 17, 1838, the heirs had disposed of their interest to Isaac G. Sillcocks, who announced, through the press, the change of ownership, as follows:

CABINET WAREHOUSE

THE SUBSCRIBER having taken the well-known Shop and Ware House in Burnet Street lately occupied by Matthew Egerton, and employed competent and experienced workmen, respectfully informs his friends and the public generally, that he is now prepared to execute all orders in the above line in a workmanlike style, with promptness and fidelity—and solicits a share of patronage.

He keeps constantly on hand, a general assortment of CABINET WARE, which he will be happy to sell on as good terms as at any other establishment in this city, or EXCHANGE FOR COUNTRY PRODUCE. ISAAC G. SILLCOCKS

—W. M. HORNOR JR.

John Jelliff, Cabinetmaker of Newark

T HE town and city of Newark has had many chair and
cabinetmakers in its day. In the eighteenth century Isaac
Alling, Matthias Bruen, and John Mann were active craftsmen,
each maintaining his independent trade on or near Broad Street.
By the turn of the century, furniture-making was evidently a
competitive and thriving business that reached far beyond town
limits. Henry B. Fearon of England after visiting New York in
1817 went on to write two years later in *Sketches of America:*

> "Chair making here, as in the town of Newark, ten miles distant, is
> an extensive business. Newark is a manufacturing town of some
> importance: carriages and chairs are made on a very extensive scale,
> chiefly for the southern markets.... The cabinet work executed in
> New York is light and elegant, superior, I am inclined to believe, to
> English workmanship. Cabinet-makers' shops of which there are
> several in Greenwich-street, contain a variety, but not a large stock.
> They are generally small concerns, apparently owned by journey-
> men,...they state their business to have been at one time good, but
> that there is now too much competition."

John Jelliff may justly be regarded as Newark's foremost
cabinetmaker. He was born at Norwalk, Connecticut, on July
30, 1813, the fourth of eight children born to Hezekiah and

Nancy Jelliff. His great-grandfather, Thomas Jelliff, had come from England in 1745 and bought a tract of land in Norwalk. John's mother, Nancy Bennett, was a Quaker who came from Huntington, Long Island.

On August 7, 1828 or '29, John was apprenticed to Lemuel M. Crane of Newark to learn "the art, trade and occupation of cabinetmaking." Presumably John Jelliff completed his apprenticeship in the late summer of 1835 for, as a "freeman" and established in his own business, he cast his vote at the first charter election in Newark on April 11, 1836. Also, he married Mary Marsh in the Dutch Reformed Church on March 16, 1836. Following their marriage, John lived for a brief period at 13 Fair Street and his widowed mother made her home with him and Mary Jelliff. The family soon moved to 206 Washington Street—a more fashionable area—and Jelliff maintained an office and shop at 301-303 Broad Street, south of Market and next door to the site of the Kinney Building. A few years later he purchased four acres of land and built a home next to the Peshine property along Elizabeth Road in a "newer" section of town. A street has since been cut through and the house is now at 70 Johnson Avenue. Jelliff was interested in the founding of Grace Church and became one of its vestrymen.

In 1838 John Jelliff and Thomas L. Vantilburg were in partnership at 333 Broad Street, near the City Hall. They advertised as "Manufacturers and Dealers in Cabinet Furniture, Mahogany Chairs, Sofas, Mattrasses, etc. Will be found at all times at their Ware Rooms, a splendid assortment of Cabinet Ware of the latest patterns, cheap for cash." In 1846, Jelliff added to his customary notice "Coffins made to order."

In spite of the fact that by 1850 other establishments were beginning to sell machine-made products, Jelliff consistently refused to make anything but hand-made and hand-carved furniture. He bought his wood at auction in Newark and let it season about two years before using it. Today there is no evidence of warping, the drawers of chests slide out and in as though they had been newly waxed. His favorite woods were walnut and rosewood, with occasional use of maple of fruit-wood as inlay. In 1847 Jelliff was awarded a silver medal by the Essex County Institute "for the best specimen of mahogany chairs exhibited." In 1850 the county census gave the estimated value of his property at $30,000.

John Jelliff has been termed a "straight-laced Yankee" and he appears to have been wary of progress in any form. One of his grandchildren recalls that he sternly objected when a bathtub was installed in his home (did Mary Jelliff have a mind of her own?). On the other hand, he believed in athletics for his seven daughters and when they married he cautioned each to keep her money separate from her husband's and thus be independent. Furthermore, he supplied them with most of their furniture. The Jelliffs had three sons but none lived to maturity. In the Museum's collection is a charming silhouette showing John and Mary Jelliff, Grandmother Nancy in Quaker garb, and three little daughters, the youngest seated on her mother's lap.

At the death of David Alling, "Fancy Chair Maker," in 1855 Jelliff took over his business which was bought by Peter G. McDermit four years later. A painting of David Alling's house and shop may be seen at the New Jersey Historical Society. The duplicate is owned by the Newark Museum and was illustrated in its *Proceedings* for October, 1954.

The partnership between Jelliff and Vantilburg only lasted five years and for another eighteen years John Jelliff continued alone, designing and carving a great deal of the furniture produced in his shop. His designs, many of which have survived on scraps of paper and the backs of envelopes, followed the styles of the period: "Gothic" associated with the 1840's; "French rococo" made fashionable in Europe and America by the Empress Eugenie in the 1850's; "Italian Renaissance." These styles must have seemed refreshingly light in contrast to the heaviness of late Empire furniture. The Museum has two side chairs in pseudo-Gothic style made in 1838 and about

Examples of Jelliff furniture; *above,* a rosewood desk made for Mrs. Daniel McMurtry, and *below,* an armchair known as a gentlemen's chair, made around 1855.

1860. A rosewood desk expressing the "French rococo" was made for Mrs. Daniel McMurtry who was Mary Roff, daughter of Stephen Roff whose tavern was on Branford Place, Newark. A double parlor set in rosewood, consisting of sofas, arm and side chairs, illustrates the "Italian Renaissance." The side chairs have short arm brackets to conform with the hoop skirts of the period. Even the carved tassels suspended from the top rails of the chairs are in keeping with the silk tassels then popular as dress trimming.

About 1860, Jelliff took as partner Henry H. Miller, who had long been his foreman and had once been a favored apprentice living in the Jelliff household. It is said that the boy's place at table was next to Mary Jelliff so she could be sure he had enough to eat. At one time John Jelliff had thirty apprentices learning the trade in his shop.

It might be well to explain here that the logical progression in trade was, first, the apprentice who spent some six or seven years learning a craft, then the graduate apprentice or "freeman" who might be the journeyman or workman hired by the day, then foreman and master craftsman. Throughout the eighteenth and first part of the nineteenth century—until factory methods prevailed—a master craftsman had his own shop where he was helped by apprentices, journeyman, and, perhaps, a foreman, depending on the size of the business.

The Newark city directory for 1865-66 carries a full-page notice under the firm name of John Jelliff & Co., "Churches, Hotels, Banks, Lodges, Offices, etc., Furnished to Order, in the best Manner, and always at the lowest Market Prices *For Ready Cash!*

After 28 years of successful business in manufacturing, he said no more than this: "Our Furniture is still made in the best manner, as heretofore, and all of it warranted as represented. Our rooms are spacious, stock large and well assorted. Give us a call before purchasing." The firm was still located at 301 and 303 Broad, near Market Street.

By 1880 the firm had moved to 794-796 Broad Street, and advertised as "Manufacturers of Parlor, Library, Dining Room and Chamber Furniture...Church, Bank, Lodge and Office Furniture, Mantel and Pier Glasses, (Best Spring Beds Made)." Jelliff and Miller continued together until 1890 when the former withdrew. Jelliff's death occured on July 2, 1893.

The fine workmanship of John Jelliff and his staff speaks for itself. Pieces made by Jelliff show that he was a craftsman of marked ability and taste, with a good sense of proportion, a keen eye for detail, and a carver's skill that should receive due recognition.   —MARGARET E. WHITE

Furniture of Monmouth County

WHILE much is recorded of the history of Monmouth County, New Jersey, both before and after the Revolutionary War, very little information has been found regarding the early cabitmakers, pewterers, silversmiths, and other artisans. Monmouth County has been primarily agrarian, and most of the early houses were farmsteads, the furnishings necessarily of the simpler sorts. Probably no cabinetmakers of the stamp of Benjamin Randolpf or Duncan Phyfe worked here, though a general statement that every cabinetmaker capable of fine work gravitated to the nearby cities of Philadelphia or New York would not be true. We do find many pieces of purely local accent that show excellent design and finished workmanship.

In the absence of labels, knowledge of the origin of many pieces can be based only on the frequency with which certain characteristics are found in certain sections. In the area of Middletown a number of well-made early tables, as well as lowboys and highboys, have been found with a distinctive Monmouth County variant of the Dutch foot, suggesting the period between 1730 and 1770.

This foot is shown in the cherry or applewood table which has

Above: A four-legged applewood drop-leaf table with a cabriole leg and the "Middletown foot."
Below left: A cherry lowboy with claw-and-ball foot.
Below right: Applewood tilt table.

a fully developed cabriole leg. This table is part of the furniture in the original Doctor Taylor house in Middletown, purchased some time ago from one of the heirs, so we believe it is unquestionably of Middletown provenance.

The characteristic pointed pad foot appears also on a six-legged mahogany table with a modified cabriole leg. The oval top is well designed to show the graceful base, and the mahogany is straight-grained and heavy, suggestive more of the Chippendale era than the Queen Anne. We believe it to have been made in the mid-1770's. In both these tables the top is secured to the frame by means of a chestnut member dovetailed across the frame at each end, extending beyond the frame, and these cross members are screwed to the top.

Another interesting detail of these tables is the addition of a four-inch piece of half-round molding on the underside at each corner of the top to "finish" the circle where the drop-leaf molding shows. Still another table with similar characteristics and construction details, but with claw-and-ball feet, was formerly in the Historical Society Museum at Freehold. It seems likely that all these tables were by the same maker.

The same "Middletown foot" occurs on a lowboy formerly exhibited at Marlpit Hall in Middletown. Similar to this and to other Monmouth County pieces in design is the lowboy shown but it has claw-and-ball feet of so-called New York type. This lowboy is cherry, with molded top and shaped corners. It was found in West Long Branch, and is believed to have been part of the original furniture of the Wardell family. Other Wardell pieces have shown up from time to time, and the old house is still in good repair.

The cabriole leg occurs again on the circular pedestal table which employs the "turn-and-tilt" principle, providing space economy with serviceability. We have seen a number of examples in Monmouth County, all having similar character-istics, so that we fell certain that they must have been the work of local makers. The tilt table shows this characteristic pedestal

Left: Applewood secretary with dovetail-corner bracket foot.
Below: Cherry low cupboard with dovetail-corner bracket foot.

with generous ball and well-turned shaft. The three legs are fully cabriole, and terminate in a rounded version of the snake foot. The four columns which make up the "bird-cage" are miniatures of the center pedestal. The wood in this table is apple, dense and heavy, and the top is made in three pieces, using narrow but full width of the log boards. A molding forms the dish top.

Another type of foot that seems a distinguishing feature of Monmouth County furniture is a straight bracket which is dovetailed instead of mitered at the corner. This is shown in the applewood secretary and the low cherry cupboard both so similar that they must have been made by the same cabinetmaker, probably in the 1750-1770 period. These pieces have all been traced to or near West Long Branch, one of the early settlements in Monmouth County. While descendants of many

A bannister-back armchair and corner chair, both attributed to Maps.

of the early families still live in West Long Branch, information regarding early artisans there is elusive and fragmentary.

We do know, however, of a cabinetmaker named Maps who worked in West Long Branch in the Revolutionary period and earlier, and we show two examples of his work. The bannister-back armchair still has its old rush seat, woven in checker design. Its stiles and front stretchers are well turned, and the shaping of the arms adds comfort as well as grace. The corner chair shows a similarity of workmanship, combining good turning and proportion, and we believe it to be contemporary with the bannister chair. Its seat is also the original rush, made in the checkered manner with four strands alternating. The cresting rail forms the arms which terminate in shaped ends. We have seen a number of these Maps chairs, including ladderbacks and children's chairs, all with comparable turnings. Maps' working life covered quite a span, and his later work deteriorated in design.

During the Empire period a cabinetmaker named Alexander Low turned out fine veneered pieces, and some heavy mahogany furniture of this period is reputed to have been made by a craftsman named Maggs. We still find the earlier pieces by cabinetmakers of the Revolutionary era in Monmouth County, and it is for these examples that collectors will continue to seek.

—ELIZABETH WYMAN

The Ware Chairs of South Jersey

S O many of the so-called rush-bottom, ladder-backed chairs can claim their origin in South Jersey, that it may be interesting to trace their history. Although not in the same class with the finer mahogany and walnut examples by the master craftsmen who followed in the footsteps of Chippendale and Sheraton, these sturdy chairs were used in most of the farmhouses as well as in the better homes of the villages throughout South Jersey. And a great number of them were made by members of the Ware family.

The first member of this family to learn the chairmaking trade was Maskell Ware, who lived near Roadstown in Cumberland County, New Jersey. Maskell was born December 13, 1766, and lived to be seventy-nine years of age. As a boy, he was apprenticed to John Laning, a chairmaker in Greenwich, Cumberland County. He was, indeed, living with the Lanings at the time of the capture of Salem by the British forces in the year 1778.

After learning the trade of chairmaking, Maskell returned to Roadstown to open his own shop. He was an expert workman. His chairs had broad lines and were well proportioned. Their

A straight chair of curly maple by Maskell in 1790 with a heavy ball stretcher in front, and rare use of a scrolled skirt for the seat. Note the careful graduation of the back slats and the ball and point finials of the stiles.

comfort is hard to surpass. The fact that so many of them have survived proves that they were well made.

Maskell Ware usually used swamp maple, curly or plain, for his frames. At times he used walnut for the wide shaped rockers. Only native material was employed and this was gathered in the vicinity of the maker's own home. As soon as the wood was dry on the outside, though still partly green, the chair was "framed up." Front and back posts were turned on an old jig pole lathe. The rungs, however, were turned of thoroughly dry wood, while the slats were hewn by hand. No nails were needed, because the parts fitted very tightly after the green posts had shrunk on the dried rungs.

Rushes for the seats were gathered in the marshes during July of each year. The triangular reeds, or "three square" as the Wares call them, were the particular rushes needed. They grow in certain marshy spots of South Jersey—Reedy Island, and near Hancock's Bridge—possibly in other places. After having been cut and carried home in bundles, the rushes were spread open like fans to cure. When the top ends were sufficiently pliable to twist, the sheaves were bound together at the end, and were spread so that the thick end could cure. Dampness meant ruin; accordingly, if a shower came up, men and boys hurried to the field to stand the rushes up like corn shocks. If favorable weather the rushes could be cured in two weeks.

Two styles of rushing were used: the "straight," in which each strand overlapped another; and the "checkered," where four strands overlapped the next four strands, making checker diagonals across the chair seat. It is sometimes thought that the straight style is the older, but I find that Maskell used the checkered seats in many of his earliest chairs. The straight chair shown is one of a half dozen made of curly maple by Maskell in 1790. This is the only example of Ware chairs I know of where a scrolled apron or skirt is used around the rush seat. An occasional example is found with a one-inch strip, or casing, binding the edges of the chair bottom. Sometimes white

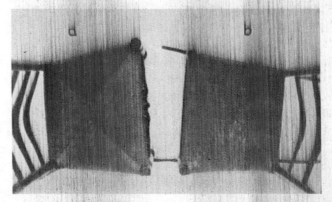

Above: Examples of rush seats of Ware chairs, straight at *"a,"* and at *"b,"* checkered rushing.

Right: A rocker made by Maskell prior to 1800 with finely shaped arms and heavy turnings at the front stretcher.

Below: Various knobs used by the Wares, all with a fine double line about the middle. The globular knob is characteristic of Maskell's work, the oval topped with a point is that of Maskell's son, John, and the elliptical, sharply pointed knob is the work of George Ware.

porcelain-headed tacks or brass tacks were used to fasten this casing to the frame. The seat has checkered rushing.

Maskell's work may be particularly distinguished by the ball turnings that he used on the front rung (or "round" as the Wares say), the turnings on the front posts, and the round knobs which finish the back posts. His patterns were distinctly globular. Other makers used pear-shaped or oval turnings.

These chairs were made for various uses. There were dining room chairs with five slats; later, with four, then three. The heavier barroom chairs had two slats with no knobs on the posts. Then there were ladies' four or five slat sewing chairs with rockers, junior rockers with three slats, and a few children's chairs and stools. Heavy five-slat straight chairs with arms and with ball knobs for feet were also made. The five-slat rocking chairs with shaped arms and rockers and ball turnings on the front rung are considered the finest of all Maskell Ware's work.

Seven sons and four daughters came to Maskell and his wife Hannah. They were: Thomas, Dec. 1792-1867; John, Jan. 1795-1870; Mary; William, April 1799-1881; Elizabeth; Hannah; Reuben, July 1806-1880; Ruth; Maskell 2nd, Aug. 1811-1905; Dan, April 1814-1901; Richard, 1816-1897.

These seven sons learned their father's trade; five of them made it their life work. It is no doubt due to the teachings of the father that so many of the sons were successful in their chosen trade, since it is a known fact that he laid much stress on the priceless value of time. A quotation which he frequently used was: "Time lost is forever lost and can never be regained."

This same Maskell had very strict ideas of right and wrong. It is told that an order for chairs had been filled for a man in Salem. A wagon was sent for the goods late on Saturday afternoon so that they could be loaded ready to start back on Sunday morning. But Maskell Ware would not allow the chairs to be taken out of the yard until Monday morning; for, said he, "Sunday is no day to parade merchandise through the country."

The sons of Maskell were, in their turn, blessed with sons,

Examples of comparative turnings used by the Wares.

a. By Thomas Ware, *circa* 1820?
b. By John Ware, *circa* 1850 or later.
c. By William Ware, *circa* 1850 or later.

In the shaping and disposition of the back slats and in the turnings, although these are weaker than those of Maskell, those produced by William appear to have clung closest to the old tradition, even though exceptionally light and dainty in construction.

many of whom learned the trade of their grandfather. It was customary for these sons to work in their father's shop until they were twenty-one years of age. In this way the business was carried on—all learning the trade and some practising it. In the next generation so many other and more remunerative occupations for young men developed that few of the Wares followed the one chosen by their ancestor.

As of the 1920's George Ware of Roadstown, New Jersey (a great-grandson of Maskell) was the only member of the Ware family engaged in making chairs. He carried on the work of his people in the old way with one exception. He used gasoline instead of foot power for his lathe. Arthur Ware of Salem, Thomas Harry Ware of Marlboro, and possibly one or two others, supplied new rush seats and repaired chairs, but they did not make them.

The designs and turnings of chairs varied with the different members of the family, though the manner of working remained the same. This may be accounted for by the fact that, after learning their trade, many of the Wares opened shops or small factories of their own in various parts of Cumberland and Salem Counties.

The knobs with two faint lines around the middle were usually used on all Ware chairs. The globular knob was made by Maskell, Sr.; those having a small, rounded top on an oval knob were made by John, Maskell's son. The long elliptical knob with the sharp-pointed piece on top is the pattern always used by George Ware.

Only Maskell, Sr. used the large balls on the front rung. Dan used smaller and more nearly pear-shaped turnings while he worked for his father, while his later work shows a decided difference. George Ware, of the present generation, has used some of the larger turned designs in his work—as did Samuel, his cousin (now deceased)—but the pointed knobs and the sharp lines easily identify such pieces.

Reuben sometimes used a large front turning on large chairs,

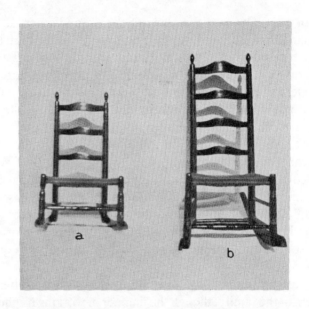

Examples of chairs made by Reuben Ware, *"a"* being a child's rocker *circa* 1830 or later, *"b"* being a sewing chair *circa* 1825, *"c"* being a rocker *circa* 1860 and *"d"* being an armchair *circa* 1828.

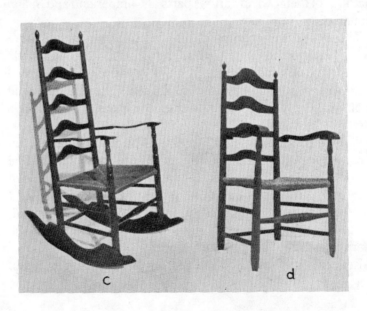

and small turning on others. Notice the thinner rungs made by William, also the plainer ones of John's and Thomas' chairs.

Thomas, the eldest son, did not use elaborate turnings on his chairs. He was fond of a decoration consisting of quarter-inch gouges arranged in groups. The posts of the stool shown are known to have been made by Thomas. He is said to have used only this turning on all of his work. John, the second son, was fond of introducing pairs of rings of convex outline. These rings were about a quarter of an inch wide. This same turning will be found variously placed on John's chairs; sometimes in three places on the front rung, and in two on the back posts and on the front posts. The turning is not deep enough to show in the picture, but all four of John's chairs pictured—the two rocking chairs, the child's high chair and the low bent back chair—carry the same decoration.

William is said to have made the lightest chair of all the Wares. Where the others used posts one and one-half or one and one-quarter inches in diameter, William turned out posts that measured three-quarters of an inch to one inch in diameter. The turnings on the front posts resemble those used by his father, but the front rung is thin. All the present Wares, when interviewed, agreed that "Uncle William made a dainty chair."

The child's rocking chair was made by Reuben, whose chairs are strong and well made. The lady's sewing chair is known to have been made by him in 1825. The posts are very heavy. Reuben's later work, about 1860, is illustrated in the five-slat rocking chair with arms. Also shown is a crude, heavy chair made in 1828. Notice the wide, heavy arms in the same design as the lighter ones of the rocker.

Maskell, Jr. and Richard learned to make chairs in their father's shop but did not follow the trade after reaching maturity.

Dan, a younger son, showed more originality in his work than any of his brothers. While all of the brothers used only swamp maple—sometimes curly maple—for their work, Dan used

Below: A late rocker of Daniel Ware, *circa* 1845 with turnings showing little of the early vigor of the heavier examples.

every kind of native wood. The proportions are excellent and the turnings the best of their particular kind. The slats in the back vary in size—a narrow one at the bottom and the rest graded to the widest one at the top. The arms are nearly three inches at the widest part and their curve exactly fits the relaxed arm and hand. They were hewn by hand from solid pieces.

The earlier rocker with the pear-shaped front rung shows a chair of curly maple, known to have been made when Dan worked for his father. The front rung or round shows the father's influence, but it is not a copy of Maskell's.

So far as is known, Dan always used the checkered style of rushing, in which four strands overlap four strands, instead of showing single laps. Many of the other chairmakers of the family used both styles, but Dan used only the one. Dan frequently used walnut for his finer chairs and, at times, combined different woods in the same chair. His tools were few and of the crudest sort. Time, thought and skill made his chairs what they are—a joy to the collector and a comfort to those who use them.

The rockers are not distinguishing features of any Ware chairs. The wide, pointed rockers were used by all the family on the earlier chairs, and the style varied but little. The narrow, plain rockers were a later style.

The designs used in chair arms vary but little in this family. Dan's arms are broad and gracefully curved, while the arms turned out by the others are, for the most part, copied from those of the father, Maskell. They are uniformly vigorous and well proportioned.   —MABEL CRISPIN POWERS

The Gardner Touch

VISUALIZE a Sunday School room of a century ago. It is registration day for the lower grades. Proud parents have brought their progeny to the door and have quickly departed. Small people are overwhelmed by excitement and confusion and begin to fidget. Meahwhile inquisitive eyes have surveyed the room for the usual tippy three-legged stools and backless benches but instead find *chairs with arms,* just like the grownups use. Along the back and seat edges are shiny brass tacks. Church windows and a star are punched out of the wood. When tried out, these wonderful chairs have no sharp edges that push and poke for back and seat are all in one, sort of *slide-y* like. The pleasure and comfort takes over, peace reigns, and the lesson can now begin.

It has been said that each man's work is a portrait of himself. In this chair the character of George Gardner is revealed: an inventive genius, a man of integrity, an artistry. His perception ensures that the "user" is united with the thing to be used. In making settees for lodges his designs guaranteed the body's comfort while perforated inscriptions inspired the mind: "VISIT THE SICK" or "FRIENDSHIP, LOVE & TRUTH," etc. A tiny

Detail of a grandfather clock with a case
made and labeled by Josiah Fithian of
Trenton *circa* 1790-1810. The entire height
measures one hundred inches, the width
twenty inches, and the depth ten inches.
Lent anonymously.

A slatback side chair attributed to Maskell
Ware of Roadstown, Cumberland County,
circa 1790-1810. The height measures
forty-five inches, the width seventeen
inches, and the depth fourteen inches.
From the collection of Robert J. Stokes.

Sunday School bench five feet long, carried the message "OUR
SAVIOUR'S HOME."

The Gardner families, ten brothers and sisters, came to
Clarksville, Hunterdon County, some time before 1863, for in
that year a Methodist Church record lists among its trustees the
names of George, William and John Gardner. These three men,
with their brothers Oliver and Joseph, had first been attracted to
Clarksville because of the commercial advantages of the branch
line of the Central Railroad of New Jersey and the healthful
atmosphere of the mountainous area.

The brothers had secured the right from a John Sperry to
manufacture his oval picture frame made of china, clay, glue
and whiteing. Increasing demand for such frames soon required
building a modern plant, one of the finest in the country—200
by 45 feet, three floors and a basement. From this factory the
frames in barrels were shipped all over the country.

Oliver and William were the practical businessmen. In the
first year of operation they reported tax payments of $18,000.
Two years later management salaries stood at $30,000 with an
overall profit of $75,000 and a plant inventory of $175,000.
Day and night shifts of workers became necessary, employing
nearly 700 persons from Clarksville and the surrounding areas.
Adult workers received from two to six dollars a day with
female personnel earning from $50 to $65 a month.

A hillside in town was laid out in planned subdivisions with
Gardner names attached for the homes built by each of the
children and their families. In the prosperity of an industrial
heyday Clarksville boomed and in honor of its benefactors the
town name was changed in 1871 to Glen Gardner, the name it
bears today.

Competition, however—and on home ground, too—brought
about reversals in production. Dr. T. Edgar Hunt and his
Hunterdon Manufactory was also producing these oval frames
and since he and the Gadrners were practically the only frame
factories in the East a price war developed which virtually

A child's Sunday school chair, 27 inches in height, manufactured by Gardner and Company of Glen Gardner, New Jersey, *circa* 1876.

ruined the industry. The Gardners bowed out, a decision which proved a blessing in disguise for now their interests could concentrate on the inventive genius of George.

On March 21, 1872, George Gardner was granted a patent on a chair seat, described as "made by gluing veneers together, so that the fibre of each layer crosses the other at right angles." With this, and additional patents, the Gardners established themselves as among the first in the country to exploit the potential of laminated wood for seat furniture. George Gardner had wisely reasoned that his invention would replace the then-popular cane seats with a product stronger, more durable, and cheaper. Wood was abundant and woodworking machinery made possible the cutting of great lengths of thin veneer inexpensively.

Gardner veneer seats would have the lightness and comfort of cane since the plywood had a similar give to it. The artist in George recognized that by perforating the wood in simple geometric designs a chair's appearance would be enhanced, its weight made lighter, and ventilation provided, all features to attract a market in mass seating.

His invention was an immediate success, receiving the First Premium medal at the American Institute fairs in New York in 1872 and again in 1873. The following year it was awarded a bronze medal at the Franklin Institute in Philadelphia. In that city's Centennial Exposition in 1876 Gardner & Company had an impressive display of chair types and optional seat patterns. An elaborate display at the Paris Universal Exposition of 1878 received great praise. The company's catalogues now contained testimonials from a variety of sources, including churches and Sunday Schools indicating pleasure with the product.

Two firms were now required for manufacturing Gardner products—Gardner Manufacturing Company supervised by William, and the Clarksville Chair Manufacturing Company supervised by George. A New York office was opened at 110

No. 3 Settee.—Suitable for Lodge Rooms, &c.

WE ISSUE A

SPECIAL CATALOGUE

—OF—

LODGE FURNITURE.

IF INTERESTED PLEASE SEND FOR IT.

No. 3 Settee.—Suitable for Lodge Rooms, &c.

Examples of Gardner benches from an 1884 catalogue.

Bowery Street and agents in Philadelphia were busy securing the eastern area business.

Under George Gardner's inventive genius more than 24 categories of seat furniture were created, each with numerous variations since variety was important in competing in a field dominated by upholstered furniture. Seating was now being produced for domestic use, for churches ("an anatomical pew"), for Sunday Schools, swivel or tilt chairs for office or library, folding chairs, settees for steamboats, railroad stations, hospital waiting rooms and lodges, reversible seats for trains, theater seats (one a fold-up type with wire rack underneath for an opera hat), and as many more types as one man's inventive mind could create.

Gardner patents were not confined solely to seating needs. The list included a twine dispenser, sewing machine cover, combination table-step ladder, boring machine, pressed wooden dish, a billiard table, air-compressor, adjustable belt-tightener, traction-rope railway, and more.

By the middle 1880's Gardner & Company faced strong competition from a number of manufacturers marketing similar products. Their enterprises came to a halt when flood waters coming down from the mountains washed away most of their factories. The families scattered, the brothers moving to New York and becoming wealthy men. Some years before George Gardner's death in 1915, at age 85, he is reported to have sold a patent for a stove device for $130,000.

Considering the thousands of pieces of furniture which Gardner & Company produced, all of sturdy construction, many examples likely exist today to entice the serious collector. The problem, as always, is where does one begin to start looking.   — ANNA WIRTZ DOMAS

Trenton
Clockmakers

E VERY school child knows of Washington's dramatic attack on Trenton the day after Christmas in 1776, and hardly a tourist visits the town today without at once asking to be shown where Washington crossed the Delaware. The early craftsmen of Trenton have been unduly neglected in favor of such picturesque events. To be sure, they were not great originators of design; but they plodded away diligently in their shops and maintained the standards of true craftsman by insisting that what was done must be well done. Some of them worked in wood, and were cabinetmakers of considerable distinction. Some were clockmakers. Some were workers in silver and in other metals, and others pioneered in pottery.

This article will discuss only the clockmakers and their achievements in one of the most exacting arts of a former day. Of all antique collectables, granting to each its own just claims to romance, there is nothing more romantic than a venerably tall and stately clock that has marked the hours and even the lives of generations gone. In the director's room of the Trenton Banking Company stood just such a clock. Colonel Isaac Smith, Revolutionary officer and the first president of this banking house, saw the hands of this timepiece turning their course over the large dial.

On the face of this clock is inscribed the name of its maker, William J. Leslie of Trenton. The case is about seven feet high and is finished in mahogany. Its design is simple, with few embellishments except a conservative scrolled top adorned with three brass balls, the middle one surmounted by the small figure of an eagle. The hours are indicated with Roman numerals, and the face is designed for declaring the phases of the moon and the days of the month, although these functions have not performed for a number of years.

The bank records show that, on April 8, 1806, the directors adopted a resolution requesting the cashier to buy "an eight-day clock" and to "cause it to be put in some convenient place in the Bank." This record refers, of course, to the present timepiece. At that period, the home of the bank was the remodeled Hunterdon County Court House, said to have been erected as early as 1719 and to have enjoyed the distinction of being Trenton's first public building.

Another tall and stately clock bearing the name of William J. Leslie graces the home of Charles P. Field, in Trenton. In so far as known, Mr. Field represents the third generation of the Field family to own the timepiece. His grandfather, Timothy Field, who operated an iron factory, is believed to have purchased it from Leslie. The clock occupied a prominent place in the office of the plant until it was rescued from a fire in the building by James D. Field, the father of the present owner. The case is similar in design to that owned by the Trenton Banking Company, except for the finials of the scrolled top.

Leslie is, in his way, as interesting as the clocks that he made. Little is known about him prior to his coming to Trenton in 1799. Probably he was a member of the family to which Robert Leslie, the Philadelphia clockmaker belonged. Early in 1799, in partnership with one Williams, he had an establishment at New Brunswick, about twenty-eight miles from Trenton. In the

Clock by William J. Leslie *circa* 1806 owned by the Trenton Banking Company.

spring of that year the firm expanded by opening a shop in Trenton in quarters on Warren Street previously occupied by Joseph Yates, an earlier clockmaker, who had removed to another part of the town. The exact location of the shop is in doubt; but what may be gleaned from advertisements suggests that it was just north of the Indian Queen Tavern, an old-time hostelry that occupied the present site of the Trent Theatre. At any rate, that was the location of the shop in 1805, for it was then advertised as the "Old Stand."

At some time prior to 1805, Leslie became the sole propietor of the business. In 1817 or early in 1818, he move elsewhere and presumably gave up his business to become a tavern keeper. His "Old Stand" was taken over by Hugh Ely, another clockmaker. In 1821 Leslie opened the Phoenix Hotel in a Warren Street dwelling that had been the official residence of President and Mrs. John Adams during the brief interval in 1799 when, owing to the prevalence of yellow fever in Philadelphia, Trenton was the national capital. In 1824 Leslie again shifted to a dwelling on the opposite side of the street, where he opened the Mansion House Hotel. When the temperance wave swept the country in the 1830's this establishment became one of the first, if not the first, temperance hotel in Trenton, and was called the "Temperance Inn."

Little is known of Leslie's personality, except that he was something of a wit. In the early 1800's those craftsmen who migrated to Trenton from such popular centres as Boston or New York, or who haild from foreign capitals, were very anxious to advertise their notable backgrounds so as to impress a new clientele. Leslie, apparently a man of considerable frankness and honesty, was equally ready to confess his won humble lineage. For example, in the *Trenton Federalist,* under date of January 28, 1805, he declared himself to be "William J. Leslie, Clock & Watch-Maker, (Not from London, Paris or Boston, but a native of New-Jersey)" and concluded a listing of his wares—and moral comments thereon—with a request for two apprentices, "Boys from the country will be preferred."

Leslie is believed to have been twice married, but the only marriage recorded is that to Ann Vandegrift, of Trenton, in 1803. In 1807-1808 he was town marshall, and a city assessor, 1808-1810. He died November 30, 1831, in the sixty-second year of his age.

Another clockmaker who possessed a sense of humor was Erastus Emmons, whose shop stood opposite the Indian Queen in the same neighborhood as Leslie's. His shop window afforded an excellent view of the old-time tippling house, where, we may be sure, very little took place of which he was not well aware. As the result of his observations he gave the tavern special mention in his advertisements. The one here quoted from the *Trenton Federalist,* July 16, 1807, is fairly typical:

WATCH MAKING

"Time is money," so saith Father Abraham, if I mistake not, in his sermon upon economy.

Such being the fact, it highly becomes all to mark well how it goes. The subscriber, therefore, again tenders his service to the public in the line of his profession.

TO MARK THE FLEETING MOMENTS AS THEY PASS

In repairing and putting into due order, watches, clocks, and time pieces, on the shortest notice, and most reasonable term, at his old stand in Warren Street, Trenton, nearly opposite the Temple of Bacchus, vulgarly called the Indian Queen Tavern, where all orders in the line of watch repairing will be thankfully received and punctually exectuted.

So, no more at present (as the girls end their love letters) from yours 'till death.   —ERASTUS EMMONS

Others who were contemporaries of Leslie and Emmons were Joseph Giles, J. L. Newton, John Parry, Joseph Yates, John Probasco, and James Huston, concerning each of whom a word.

Joseph Giles, who came from Boston, probably in the summer of 1804, opened a shop in Warren Street, under the

Clock by William J. Leslie owned by Charles P. Field of Trenton. The case for this clock, as well as the one previously illustrated in this article, have yet to be attributed to any known cabinetmaker. Both appear to be of the same hand.

printing office of the *Trenton Federalist.* In the paper for October 21, 1804, he announced his change of location:

> Joseph Giles, clock and watchmaker, respectfully informs his customers and the public that he has moved next door to Thomas M. Potter's Medicine Store, in Market Street, where he continues the business of Clock Making and watch repairing, which he will execute on the most reasonable terms.
>
> N.B. He will warrant his work to run well for one year, the cheapest kind of watches.

About the same time, J. L. Newton, "watchmaker and gilder from London," opened a shop in the town.

John Parry was a Philadelphia clockmaker who temporarily removed his business to Trenton in 1799 during the prevalence of yellow fever in his home city.

Joseph Yates was a member of the partnership of Yates and Kent, clock-and watchmakers, jewelers and silversmiths, who opened a shop in Trenton in the spring of 1789. For unknown reasons Kent presently retired. Yates continued as a clock- and watchmaker until 1803, when he removed to Freehold, New Jersey.

Probasco had a shop in the town for many years, where, it is said, Trenton's first town clock was produced. James Huston, an ingenious craftsman employed by Probasco, is named as the maker of this timepiece, which originally occupied a place in the steeple of the First Presbyterian Church. Later it was removed to the City Hall, where it did duty for many years. Huston died in Montreal, Canada, in 1822. For a number of years Probasco was the official custodian of the clock at a salary of $20 a year.

Hugh Ely, who took over the "Old Stand" near the Indian Queen Tavern first occupied by Yates and later by Leslie, was a native of Bucks County, Pennsylvania. He was born November 5, 1783, son of John and Margaret (Richards) Ely of Solebury. For a number of years he resided at New Hope, Pennsylvania, where he opened a shop early in 1800. A history of the Ely-Ryell-Stayce families compiled by Reuben P., Warren S., and

Daniel B. Ely says, "He was considered an expert in the manufacture of tall 'grandfather's clocks.'" The same volume further informs us that "many of his manufacture are still in use in his native county and elsewhere." Captain John S. Baily, of Buckingham, Pennsylvania, in his paper entitled, *The Early Clockmakers (Bucks County Historical Papers,* Vol. 1) mentions an ingenious clock Ely made for his step-brother. It "played the old familiar tunes of Yankee Doodle, Nancy Dawson and Beggar Girl."

Ely married Hannah, daughter of Isaac Wilson. He died in Trenton January 6, 1829.

One of the earliest Trenton clockmakers was Jacob Maus, who probably came from Philadelphia. It is likely he was in the town prior to 1780. June 1781 his shop was broken open and robbed of a number of articles. The following year he was located at the northeast corner of Queen and Second Streets (Broad and State Streets), now one of the busiest corners of the city. In the spring of 1784, he was doing business in Warren Street opposite the Indian King Tavern, a hostelry north of the original site of the Indian Queen.   —HARRY J. PODMORE

Isaac Brokaw, Jersey Clockmaker

IN the homes of many old families of Somerset, Middlesex, Union and Essex counties may still be seen tall case clocks, popularly known as grandfather clocks, the handiwork of Isaac Brokaw. Of graceful design and artistic finish enhanced by the patina of age, they display a dignity of which their owners may well be proud. Although the works are generally incased in solid or veneered mahogany with little or no ornamentation, some are found decorated with exquisite inlays combining box, ebony, tulip, amethyst or other rare woods. Only infrequently do we meet with cases of walnut, curly or birdseye maple.

Isaac, one of the five sons of John and Sarah Brokaw's family of nine children, was born in Hillsborough Township, Somerset County, New Jersey, in 1746 and died in Rahway in September 1826. He was married about 1766 to Elizabeth, daughter of Aaron and Elizabeth (Hatfield) Miller, of Elizabethtown, New Jersey.

It was with his future father-in-law, clockmaker Aaron Miller, that Brokaw learned his trade. As apprentices were generally indentured between the ages of fourteen and sixteen, it may be assumed that he began his apprenticeship not earlier than 1760 or later than 1762. It would appear, in his case, that the relationship existing between master and 'prentice was more like that of father and son. This is suggested not only because of Isaac's marriage to his master's daughter, but also by the provisions of Aaron Miller's will, which leaves "[to my] son Cornelius and my son-in-law Isaac Brokaw my clockmaking tools."

That Isaac was taught by one of considerable versatility in the field of mechanical arts is disclosed by the following announcement:

> Aaron Miller, clockmaker in Elizabethtown, East New Jersey, makes and sells all sorts of clocks, after the best manner, with expedition:—He likewise makes compasses and chains for surveying; as also church bells of any size, he having a foundry for that purpose, and has cast several which have been approved to be good; and will supply any person on a timely Notice, with any of the above Articles at very reasonable rates.

Shortly after his marriage, Isaac moved from Elizabethtown to his native village in Hillsborough Township, where he embarked upon the business of clockmaking. Inasmuch as we find an Isaac Brokaw described as a "silversmith" who had an account with John Vanderveer, merchant of Somerset County, running from 1769 until 1771, the question arises: Did Isaac combine silversmithing with clockmaking, or was the silversmith a different person?

Although the writer has never seen a Brokaw clock bearing any indication of its Hillsborough origin, it is definitely established that Isaac was making clocks in that place early during the Revolution.

> The Province Congress in 1776 ordered that the Committee of the Township of Hillsborough, in the County of Somerset, do leave in the hands of Mr Isaac Brokaw, clockmaker, thirty pounds weight of lead, he having represented to the convention that he could not carry on his trade without such quantity. Saturday, July 27 [1776].

After the deaths in 1779 of both his father-in-law Aaron

Miller and his brother-in-law Cornelius Miller, also a clock-maker, Elizabethtown was bereft of persons in this business. Embracing the opportunity thus afforded, Isaac promptly moved to Elizabethtown and proceeded to occupy the old shop in which the days of his apprenticeship had been spent. Here he continued to ply his trade until 1788 or 1789 when he moved to Bridgetown, now part of Rahway, leaving his son John in charge of the shop in Elizabethtown. After moving, he continued to make clocks until about 1816, when he turned over the business to his son Aaron.

Isaac and his wife Elizabeth (Miller) Brokaw had four children, John, Aaron, Cornelius and Ann. The sons followed in their father's footsteps, learning from him the art of clock-making. John was born in Hillsborough Township in 1767, was married August 10, 1788, to Rebecca, daughter of Andrew and Sarah (Ross) Miller of Westfield, New Jersey.

He worked with his father in the Elizabethtown shop, taking over the business in 1788 or 1789. An item in *Antiques Magazine* of May, 1944, refers to a tall clock bearing the inscription "John Brokaw, E. Town." Penciled or scratched inside the case is the date May 5, 1803, below which are initials "J.B." These notations may indicate the date when the clock was made or sold. Upon his father's retirement about 1816, John moved to Rahway where he continued to make and repair clocks. The date of his death is not known to the writer.

Aaron Brokaw, born in Hillsborough Township, June 23, 1768, was married about 1790 to Elizabeth, daughter of Phebe Tooker (Tucker?). He continued clockmaking until his death in Rahway, December 18, 1853. A direct descendant has stated that Aaron acquired all of his father's tools, among which was an ingenious gear-cutting machine that Isaac had devised early in his career. Upon Aaron's death, this device, together with a chest of tools, was acquired by one Patrick Clark, a repairer of clocks and watches who died at Scotch Plains in March 1887.

Cornelius Brokaw was born in Hillsborough Township

September 27, 1772, died in Plainfield, N.J., April 9, 1857, and is buried in Rahway. He was married to a daughter of Daniel Tucker, who died April 1817. His second wife was Martha Miller, daughter of Jonathan Terry, and widow of David Miller. For many years he made and repaired clocks, either alone or with his brother Aaron. Several clocks bearing his name have been seen by the writer. Sometime prior to 1846 he retired from business and moved to Plainfield.

Since the mechanisms of the clocks made by Isaac Brokaw and his sons vary little, if at all, in design or fabrication, why is there such diversity in the design and ornamentation of their cases? This is due to the fact that the mechanism alone was made and assembled by the clockmaker, whereas the case was built by a cabinetmaker in accordance with the design selected from illustrations in his books, or made from original designs incorporating the ideas of the purchaser. Doubtless in many instances cost was a deciding factor as to whether the case should be plain or ornate.

While it is probable that cases for Isaac's and his sons' clocks were constructed by various cabinetmakers, only a few bearing their labels can, with any degree of certainty, be identified. These are Richardson Gray, Abraham Rosett, Rossett & Mulford, and John Scudder.

That Richardson Gray of Elizabethtown made cases for some of the first clocks constructed by Isaac Brokaw after his removal from Hillsborough Township to Elizabethtown in 1779 is indicated by a clock which bears his label and has pasted on the inner side of the pendulum door a bill of sale for the clock, signed by Brokaw and dated Elizabethtown, March 22, 1780. Other Brokaw clocks with Gray's labels have been seen, but without indication of the date when the clock was made. However, we know they were all made prior to June 1803, because late in that month Gray sold his business and stock to Burrows & Howell. Richardson Gray, son of John and Amy (Richardson) Gray, was born in 1754 and died June 21,

1818, in his sixty-fifth year. His wife Elizabeth was born 1755 and died January 9, 1831, in her seventy-seventh year.

Although Burrows & Howell may have made cases, none has been found with their name. Shortly after Gray disposed of his business, a newcomer, Abraham Rosett, established a cabinet shop in Elizabethtown and his label has been found in Brokaw clocks. In the initial announcement of the opening of his shop he used as its preamble an innovation unique in the advertising of that day—a paraphrase of Hamlet's soliloquy:

> To brag of not to brag…that is the question, whether it is nobler to be passive and patient, wait the calls of custom, or swell the columns of a newspaper with feats of workmanship beyond compare.
>
> A. ROSETT, CABINET-MAKER
> *Near the Stone-Bridge*
>
> Having, since his residence here, received a small share of patronage unasked for, though he trusts not unmerited, acknowledges the favor, and solicits a continuance, hoping by a proper attention to business to claim a larger share, which will enable him to open, upon a more extensive scale, and thereby advance his own interest, to the satisfaction of those who may honor him with their commands.
>
> Furniture finished in as much taste, on as short notice, and at as light a rate as may be had anywhere—Produce received in payment—Mahogany boards, plank & joists for sale. Elizabethtown, Feb. 13, 1804.

On March 12, 1807, he published the following announcement:

> The subscriber having taken into partnership Abraham Marsh Mulford, the cabinet making business formerly conducted by him will, in the future, be carried on under the firm of Rosett & Mulford, at the same place where continuance of favors are still solicited…
>
> —ABRAHAM ROSETT

A notice in the local paper discloses that this association lasted only one year: "The partnership of Rosett & Mulford will expire on the 12th day of March next—a settlement of their accounts will of course be necessary. The business will be

One of the grandfather clocks made by Isaac Brokaw at Rahway (Bridge Town).

continued by the subscriber at the same place. Abraham Rosett." A clock by Isaac Brokaw has been seen bearing the Rosett & Mulford label. Rosett continued in business until his death. He was born in 1781 and died at Elizabethtown April 8, 1815. His wife Susan was born in 1786 and died in New York City April 26, 1847. Abraham Marsh Mulford was born May 8, 1794. He was married to Jane, daughter of John Burrows, January 31, 1808. She was born in 1788 and died May 13, 1850. Abraham died March 9, 1863.

Although John Scudder's label has been found in several cases made for Isaac Brokaw clocks, and in one or more cases made for his sons John and Cornelius, little is known of his life. He was born in Westfield, New Jersey, about 1773, and since he occasionally suffixed "Jr." to his name, it may be suspected that his father's name was also John. He was married first on January 29, 1794, to Chloe Sayres. His second wife, to whom he was married on March 24, 1811, was Susanna Miller. Sometime after 1815 Scudder and his family moved to Ohio.

While the foregoing is offered merely as a compendious account of an early artisan, it is noteworthy that in 1776 at the early of thirty, Isaac Brokaw's repute and competence in the field of clockmaking were recognized by the Provincial Congress. He attained the disinction of being the first to pursue his art in Hillsborough and Rahway, and was the second in Elizabethtown to ply at that craft. That his proficiency was inherited by his sons is attested by their having continued the family name in the annals of New Jersey clockmaking until 1853, a total period of over three-quarters of a century.

—ELMER T. HUTCHINSON

Glassware

Wistarberg and South Jersey Glass

A S I look back about ten years, to the beginning of my interest in early American glass, the field was virtually divided into two principal sections—*Stiegel* and *Wistarberg*. Of course, there was Sandwich glass; also bottles and flasks—the former generally dismissed as pressed, late, and of slight interest and little value, and the latter as junk, which only a "loon-a-tick" would think of collecting.

There were a few pioneers in the field of American glass, like the late Alexander Drake and Edwin Atlee Barber, who collected flasks and bottles, appreciating, probably, the wide and beautiful range of colors and the interesting designs found not only in the earlier plain and pattern-molded flasks, but also in the whisky flasks and bar bottles appearing after 1812 and blown in two-piece molds, in which designs of historical, patriotic, political, and similar import were cut. Perhaps these pioneers in a field of collecting held in contempt by the discriminating (spelled with very large capitals and pronounced with great relish) collectors of early glass—so-called *Stiegel* and *Wistarberg*—sensed, dimly perhaps, that the lowly and despised flasks, many of which bear names of the glass factory

Figure 1: Characteristic examples of South Jersey glass.

in which they were made, might prove connecting links in proving fine pieces of Stiegel and Wistarberg to have been blown at a time and place far removed from the day and locality of Baron Stiegel and of Caspar Wistar and his son Richard.

As for Sandwich, likewise dismissed with a shrug of disdain by the discriminating collector (again in large capitals) of early American glass, it came eventually into its own in so far as popularity was concerned; but even with the remarkable range which developed three or four years back for the *lace* and *snakeskin* glass, colored lamps, candlesticks, cup plates, and the like, few collectors realized that some of the finest blown glass produced in this country was made at Sandwich, as well as at the plants of the New England Glass Company, and at certain Pittsburgh factories, which likewise made much of the pressed glass generally classified as *Sandwich.*

The exquisite contact three-section mold glass of the finest types and patterns, described in the brief article by Helen A. McKearin in the August, 1924, number was, of course, generally collected by the early American glass collector of ten to twelve years ago; but it was quite generally, though erroneously, written and spoken of as Stiegel. It is interesting to note, in passing, that data which has come to hand during the past year or so identifies Sandwich as undoubtedly one source of some of the finest of this glass.

EARLINESS A MATTER OF TYPE, NOT OF DATE

S O much in the way of very sketchy and general comments regarding the field of early American glass; and let me make clear at the outset—*when I speak of early American glass I refer to type, pattern, decorative technique, and quality of glass, rather than to date.* The collector of Americana does not think of the period from 1825 to 1860 as *early,* and chronologically it is not; but, in the field of American glass, many of the finest specimens, bearing every apparent indication of eighteenth century production, were blown in relatively obscure factories scattered throughout the New England states, New York, Pennsylvania, New Jersey, Ohio, Maryland, and that part of what was then Virginia but is now West Virginia, during the early and mid-nineteenth century period.

In the choicest collections, those privately owned and those in our museums, many of the best specimens of early American glass, referred to as *Stiegel* or *Wistarberg,* were actually produced during that much later period. Nor does this fact detract one jot or tittle from their interest or their beauty in form, color, and design; neither does it lessen their rarity.

WISTARBERG AN OVERWORKED TERM

WITH the exception of *Stiegel,* not any word in the realm of American glass has been as loosely used and greatly abused as *Wistarberg.* At first every fine piece of green, blue or amber glass too heavy to qualify under the supposed Stiegel distinctive quality of lightness in weight, and all those pieces with certain decorative characteristics, such as the crimped foot, threaded neck, and superimposed layer of glass tooled into a frieze-like effect sometimes called lily-pad, were Wistarberg. Collectors and museums bought and cherished them as such. South Jersey many of these specimens undoubtedly were, but I doubt that there are half a dozen pieces of glass in existence which can be *authenticated* as the product of the factory of Caspar Wistar and his son Richard.

For years Boston pickers, traveling every week from Charles Street, gathered such pieces from private homes or from shops of small dealers throughout the highways and byways of Massachusetts, Connecticut, New Hampshire, New York, Pennsylvania, or wherever their quest for the antique led them. They were, quite naturally, not particularly interested in early American glass from the standpoint of study and investigation; and consequently expended little or no effort to secure infor-

Figure 2: South Jersey glass including deep blue vase of a late form; clear, light blue bowl of earlier make; and pitcher by Joel Duffield at the Whitney Glass Works which, while a nineteenth-century piece, is a beautiful specimen of South Jersey glass.

Figure 3: Typical pieces of the Whitney Glass Works, all heavy, amber examples similar in color and quality to the flasks which the Whitney people made for many a brand of whiskey in the days when good liquour was the rule—and cheap.

mation as to the history and probable origin of their finds. Collectors wanted Stiegel and Wistarberg, and therefore, Stiegel and Wistarberg these pieces were.

We know quite definitely that the commercial products of the Wistar factory were window glass, bottles, snuff cannisters, and so on; and this is true also of the the factory of the Stanger Brothers, which started at Glassboro, New Jersey, about 1775,* and of various other factories which came into being throughout South Jersey between 1775 † and 1850.

The lovely bowls, pitchers, mugs, vases, candlesticks, and the like, which were blown in these factories, treasured and handed down to posterity, later to delight and enchant the collector of early American glass, were the products of individual workmen, blown offhand for themselves, their families or friends, in accord with the prevailing custom of permitting workmen to use for their own purposes the fag-end of the pot of molten glass. This same custom prevailed in practically every bottle or window-glass factory which operated between 1775 and 1850 throughout the New England states, New York, Pennsylvania, Maryland, Ohio, and Virginia, as well as in New Jersey.

THE EMERGENCE OF "SOUTH JERSEY"

ABOUT sixty years ago, at the time of the sale of Dr. Pleasant Hunter's last collection, in November, 1920, at the American Art Galleries, many thoughtful students of early American glass began to realize that not all of the glass called *Wistarberg* could possibly have been made in and survived from the original factory of Caspar Wistar and his son Richard. From that time on, therefore, glass of this type began to be spoken and written of under the more general term of *South Jersey;* but, naturally, many of the finest examples still were,

---

*It is now known that the glassworks was built on land acquired by Solomon Stamper by 1780 and was blast by 1782.
† 1780's.

and are today referred to as *Wistarberg*. In an introductory note in the auction catalogue of Dr. Hunter's sale, J. B. Kerfoot writes most interestingly of South Jersey glass, and from him I quote as follows:

> The first South Jersey glass factory was established near the village of Alloway, in Salem County, in 1739, by Caspar Wistar of Philadelphia; the small settlement that grew up around the works being known as *Wistarberg*. In 1775 another factory was started at what is now Glassboro by two of Wistar's workmen. Between then and the early 1840's a great number of factories—small and short-lived for the most part—were started throughout this section and along the Mulliga River; most of them established by Wistar workmen or their descendants, and all of them manned by workmen trained in the Wistar tradition and technique. Under this tradition the right to use the fag-end of each pot of molten glass for their individual purposes was a recognized perquisite of the workmen. And, as a matter of fact, practically all the pieces now collected as *Wistarberg* or *South Jersey* glass are of this latter origin, the commercial output of all these factories having consisted of window glass, bottles, snuff canisters and other similar hollow ware. Again and again, as a matter of proved and indisputable fact, three generations of these workmen continued for more than one hundred years to make for themselves and their friends the same range of pieces unaltered in form and indistinguishable in technique. So that, so far as concerns these wholly true-to-tradition specimens, the attempted differentiation between *true Wistarberg* pieces and *South Jersey* pieces is utterly futile and meaningless. But, call them what we will and date them as we choose, their rarity remains the same. About 1850 a complete change of fashion seems to have taken place under the influence of which the earlier forms more less wholly disappeared. Previous to this, but for how long back of 1840 it is not yet possible to say, slight modification of technical treatment and a decided fondness for color stunts had been creeping in, although the earlier *forms* were retained unaltered.

OLD FORMS APPEAR IN LATE SPECIMENS

HOWEVER, bear this in mind: while it is self-evident, when you find, say, a glass pitcher showing certain characteristics in shape or decoration which were not encountered in our china or silver before 1830, that the pitcher can hardly be earlier

Figure 4: Work from various South Jersey factories including, the Isabella Glass Works, the Whitney Works, and the Waterford Works.

Figure 5: The globular bowl is New York State work of South Jersey character, the others are of South Jersey origin.

than that date, it is not at all unusual with glass, not the commercial product but that blown by individual workmen, to find very early forms or decorative features faithfully copied many, many years later. I know this to be true. I have specimens in which very early South Jersey characteristics are followed, but which I know to have been blown by individual workmen in New York and New England factories *after 1830*—pieces which would readily be accepted as early South Jersey, and, in some cases, even as Wistarberg.

What I am trying to set forth is that in the identification or attribution of early American glass there is not any royal road to learning. It is only the occasional and exceptional rule which may within itself tell its own story. *Generally speaking, it is not possible from the color, quality, form, or decorative technique of a piece of glass to determine the particular factory of its origin.* Fortunately, however, for the student and real collector of American glass, one thing with respect to these individually blown pieces is generally true—they were owned and remained in the the vicinity where the factory which produced them was located. Most of these factories operating between 1825 and 1860* were located in what were then, and still are, small villages or rural communities; and from the direct descendents of the men who worked in such factories or the friends of the workmen, to whom individually blown pieces were given, it has been possible to obtain many interesting examples authenticated beyond a doubt as to the factory where they were produced.

THE RELIABILITY OF FAMILY HISTORY

FAMILY history going back only one or two generations with respect to such pieces of glass found in the immediate vicinity of the factory is generally accurate with respect to the attribution. Thus, we have been able to classify with certainty interesting examples from the factories which were located at Keene, Stoddard, and Lyndeboro, in New Hampshire; West-

*Between about 1810 and 1860.

ford, East Willington, Coventry, and New London, in Connecticut; Redford, Redwood, Sand Lake , Saratoga, Cleveland, Bristol, and elsewhere, in New York; Whitney Glass Works, Isabella Glass Works, Waterford, Coffin & Hay, and others in New Jersey.

However, when it comes to eighteenth-century factories, like that of Caspar Wistar and his son Richard, family history becomes, in most instances, a dangerous and uncharted sea upon which to embark for the port of attribution. The colors, shapes, and decorative features which we believe characterize pieces blown by individual workmen in the factory of the Wistars undoubtedly were reproduced by the same and other workmen in many later factories, and I do not know of any way of distinguishing a Wistarberg piece from a similar piece made years later in another factory. Hence, my expressed doubt as to there being in existence half a dozen pieces which can unquestionably be attributed to the Wistar factory.

CASES IN POINT

L ET me illustrate: I have in my collection what has been for several years considered one of the finest and earliest of South Jersey blue glass bowls, with circular crimped foot. It was in the early collection formed by Messrs. Kerfoot and Hunter when they first became interested in Wistarberg glass. It passed into the hands of a well-known student and collector, was exhibited with other rare examples of South Jersey glass in the Metropolitan Museum, and was considered a Wistarberg piece. It had characteristics which have been held to distinguish the earliest South Jersey glass; yet, not very long ago, I secured its exact counterpart in everything except color, in another bowl— of beautiful clear amber—which has a well-authenticated history of having been blown by William Coffin himself, in the factory of Coffin & Hay,* at Hammonton, New Jersey. *And that*

---

*The factory started by 1820, but the firm name of Coffin & Hay dates from 1836, when the works was operated by both Coffin's son, Bodine, and by his son-in-law, Andrew K. Hay, as Coffin & Hay.

South Jersey glass done at various works during the nineteenth century. *From the Collection of the New Jersey State Museum.*

A blue iridescent glass vase made at the
Durand Art Glass Company in Vineland
circa 1925-1932. Its height measures
seven and one-quarter inches, the
maximum diameter is five and one-quarter
inches. *Lent anonymously.*

factory did not start until 1820. This does not prove that the blue bowl was made in the factory of Coffin & Hay—it may be a Wistar piece—but it does go to show that one cannot, from the evidence of the glass itself, say that certain pieces are, or are not, Wistarberg.

In one of the auction sales, a few years ago, appeared a dark amber pitcher with superimposed decoration of the so-called lily-pad type. It is, I think, the largest and one of the finest pitchers of that type and color in existence. Everyone seemed to consider it Wistarberg beyond a doubt. Just how they could be so certain, I could not figure out. I have seen pitchers similar in color and decoration which were made in New Hampshire factories. This particular pitcher showed signs of great wear, but I have seen just as great wear on a piece which I know to have been made after 1800. There was nothing in the way of history or record to connect the piece with the Wistarberg factory; in fact, it was picked up in New York state, far from the Jersey line, and there was no record of its having come from South Jersey. I am not speaking thus of the blue bowl or of the amber pitcher in any way to disparage them. To what particular factory you attribute them does not add to or take from either piece an atom of the beauty and rarity it possesses by and of itself. I merely wish to illustrate with respect to Wistarberg glass how impossible it is, in almost every instance, to prove the attribution.

GENERAL TERMS SAFEST

WITH the more general term of *South Jersey,* we are treading on firmer ground: firmer, first, because the term is general, indicating a type of glass instead of examples of the product of one factory which ceased to exist at such an early date that attribution, based on any family history, becomes, in ninety-nine cases out of one hundred, an attempt to weave the fabric of identification to the pattern of one's own desire; and, secondly, because the general term applies to the product of a large number of factories scattered throughout a certain section

Figure 6: Glass from Redwood, New York.

Figure 7: Light green turquoise examples from Redwood, New York.

or district, operating, probably, with a continual interchanging of workmen and handing-down of methods and technique from father to son and grandson, so that, for generations, the same general shapes, colors, and decorative features were produced almost unaltered, though they were eventually modified more or less in keeping with the commercial glass, china, and metal ware of the day.

In the third place, we are on firmer ground because these factories came into being many years after Casper Wistar's day. In like manner, they were engaged in the manufacture of window glass, or, as with most of them, of bottles, whiskey flasks, snuff jars, medicine phials, and such. Bowls, pitchers, mugs, and similar articles were not a commercial product, but were individually blown pieces, frequently, in fact generally, cherished and handed down in the families of the workmen who made them, or of the friends and relatives for whom they were made. Consequently they remained, as a rule, in the vicinity of the particular factory where they were produced, traveling only as the occasional family was uprooted from its native soil. Attribution based on family history going back only two or three generations does not become lost in the limbo of uncertainty which obscures practically every attempt at attribution to a specific factory as early as that of the Wistars.

MOST SOUTH JERSEY GLASS AFTER 1800

I THINK we must concede that by far the greater proportion of South Jersey glass, including much of the finest in quality and what we consider early in form and feeling, was blown *after 1800*. Prior to that date we have, I believe, only two factories to draw from—the original enterprise of Wistar, continued by his son Richard; and the factory at Glassboro, founded by the Stangers, which, after the failure and imprisonment for debt of the original founders, was, in 1781,* acquired by Colonel Thomas Heston, and during the following years passed through

---

*1784, by October.

Figure 8: Wine or spirit bottles.

Figure 9: South Jersey glass from Glassboro.

various ownerships, until, in 1835, Thomas H. Whitney purchased an interest in the factory, which was then known as the Harmony Glass Works. *American Bottles Old & New,* by William S. Walbridge, and Barber's *American Glassware* give the Whitney date as 1837.

From about 1815 on there were many factories in the South Jersey districts, the advent of the hinged molds for producing fancy bar bottles and whiskey flasks having apparently given a great impetus to the business. It is among pieces produced by workmen in these factories (including, of course, the Stanger-founded glass works) and during this period, we must place the great bulk of our South Jersey glass. As a rule, specimens found in the section where these factories operated and showing typical characterisitics of form, color, and decoration, may safely be accepted as South Jersey, even though we know that pieces similar in color and general characteristics to South Jersey glass were made in New York and New England factories of contemporary period. In case of many of these specimens—particularly those made in the bottle factories after 1820—family history may be accepted with a fair degree of safety, particularly when the source as well as the characteristics of the glass itself bears out the attribution. Unfortunately for identification as to specific factories, much of the fine South Jersey glass was picked up in the early days of American glass collecting when practically everything found in that section was called *Wistarberg.* Apparently the possibility that such early-looking pieces were blown by workmen in the various comparatively late bottle factories was not sensed at the time. Hence the opportunity to secure specific attributions was, in most instances, irretrievably lost.

Many of the best of these South Jersey examples were dispersed during the Frederick William Hunter Sale in January, 1920. Some marvelous specimens were in the collection formed by Miss M. I. Meacham not long after. Some of them may well have been examples from the Wistar factory, or that of the

Figure 10: Free-blown pitcher from near Salem, New Jersey.

Figure 11: Large pitcher with "lily-pad" decoration.

Stangers. But these two collections have been scattered, and with very few specimens, in so far as I know, was any definite history supporting any attribution, handed on. Some of the finest examples were acquired by the Metropolitan Museum of Art in New York City and may be seen there.

Fortunately, from time to time, South Jersey pieces have been picked up there by an occasional collector or dealer interested in identifying the factory which gave birth to them; and such specimens are of great value to us in our study of American glass. I have been particularly fortunate in acquiring a few interesting examples with what I believe to be, in most instances. At this point, I would do well to illustrate a few such specimens which can be accepted as actually being South Jersey glass.

ILLUSTRATIONS

FIGURE 1 shows characteristic examples of South Jersey glass. The pitcher in the top row is a lovely shade of blue, light in tone—what I call a steely blue. It shows the modification in form and decorative technique which appeared toward the middle of the nineteenth century. The amber bowl next to the pitcher and the three pieces in the middle row are also shown in other illustrations accompanying this article. The vase at the right end of the top row is actually a dark olive amber, quite similar in shade to many of the pieces made at Keene and at Stoddard, New Hampshire; Coventry and East Willington, Connecticut; and certain of the New York State factories. The blue bowl on circular, crimped foot in the bottom row is the one referred to in the text as having been in the early collection found by Messrs. Hunter and Kerfoot and considered a Wistarberg piece. Its amber counterpart beside it is the bowl said to have been made by William Coffin himself, in the factory of Coffin & Hay, founded at Hammonton, New Jersey, in 1820.*

---

*See footnote under "CASES IN POINT."

In Figure 2 are shown three pieces. In color they are typical South Jersey blues. The pitcher, with its threaded neck and crimped foot, is a particularly fine example and was made by Joe Duffield at the first Whitney factory—so says family history. By *first* is probably meant the factory of the period beginning in 1835 when Thomas H. Whitney purchased an interest in the glass works, as distinguished from the period beginning about 1842, when he acquired entire control and, with his brother Samuel A., formed the firm of ·Whitney Brothers and changed the name to Whitney Glass Works. The small vase is also a Whitney product. The bowl is a lighter shade of blue than either of the other pieces, and I do not know in what factory in South Jersey it was made; but it might easily be of a much earlier period.

The pieces in Figure 3 are also specimens from the Whitney Glass Works. They are a clear deep amber in color, and the vases, nine inches tall, while very rare and unsusual, are —quite patently—relatively late.

Figure 4 shows some very interesting examples of South Jersey, all with specific factory attributions. The small doubled-colored pitcher at the left is of heavy glass, light green and opaque white, and was made at the Whitney Glass Works about 1850 by one Jacob Montcuef. The mug, similar in color and character of glass, was made at the Isabella Glass Works, New Brooklyn, New Jersey. The pitcher next it is typical South Jersey light green glass. It was made at Waterford, one of the bottle factories. This specimen is quite unusual in shape, the short squatty body resting on a crimped foot and merging into a very broad, cylindrical neck with flaring rim. The applied decoration is also unusual, a sort of wave-like effect covering just the very lowest part of the body, while three long filaments are carried upward over the body and on to the neck in a form one can almost fancy as the heads and necks of long sea serpents arising from an uncharted and mysterious sea of glass to leer at the poor investigator who has embarked upon an uncertain and danger-beset voyage of attribution. The taller pitcher, next to that of my sea-serpent fantasy, is a lovely light green with turquoise tint. It is an attractive shape with heavy crimped foot. The simple decoration encircling the neck is similar to that of the pair of amber vases in Figure 3 and is, I think, late. This pitcher was made at Waterford. The lamp is a rare piece, turquoise green in color. It was made at the Isabella Glass Works, about 1840 by Julius Stanger, and was purchased from an heir and descendant, a Miss Stanger of New Brooklyn, New Jersey.

In Figure 5 is an interesting pitcher, showing a two-colored effect in light green and opaque white. It shows a late form and this is borne out by the coin, dated 1873 imprisoned within the hollow of the stem. The bowl of straight-sided cylindrical form at the left is a very unusual rich yellow green color. I know of nothing of its history other than it was found in South Jersey, but I have seen a similar bowl, of similar glass and color, which is attributed to the Isabella Glass Works. The sugar bowl at the extreme left is a beautiful shade of light green, with turquoise tint, typical South Jersey glass, *but I happen to know that it is a New York State product,* probably made at Redwood, Jefferson County, as it was found in the vicinity of that place. Originally it no doubt had a cover and I know that it had smalled applied looped handles on the sides, which were broken off.

In Figure 6 are a bowl and pitcher which, a few years ago, would have been accepted as unquestionably Wistarberg; but they are New York State glass, made at Redwood, fully one hundred years after Caspar Wistar founded his glass works. They are a lovely light turquoise green in color. The bowl, resting on a circular foot, is very graceful in form and measures nearly twelve inches across the top. The pitcher, made to go with the bowl and matching it perfectly in color and decoration, holds fully two and one-half quarts.

In Figure 7 are two of the finest pitchers of this type I have ever seen. The color is even finer than that of the bowl and pitcher. The larger holds better than two quarts; the smaller

Figure 12: Aquamarine creamer of South Jersey make.

Figure 13: Free-blown pitcher from Millville, aquamarine in color.

about a pint. They, as well as the plain bowl on circular foot at the left, were made at the Redford Glass Works, located in the little hamlet of Redford, not far from Plattsburg, New York. Let me say right here that as far as my own observation and study go, there is, generally speaking, nothing in the character and color of the glass itself to distinguish Redford pieces from Redwood or from those of several other New York State factories which came into existence during the early or mid-nineteenth century. I have been extremely fortunate, however, in securing for my own collection many pieces found in the immediate vicinity of these various factories and purchased from families whose fathers or grandfathers worked in them. Such specimens, absolutely authenticated, have been of inestimable value to me in my study of American glass.

THE glassworks founded by Caspar Wistar in 1739, and continued by his son Richard until about 1780, was the first glasshouse in America to operate with any degree of commercial success over a long span of years. The works was located about eight miles slightly southwest of the town of Salem, New Jersey, not far from the main road between Greenfield and Salem where it crosses the Alloways Creek about twelve miles from its mouth.

The commercial products of the Wistar works were window glass, wine and spirit bottles, and similar wares. Undoubtedly, as in all the early glasshouses, individual workmen made pieces of hollowware such as bowls, pitchers, and so on for their own use, or as gifts to friends, and possibly to a limited extent for local sale. The metal of the hollowwares which have been attributed to the Wistar factory, or to that of the Stangers, was ordinary bottle glass, and in colors aquamarine, a shade of dark blue, and of course the olive-greens and ambers encountered in wine and spirits bottles.

Fragments of glass usually in light green, olive green, and shades of dark amber have been excavated on the site of the

Wistar glassworks. Such fragments have largely been from wine and spirits bottles similar to those shown in Figure 8. Reports have come in from time to time of authenticated examples of glass made at the Wistar glassworks, but personally I have never seen a piece of glass that I could be absolutely certain was Wistar. A pair of candlesticks was illustrated in *Antiques* in October 1950 *(p.291)*, which had been acquired about fifteen years ago in Woodbury, New Jersey, from descendants of early settlers; they were reluctant to part with them because they had been blown by ancestors who had worked in a glass factory at Alloway in the eighteenth century. These candlesticks are definitely of eighteenth-century type, and may have been made at the Wistar factor.

The glassworks started by the Stangers passed through various ownerships, and in the 1830's was acquired by the Whitneys and subsequently known as the Whitney Glass Works. The largest and most successful of the South Jersey glasshouses, it was acquired in 1918 by the Owens Bottle Company.

From the beginning of the nineteenth century and throughout a period of several decades there were many glasshouses throughout the southern part of New Jersey, engaged for the most part in making utilitarian wares such as window glass, bottles, and flasks. In practically all of these glasshouses, individual workers continued to make milk pans and bowls, pitchers and mugs, and other hollowwares in the so-called South Jersey tradition.

A superimposed gather tooled into swagging or some similar design on the body of a pitcher or bowl, threaded neck, and crimped foot were characteristic South Jersey decorative techniques, following styles encountered in Spanish or other Continental glass which in turn copied techniques of the ancient glassmaker. However, we feel today that in all liklihood the so-called "lily-pad" design in the superimposed gather is an American idiom which probably did not appear until after

Figure 14: Pitcher of dark amber non-lead glass from Bridgeton.

1800. Examples of this superimposed lily-pad are shown in Figures 11 ad 12.

The pitcher in Figure 14 is a typical example of the decoration of threading in a contrasting color, hooked into a design of swirls and looping and rolled into the body of a pitcher, bowl, or mug that was used in the nineteenth century in South Jersey glasshouses. This type of decoration was used extensively in certain English glasshouses and in America at the works of the Boston and Sandwich Glass Company, New England Glass Company, and in Pittsburg and Wheeling glasshouses.

From about 1820 to the 1870's, historical bottles and flasks were a minor commercial product of many of the South Jersey glasshouses.

Wine or spirits bottles, of dark olive-green (black) bottle glass are shown in Figure 8, typical of the bottles which were a commercial product of Caspar Wistar and his son Richard. The two at the left are the early type in vogue during the first twenty years of Wistar's glasshouse, and the one at the right shows the development to taller, more slender form in vogue during the later years of the Wistar glasshouse. *Left;* height is 6⅞ inches, greatest diameter is 5⅜ inches. *Center;* height is 10 inches, greatest diameter is 5⅞ inches, marked on seal is W. LUDLOW. *Right;* height is 9¾ inches, greatest diameter is 4¾ inches with a seal that is marked S. COLTON with date *1776.*

Figure 9 shows fine examples of South Jersey glass probably dating from the last quarter of the eighteenth century. *Left,* free-blown sugar bowl and cover in clear deep green glass, found in a private home near Glassboro. *Right,* free-blown clear deep green pitcher with applied strap handle and thumbpiece in contrasting deep olive-amber (black) glass, formerly in the collection of Louis C. Myers.

In Figure 10, one of a pair of free-blown deep yellow-green pitchers is shown, with applied threading on the neck, heavy circular foot, and solid handles with crimping at the base. It was purchased in Burlington County in 1919 from Benjamin Budd, in whose family the pitchers had been handed down for several generations, and who stated that they had been made in a very old glasshouse near Salem, New Jersey. The glass is the typical bottle glass encountered in some of the early South Jersey products. This pair of pitchers may have been made either at the Wistar glasshouse or at that of the Stangers, but in the absence of definite history there is always the possibility that pieces exhibiting such eighteenth-century form and techniques were made in one of the early nineteenth-century glasshouses in Salem County. Note the similarity in form to the pitcher shown in Figure 11.

This large pitcher (Figure 11), is one of a pair, in deep green glass, with superimposed "lily-pad" decoration of the type more regularly encountered in pieces made at some of the New York State glasshouses, such as Redwood, Redford, and Harrisburg, and also in Stoddard, New Hampshire. Purchased in South Jersey about twenty years ago, and subsequently acquired by the late George Horace Lorimer, it is now in the Lorimer collection at the Philadelphia Museum of Art.

Figure 12 shows a small aquamarine creamer with superimposed "lily-pad" decoration of the type usually encountered in South Jersey pieces. —GEORGE S. McKEARIN

Sidelights on the Wistars and their Glass-House

I N Philadelphia, May 9, 1724, a bill was passed as follows:

> *Entitled* an Act for the enabling of John Cratho, Merch't, Caspar
> Wistar and Nicholas Gateau, to Trade and Buy and Hold Lands in
> this Province.

The Caspar Wistar referred to therein had come to this
country when twenty-one years of age, and in the year 1717. He
was a German Palatine, but, soon after settling in Philadelphia,
he joined the Society of Friends and married a Quakeress.
Wistar first engaged in the business of making buttons, and so
assured was he of their quality that he gave with them a several-
year guarantee. Whatever he attempted was carried out with
marked success and his foresight led him to enter the glass
industry.

July 31, 1740, letters to Thomas Hill, Secretary to the Lords
Commissioners for Trade and Plantations, from one Charles
Carkese, noted the erection of a glass works eight miles from the
port of Salem in West Jersey by one "Caspar Wester, a
Palatine, the glass house being brought to perfection so as to
make glass."

By 1748 both Caspar and his son Richard were actively interested and at work. In the year 1752 the father died and Richard inherited the business.

The new owner lived in Philadelphia. Associated with him, and living about year 1767 at the glass-house on Alloway's Creek, were Martin Halter and Hugh Blackwood. Later, though perhaps even during the above-mentioned period, Benjamin Thompson managed the manufactory. For two or more years after the elder Wistar's death, the business continued to grow, but the furnaces turned out the same sort of crude glass.

It will be interesting for those of today who seek specimens of Wistar glass, to know how the product was regarded in Colonial times. Those persons who are not of the collecting fraternity, and who look askance when one muses on the charms of Wistarberg, who see nothing to enthuse over in the robust little bottles all so alike in shape, and who discover no beauty in the whorled or the double-dipped glass—such persons would no doubt agree with the ideas expressed by Governor Franklin.

June 14, 1768, writing from Burlington, New Jersey, to the Right Honorable Earl of Hillsborough in regard to the industries in the Colony, Franklin referred to the factory as one where were made "Bottles and very coarse Green Glass for Widows used only in some of the Houses of the poorer Sort of people".

The profits from this factory had been insufficient to induce others to follow in the glassmaking industry, although there had been at that time talk of others starting, since Parliament had laid a duty on glass. Notwithstanding this duty, however, Franklin considered that America would continue to secure glass from abroad, because fine glass could be made there cheaper than here.

It may have been this duty which encouraged Richard Wistar. It may be that from then on he imported a higher grade of foreign artisans to work exclusively for him in producing a greater variety of wares; or, again, it may have been that, in spite of the quality of American-made glass, Americans would not pay the price for the imported article as the Governor had so confidently expected. In any case, the factory thrived.

As for the work, a good share of it was turned out by men—many of them ex-soldiers—who spoke Dutch, French, and Portugese, but very, very little English; men often homesick for their native land, hugely dissatisfied, anxious to start at something for themselves, considered slaves, bound by a period of time to these Wistars. They were constantly deserting.

Richard Wistar was observing. The entire age for that matter was an observing age, and Richard Wistar could give the most minute details regarding men employed by him at the glasshouse. He kept in touch with the intimate details of their lives as well as the interests of their families. No doubt, too, realizing that there would be desertions, with consequent loss of labor and money to him, he made especial effort at remembering the idosyncrasies of his men. The following advertisements are of interest in this connection:

> Twelve Dollars Reward. Run away on the Second of this Instant from the Glass House in Salem County West New Jersey, a Dutchman named Philip Jacobs, about Five Feet Six or Seven Inches High, light Grey Eyes, sandy Hair, thick Lips, speaks but little English; had on when he went away a blue Cloth Coat with Metal Buttons, red Plush Jacket striped Ticken Trowsers, good Shoes with large Brass Buckles and a Castor Hat about half worn; took Sundry other Things with him, also a Fiddle upon which he is much addicted to play; both his Legs are sore.
>
> November 6—1767.   RICHARD WISTAR, Wistarburgh

> Ten dollars Reward. Run away from the Subscriber's Glass House in Salem County, West Jersey, a Dutch Servant Man, named ADRIAN BRUST, about 27 years of Age, 5 feet 7 or 8 inches High of a pale Complexion has short light Hair, two Moles on his left Cheek and on his right temple a Scar, also on one of his Feet near his Ancle which is but lately healed, and the Shoe mended where the Cut was. Had on when he went away an old Felt Hat, a lightish coloured Upper Jacket with Brass Buttons, this Country

make, about half worn with a Patch on one of the hind flaps where there was a Hole burnt; an under one with flat Metal Buttons, both of Linsey. Leather Breeches, Grey Yarn Stockings, good shoes with Brass Buckles, A good Shirt, and generally wears the Bosom Part behind.

A third advertisement refers to another "Dutchman" and describes certain blue-flowered buttons of metal, brass buttons, a Dutch pillowcase and a silk handkerchief, as well as a piece of linen for shirts, carried away by the deserter, who might further be identified by a scar located on the sole of his foot.

Two things in these advertisements are of particular interest: first, the gay buttons which Wistar was wont to describe as adorning the garments of his runaways; secondly, the men deserting were scarred. It may be that these men (ex-soldiers) bore the marks of battle; it may also be that the acquired their wounds through carelessness in their glass-house work.

While there is no record to prove it, Richard Wistar or his manager may well have been the person responsible for the suppresion of the fairs customarily held at Salem within a few miles of the glass-house. These events were considered most "inconvenient and unnecessary." Horse racing was held, and one may easily imagine how vigorously the men discussed John Budd's famous horse there at Salem. Swan was "a black horse, fifteen hands one inch high, one white foot, a snip on his nose and a small star on his forehead. Learnt to pace and goes fast as any horse in the continent—trots and gallops very light and runs fast. He is as handsome as any horse in America."

Fairs were unnecessary and inconvenient, but quite to be approved were the building of roads, erection of bridges, causeways, and so on. Benjamin Thompson was appointed to collect subscriptions in their behalf at the glass-house.

By 1771 visitors from remote sections were coming to the famed place at Allowaystown. William Shute and Jacob Paullin started a stage route between Piles Grove (adjacent to the glass-house) and Philadelphia. "Prices for passengers or lumber per 100 weight carried the whole distance into Piles Grove for three shilling nine pence and those gentlemen or ladies favoring them with their custom could depend on good usage and utmost care." These two above "humble servants" promised to carry them to the glass-house.

Then suddenly the business established after years of labor faced its most critical period, the Revolutionary War.

Wistars—Caspars, Richards, Daniels, Bartholomews, Williams, and Johns, all related to the Palatine Caspar—are mentioned frequently in the records of the Revolution. At first, on account of business or their Quaker religion, many were excused, only to take their places later in the different battalions of the Philadelphia militia. A letter from Colonel Samuel L. Miles, of New York, in November, 1776, to William Wistar, Merchant in Philadelphia, mentions a Captain Wister as being there in New York.

Where hitherto he had steadily acquired land, by 1778-79 Richard Wistar was placing for rent and sale various sections throughout West Jersey—lands rich in orchards of cherries, pears, apples, plums; fertile meadows and vast beds of asparagus. He was not even now a poor man, but he was past middle life and too worn by war to cope with the necessary readjustments. Before him was a dreary outlook for the glass industry. In October of 1780 Richard Wistar put the glass manufactory up for disposal through the *Pennsylvania Journal:*

The GLASS MANUFACTORY in Salem County West Jersey is for sale with 1500 Acres of Land adjoining. It contains two Furnaces with all the necessary Ovens for cooling the Glass, drying Wood etc. Contiguous to the Manufactory are two flatting Ovens in Separate Houses, a Storehouse, a Pot-house, a House fitted with Tables for cutting of Glass, a Stamping Mill, a rolling Mill for preparing of Clay for the making of Pots; and at a suitable distance are ten Dwelling houses for the Workmen; as likewise a large Mansion House containing Six rooms on a Floor, with Bake-house and Washhouse; Also a convenient Store-house where a well assorted retail Shop has been kept above 30 years, is as good a stand for sale of goods as any in the County, being situated one mile and a half from a navigable creek where shallops are loaded for Philadelphia, eight miles from the county seat of Salem and half a mile from a good mill. There are about 250 Acres of cleared Land within fence 100 whereof is mowable meadow, which produces hay and pasturage sufficient for the large stock of Cattle and Horses employed by the Manufactory.

There is Stabling sufficient for 60 head of Cattle with a large Barn, Granery and Wagon House. The unimproved Land is well wooded and 200 Acres more of Meadow may be made. The situation and covenience for the procuring of Materials is equal if not superior to any place in Jersey.

For terms of Sale apply to the Subscriber in Philadelphia.

—RICHARD WISTAR

Before he could sell the factory representing his life-work, Richard Wistar had passed away.

In the Chersterfield Friends' *Marriage Records,* on the seventeenth day of the tenth month, 1781, appears the marriage of John Wistar of Upper Alloways Creek, Salem County, son of Richard and Sarah deceased, to Charlotte Newbold of Mansfield, daughter of Clayton and Mary Wistar. Family witnesses of the ceremony included Mary B., Richard, Caspar, Jr., Thomas, Elizabeth, and Sarah. John continued with the factory for a time—then all record of it gradually ceases.

On January 15, 1799, one John Wister, Jr., merchant, married the "amiable" Jane Richards, both residents of Philadelphia, and one Robert Wharton, Esq., performed the ceremony.

There is one point not quite clear to Wistar admirers, and that is the relationship between Richard and the famous Dr. Caspar Wistar. The impression has been quite general, and was considered correct by the Editor of the New Jersey Archives, that Dr. Caspar was also a son of the founder of the glass industry who died in 1752; but this cannot be if we are to believe the folowing notice copied from the *Niles' Weekly Register* of Baltimore for January 31, 1818:

Died at Philadelphia on the 21st. inst., Dr. Caspar Wistar age 56, a first rate physician and professor of Anatomy in the University of Pennsylvania. He has long been famous in the Medical world and was exceedingly well versed in the Sciences generally. His decease is a public calamity!

Dr. Caspar was an author, and was at one time president of the Philadelphia Philosophical Society. A letter in regard to the appointment of an inspector of pearl ashes, dated March 31, 1790, is jointly signed by Drs. Hutcheson and Wistar, and the latter appears as "Caspar Wistar, junr."

A hundred years and more have passed. Where once stood the first successful flint glass manufactory of this country only a commanding buttonwood tree remains as sentinel. The objects from the Wistar glass-house are still being diligently sought for and admired, cherished, and preserved. Their testimony is mute but none the less effective in regard to that tireless, sagacious, and most successgul gentleman, Richard Wistar of Wistarberg.

—HORTENSE FEA SICARD

Jersey City Glass

JERSEY CITY was a tiny village when George Dummer established his glass works there in 1824. The census of the following year reveals that there were but 23 freeholders and 82 taxable inhabitants. His glass works were located at what was better known as Powles Hook (Paulus Hook), a point of solid ground that extended out into the Hudson River directly opposite lower Manhattan.

Having learned the glass cutter's trade in the Hamilton Works a short time before 1821 in Albany, Dummer opened a retail glass store at 110 Broadway, Manhattan. Being a creative artist, rather than a mere merchant, he grew restless and in 1824 moved across the river to the infant Jersey City, where he built what was then one of the larges glass factories in the United States. From the day its fires were first ignited in 1825, until March 1866, they had never been extinguished.

The glass house, as it was known, covered 14 city lots. The yard, used for storage, stables, carpenter, tinsmith and blacksmith shops, was 15 lots in extent, opposite the factory.

In founding the firm of George Dummer & Company, Joseph K. Milnor and William G. Bull, in addition to Phineas C.

Dummer, a brother of the founder, were taken in as partners.

Two years after its extablishment, the new firm received "honorary mention for the splendid collection of cut glass" along with such noted competitors as McCord & Shriner, Philadelphia; Jackson & Baggor, New York; New England Cut Glass Company, Boston; and Bakewell, Page & Bakewell, Pittsburgh at the Franklin Institute's prestigious exhibit in Philadelphia. The judges stated, "These articles are so well and extensively made as to prove, beyond all question, that this country need not remain tributary to foreign manufacturers; and they state without hesitation that there was not an article exhibited that would not do credit to any foreign establishment."

Dummer was a master craftsman and took pride in his products. The old Jersey City *Argus,* in its obituary of Phineas in September, 1875, recalled that the brothers "turned out the finest specimens of glassware in the country," adding that their wares "carried off the highest medals in Philadelphia and New York City industrial exhibits." They did, indeed, since the list of awards received was impressive. In 1835, certificate of honorable mention from Franklin Institute for astral lamp shades, some of exceptional size; in 1838, the Franklin's silver medal, being the first prize, for four pairs of fluted decanters, described as "the very best articles of Cut Glass exhibited, both for quality of the metal and beauty of the cutting." In 1843, the Jersey City firm, now known as P. C. Dummer & Company again received the first prize at the Franklin Institute exhibit in Philadelphia for a "cut glass bowl, of graceful form and good finish, and of superior quality of material" and was further recognized as having "the best display of glassware in the exhibition."

One of the most coveted awards came to the Jersey City glass makers in 1837, when they walked away with a gold medal for the "best specimens of cut and moulded glass from the American Institute of the City of New York at its annual fair.

A pair of glass pitchers from the Dummer-Lyman Glass Factory with fanned rims.

The following year the same organization presented Dummer with its siver medal.

A highpoint came when what is now New York's Bryant Park, Sixth Ave. and 42nd Street, became the site of the famous Chrystal Palace, a huge dome-shaped glass structure, where in October 1853 was held an international exhibition that drew thousands to see the best and most stylish products of the world. Glass makers from every corner of the globe competed, but Jersey City Glass Works came away with the gold medal for the "best cut plain and colored glass."

The firm's sales rooms advertised "All kinds of Cut Decanters, Tumblers & Wines, Champaignes, Jellies and Claret, Salts and Stands, Butter Coolers, Hall Lamps, and Candle Shades." For those who could not afford the best, the Dummers produced "plain and moulded glass of all descriptions." In addition, they manufactured flint and green-glass for druggists, such as fancy bottles and vials. The Jersey City firm was unusual, since it was making both expensive and ordinary glass for householders, as well as glass ware for commercial purposes.

Proud of his craft, Dummer brought from England the best glass "gaffers" he could find, and introduced modern machinery, including 32 steam-powered cutting wheels. To induce his workers to remain, he built housing for them and opened a "company store." At its peak, the glass works employed 150 persons. Always seeking to improve methods, both George and Phineas Dummer were innovative. The latter received a patent "on the construction and use of moulds with a core for pressing glass into various useful forms; called Dummer's scallop or coverplate."

While the Dummer's were kept busy with their glass works, they found time to branch out into the pottery field. On December 10, 1825, under an act of the New Jersey Legislature, the Jersey Porcelain and Earthenware Company was incorporated. The incorporators were George Dummer, Tim-

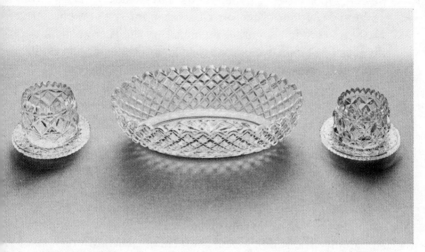

Cut-glass from the Dummer Glass Company of Jersey City, an oval dessert bowl and containers with saucers.

othy Dewey, Henry Post, Jr., William W. Shirley, and Robert Abbatt. Again, though in a different field, this establishment won tops honors from the Franklin Institute in 1826 for "the best china from American materials." The factory was located in Jersey City.

George and Phineas Dummer lived close by their factories. George, who died in 1853, was President of the Board of Selectmen of Jersey City, under the 1820 charter, serving from 1826 to 1831; and when the city was granted a new charter in 1838, making it a separate municipality, he served as mayor. Phineas C. Dummer was sixth to hold the office, serving as chief executive from 1844 to 1848.

Over the years, the firm changed its name several times. George Dummer & Company by 1830 was known as P. C. Dummer & Company. In 1843, it was Dummer & Lyman (the partners being George Dummer, Jr. and George Dummer Lyman), 1848: George Dummer Lyman & Company; 1851: George Dummer & Company; 1856 to 1862: Augustus O. Dummer. About 1862, the glass works was bought out by Reed & Moulds. They continued at the old stand, until the financial situation following the Civil War forced them out of business. Apparently, the buildings and land remained in the family, since the property was sold by Phineas' son-in-law, Solomon Alofsen on Feburary 1, 1867. He had sold the "yard" on October 30, 1862 to the New Jersey Sugar Refining Company, and now this outfit wished to expand. They bought the glass works, itself, demolished it, and on its site erected a huge sugar house. Demolition was underway of February 19, 1867, since the public library of Jersey City possesses an original picture, showing the famous old manufactory on the day before the wrecker's ax fell.

If you should come across a piece of glassware from the old Jersey City Glass Works today, you will have a collector's item, since it is very rare. A few pieces are in the hands of private collectors, but the best place to view specimens is in

A cut-glass pitcher from the Dummer Glass Company with the characteristic
level cut from the top of the handle.

leading museums. The New Jersey Historical Society, Newark is fortunate in having several pieces. Outstanding is a plaster of Paris "cast of the seal of the Society, sunk in a ball of flint glass," as a paper weight. Solomon Alofsen was the donor to the Society in 1868.   — J. OWEN GRUNDY

SECTION FIVE

Pottery

The Pottery
of New Jersey

THE pottery industry, which has reached such a marvellous growth in Trenton as to gain for that city the title of the "Staffordshire of America," had its actual beginning there in 1852, when Messrs. Taylor and Speeler commenced the manufacture of yellow and Rockingham wares. At the present time the establishments engaged in Trenton in the production of all grades of ware, from common pottery to majolica, and from white granite to the finest porcelain, both plain and decorated, number thirty-seven, having the capacity of producing in value about five million dollars' worth of wares per annum. The central location, superior railway, canal, and river transportation facilities, and close contiguity to the clay deposits of New Jersey, have all contributed to the concentration and enormous development of the manufacture at this point. Interesting as is the subject to the ceramic student, we must of necessity confine ourselves to a review of the history of the most important and representative of these establishments.

We can but briefly allude to the difficulties encountered by the early potters in seeking the various clays necessary for the production of white wares, as well as the feldspar and flint required in the manufacture of these goods. It must be remembered that no mines, except of the common New Jersey fireclays, had been developed at that time. Many thousand miles were travelled by the first potters of Trenton in search of suitable kaolin. The first deposit was found near Hockessin, Delaware, and was known as the Graham mine. This afterwards changed hands and several other mines were developed in that section, the most notable being that operated by Israel Lacy. Another deposit was discovered a few years later at Brandywine Summit, Delaware County, Pa., and worked by the National Kaolin Company. This clay was probably the best used in the early years of the industry and is still largely in demand. The first flint used in Trenton for the production of white ware was picked up in Pennsylvania and in different places near Trenton, wherever a piece could be found on the surface. Later, the vast quarries of Harford County, Maryland, on the Susquehanna, were discovered, and the bulk of this material has come from that section. The first feldspar mines operated were in Connecticut, near Hartford. A number of mines have since been developed in that State, in Maine, Pennsylvania, and Maryland, and kaolin deposits of fine quality are at present in course of development in North and South Carolina, Florida, and various other sections of the country. When it is realized that the clay and mineral mines of England have been worked for perhaps three hundred years, while in this country the raw materials have not been developed in a systematic way until within the past forty years or so, we can more fully appreciate the obstacles which our potters have surmounted in bringing the industry to its present condition. Until a comparatively recent period each pottery manufactured the same class of wares, white granite, and C. C. or cream color, and to a limited degree, decorated toilet ware. Of late there has been a great diversification and specialization of the business, so that now a number of manufactories produce sanitary and plumbers' earthenware exclusively; others make nothing but

Baseball Vase, *circa* 1876, by Issac Broome for Ott and Brewer Co., Trenton, New Jersey.

vitrified china, while some confine their productions to semi-porcelain and white granite, and a few have embarked in the manufacture of the finer grades of porcelain. To all of these establishments extensive decorating departments have been added.

The Glasgow Pottery was established in 1863 by Mr. John Moses, who has ever since been prominently identified with the pottery business in Trenton. He was born in County Tyrone, Ireland, in 1832, and came to the United States at the age of twenty. He first served an apprenticeship at the dry-goods business in Philadelphia, where he acquired a practical business training. In the year first mentioned above, he rented a pottery with two small kilns that had been used for making yellow and Rockingham wares, and immediately commenced the manufacture of cream-colored ware, shortly afterward extending the business to the production of white granite or ironstone china. At the time he introduced decorations on table and toilet sets there was only one man in Trenton who understood this branch of the art, who did all the decorating for the ten potteries in operation. The first ornamentation attempted was the application of plain color bands, then gold lines, and by a gradual development the more elaborate decorations were finally introduced. The capacity of the factory was increased as the growth of the business required, and in a short time Mr. Moses was successfully making wares fully equal to any made by the practical English potters who were his competitors in Trenton. His present productions are dinner, tea, toilet, and decorated wares of every description. The name of the Glasgow Pottery is widely known throughout this country in connection with the John Hancock cups and saucers used at the Centennial Tea Parties, which were made extensively just prior to the Exhibition of 1876. Mr. Moses is also a larger producer of white granite and cream-colored wares, thin hotel and steamboat china of excellent grades, and has always taken an active part in upholding the protective tariff on American crockery before the Ways and Means Committee of Congress.

THE ETRURIA POTTERY.

THE OTT & BREWER COMPANY, of Trenton, N.J., now operate the factory which was built by Messrs. Bloor, Ott, & Booth, in 1863. Mr. John Hart Brewer, president of the company, entered the firm in 1865, and, being an artist himself of considerable ability, soon made his influence felt in the improvement of methods and elevation of standards. Until 1876 the chief products of this factory consisted of white granite and cream-colored ware.

The first attempts in the manufacture of "Belleek" egg-shell china were made by Mr. Brewer in 1882, in conjunction with Mr. William Bromley, Jr., but these early trials were not entirely satisfactory. Encouraged by partial success, however, Mr. Brewer induced Bromley to send for his father, William Bromley, and his brother, John Bromley, who, with two or three other hands, came over in the following year from the Belleek factory in Ireland. Mr. William H. Goss, of Stoke-on-Trent, invented this body some thiry years ago, at which time the elder Bromley was acting as his manager. Messers David McBirney and Robert Williams Armstrong were then attempting to make first-class ceramic goods at their recently established manufactory in the village of Belleek, county of Fermanagh, Ireland. Mr. Armstrong induced Bromley to take a number of Mr. Goss' best workmen to Ireland and introduce the egg-shell porcelain there. The ware produced at that factory has since become world-famous, being characterized by extreme lightness of body and a beautiful, lustrous glaze.

The ware now manufactured by the Ott & Brewer Company at the Etruria Pottery is made entirely from American mater-

Above: A white granite jardinière from the Ott & Brewer Company.
Below: Semi-porcelain plate, cobalt blue border and gold printed tracery, of the International Pottery Company.

ials, and is a vast improvement over the body and glaze first introduced by the Bromleys in the 1920's. The rich iridescence of the nacreous glaze is fully equal to that of the Iris Belleek which is produced from salts of bismuth colored with metallic oxides; in delicacy of coloring and lightness of weight the Trenton ware is even superior. A dozen cups and saucers, making twenty-four distinct pieces of the ordinary size, almost as thin as paper, weigh just one pound avoirdupois, or an average of only two thirds of an ounce each. A large variety of forms of this porcelain are produced, in both ornamental and useful designs. The larger vases are usually simple in outline and of the same comparative lightness as those of smaller size. They often possess pierced necks, feet, and handles, and are elegantly decorated in enamels, gold relief, and chasing.

A triumph of the potter's skill is a Belleek ostrich-egg *bonbonnière,* in two segments, which is exquisitely perforated or honey-combed over its entire surface.

In addition to art porcelains, this factory produces a great quantity of granite ware and opaque china, in dinner, tea, and toilet sets, which are both print-decorated and hand-painted. A *jardinière* of white granite, which is here figured, is a refined example of artistic decoration in quiet tones.

In presenting a biographical sketch of Mr. Brewer, we cannot do better than quote from the *Pottery and Glassware Reporter,* of June, 18, 1891:

"In 1873 Messrs. Ott & Brewer bought out the interest of Mr. Bloor, who removed to East Liverpool, where he subsequently died. The young member of the firm, then in his twenty-ninth year, filled with enthusiasm for his business and inspired with the patriotic sentiments pervading the preparation for the 1876 Centennial Exposition, at once began to show the possibilities of his craft, and the result was a showing at Philadelphia that was a revelation both to the American people and their foreign competitors. In the preparation and organization of the American pottery display, Mr. Brewer took an active and leading

Examples of Ott & Brewer decorated Belleek vases.

part, and subsequently took a prize at the Paris Exposition, where he also exhibited. About this time he first manufactured vitrified hotel china, and several specimens still in his possession testify to its excellent quality. It was, however, left to others to make its manufacture a commercial success. Mr. Brewer, like the early potters of the English and French schools, has been more interested in achieving practical success than in making money, and, as a consequence, is not as wealthy as some of his more conservative contemporaries. He has spent many thousand dollars in arriving at the present stage, and the American industry generally has shared in its benefits.

"The United States Potters' Association, which has done much to unify, strengthen, and advance the pottery interests of this country, was suggested and successfully organized by Mr. Brewer, who was for some years its secretary, and subsequently became its president. His familiar face is seen at every convention, and it is hard to tell when he is at his best: in the serious discussions of the convention, or when, as toastmaster at the banquet, the speakers are introduced with witty and appropriate remarks.

"In 1857 he was elected to the New Jersey House of Assembly in a district that usually went Democratic, and subsequently became a Representative in both the 47th and 48th Congress, where he speedily became recognized as one of the most intelligent exponents and advocates of the tariff question, and gained a national reputation.

"Mr. Brewer is a thoroughly practical potter, familiar with all the details of the industry, acquainted with all its ups and downs during the past twenty-six years, and always taking an active interest in anything related to its advancement. In the recent efforts to cultivate the spirit of practical art by offering prizes to the various art schools he has been prominent. His genial manners and kindly disposition have endeared him to all he has come in contact with, and even in the heat of political strife he has commanded the respect and friendship of his opponents. No employer is more popular among his employees, and no manufacturer more respected among his colleagues.

"Mr. Brewer was born in Hunterdon County, N.J., March 29, 1844, and is a lineal descendant, on his mother's side, of John Jart, one of the signers of the Declaration of Independence."

A short time previous to the Centennial Exhibition, Mr. Isaac Broome, an American sculptor, who had already gained considerable reputation as an artist of ability, was engaged by Messrs. Ott & Brewer to design and model a series of works in parian for that occasion. These attracted much attention, both on account of their originality of form and artistic treatment. A tea set, ornamented with raised designs and portrait busts of General and Mrs. Washington, was particularly noteworthy. His "Fashion" vases, embellished with figures in low relief, illustrate the styles of the last and present centuries. They are unique in form and, like all of Prof. Broome's work, characterized by conscientious attention to detail and careful finish. One of the most spirited designs of the series is the base-ball vase which was suggested by Mr. Brewer and worked out by Mr. Broome. It is suggestive throughout, in all of its harmonious details, of the American national game. From a pedestal rises a gradually tapering vase, of which the lower portion is formed of a series of bats banded together by a strap, while the upper portion is embellished with figures of ball-players in low relief. The cover represents a base-ball, surmounted by the American eagle, and around the projecting ledge of the base are arranged three players in life-like attitudes. The modelling is faultless and the figures are full of action.

A pastoral vase, by the same artist, is no less meritorious, though of an entirely different character. The rustic decoration, in low relief, is well suited to the form, and the goat's head handles are in keeping with the other ornamental details. A faun's head bracket, of classic conception and excellently modelled, forms an appropriate support for the vase.

Right: Pastoral vase and bracket; both modelled by Broome.

Probably the most pretentious piece of work which Prof. Broome has done for the Etruria Pottery is the parian bust of Cleopatra. This alone would be sufficient to place him in the front ranks of American sculptors, and is one of a large number of heads which have been modelled by him. Busts of public men have been made from life or the best portraits obtainable, and are faithful lilkenesses of the originals. The parian ware of the Etruria Pottery is soft and mellow in texture and a close imitation of the finest statuary marble.

T HE BURROUGHS AND MOUNTFORD COMPANY commenced business in Trenton, in 1879, in what was formerly the Eagle Pottery. Their specialties are vitrified, thin, and hotel china, decorated table and toilet sets, and underglaze printing on pottery and porcelain. The mechanical application of decorations is the distinguishing characteristic of one line of their art potteries, which, while closely imitating the more expensive methods of hand-painting, enables them to produce highly artistic effects at a greatly reduced cost. The bold ornamentation of their *jardinières,* umbrella-jars, punch-bowls, and vases, after the Doulton, Royal Worcester, Limoges, and Adderley methods, bears a striking individuality of its own. Probably their most beautiful pieces are those on which raised gold designs are applied by hand to an exquisite mazarine blue. One of the finest examples of this class is a large vase thiry-six inches in height, with silver and gold raised paste work, on a solid blue ground, executed by a Japanese artist. The accompanying illustration shows this piece mounted on a four-inch pedestal, between two vases of ordinary size.

White tiles of a fine quality, with underglaze blue printed devices, as well as embossed and enamelled art tiles, are also made here to some extent.

One of their latest styles of ornamentation, as applied to *jardinières* and vases, is the outline printing of human figures and scenes which are filled in by hand in colors, over the glaze.

Mazarine blue vase with gold design of the Burroughs and Mountford Company.

The effect is exceedingly rich and artistic, and by this process very creditable substitutes for the more expensive imported ceramic paintings are placed on the market at surprisingly low prices.

THE GREENWOOD POTTERY COMPANY was incorporated in 1868, the present officers being Mr. James Tams, president, and Mr. James P. Stephens, secretary and treasurer. The business was established in 1861, under the style of Stephens, Tams & Co. Mr. Tams came from Longton, Staffordshire, England, where, at an early age, he learned the pottery business in all of its branches. Until 1876 they made white granite or stone china ware, since which date they have been making a specialty of the manufacture of vitrified and translucent china for hotel, steamship, and railway lines. They are also producing at the present time thin china table ware of a superior quality, with overglaze and underglaze decoration, for domestic purposes, porcelain hardware trimmings, and electrical, telegraph, and telephone insulating supplies. Some years ago they added an art department to their extensive establishment, and their productions, consisting of vases, plaques, and other ornamental designs, richly decorated in the Royal Worcester style, are characterized by elegance of form, of which, it is said, no duplicates are made. The best pieces possess an ivory finish and white enamel, raised gold, silver, and bronze effects. Their mazarine blue is particularly noteworthy, being exceedingly rich in tone and remarkably fine and even in texture, and has been favorably compared with the *Bleu de Roi* of European factories. Another style of decoration, which has been practised here to some extent is *pâte-sur-pâte* or clay upon clay.

The plant of the company consists of seventeen large kilns, with an annual producing capacity of over half a million dollars. The experience of this company, in introducing their vitreous hotel china, reveals the extent of that deep-seated prejudice which existed in this country some years ago against everything made in America, but the superior merits of the ware were finally recognized and it has now largely taken the place of imported china.

The mark used from 1865 to 1876 was the coat-of-arms of the State of New Jersey above the words "Ironstone China" and "G. P. Co." This was printed in black under the glaze. The first table porcelain made at this pottery was stamped "G. P. Co."

THOMAS MADDOCK first made plumbers' sanitary ware in 1870, and still continues to manufacture it exclusively. At the American Institute Fair, held in New York in 1879, he exhibited an interesting large Grecian vase of stoneware, decorated on one side with a drawing of an ancient Egyptian potter at work. The names of half a dozen governors of as many States were written on the biscuit, who were present when the piece was being made.

THE DELAWARE POTTERY.

IN 1880 one of Mr. Maddock's foremen went to the Enterprise Pottery and introduced these specialties there. Mr. Oliphant was then interested in the latter factory, but withdrew in 1884, and started the Delaware Pottery in partnership with three of his sons, in conjunction with Mr. Thomas Connely, recently from the Belleek works, Ireland, and Mr. Charles Fay. Messers. Oliphant & Co. manufacture plumbers' appliances and sanitary specialties, druggists' and jewellers' supplies. These wares have justly acquired a wide reputation for excellence of quality, design, and decoration. Their Wedgwood ware mortars and pestles are characterized by extreme hardness of body and smoothness of finish.

About 1886 Mr. Connelly commenced experimenting in Belleek china. He succeeded in producing some exquisitely thin trial pieces of the finest grade, but the ware was never made in sufficient quantity to place upon the market. The few pieces which were produced, consisting of small ewers, cups, and saucers, were fired in the large kilns with the sanitary ware. This branch of the business was not developed beyond the experimental stage, although at the time of Mr. Connelly's death, in 1890, success was assured.

THE INTERNTIONAL POTTERY.

IN 1878 Messrs. James Carr, of New York, and Edward Clarke, of England, commenced the manufacture of cream-colored and white granite wares, as the Lincoln Pottery Company, in the old Speeler works, one of the first potteries built in Trenton for the manufacture of Rockingham and yellow wares. Mr. Carr retired within a few months, and Mr. Clarke, with others, founded the International Pottery Co. In 1879 the business was purchased by the present propritors, Mr. William Burgess, now United States Consul at Tunstall, England, in the pottery district, and Mr. John A. Campbell, who have with varying sucess, for some years previous to 1888, when a new body, of exceptional standing qualities, was produced, and has been made to the present time. The specialties of these works are toilet and dinner sets of artistic and novel shapes, in semi-porcelain body, in royal blue, still blue, and gray underglaze colors. Their flown blue services, produced within the past two years, are of exceptional merit and have been pronounced equal in all respects to the best of the kind produced in England. While no special effort has been made in the direction of decorative designs, many of their pieces are characterized by elegance of form and a richness and depth of blue ground seldom surpassed in this country or abroad. Their royal blue "Wilton" dinner service is especially praiseworthy, The International Pottery Co. also produces porcelain of a fine quality, white granite, and other grades of ware, with embossed gold, enamelled, and vellum-finished decorations. The mark used on certain patterns of underglaze ware is the circular stamp enclosing the names of the members of the firm, which is impressed in the clay. This and their Rugby flint china mark, which is printed under the glaze in brown, are here given.

They are now stamping all of their porcelain goods in blue color: Royal Blue/B—C/Porcelain.

The mark used on their ironstone china is the same which was formerly employed by Messrs. Carr & Clarke, and afterwards used in a modified form by Mr. Carr at his New York factory.

THE WILLETS MANUFACTURING C.

AMONG the most extensive establishments in the Eastern States is that of the Willets Manufacturing Company of Trenton, N.J. The present proprietors, Messrs. Joseph, Daniel, and Edmund R. Willets, three brothers, succeeded to the business in 1879. The factory was erected in 1853 by William Young and Sons, who at first made Rockingham and common ware. At the Centennial Exhibition, William Young's Sons did a display of crockery and porcelain hardwared trimmings, at which time the plant included only four kilns. The business has since grown to such an extent, under the present management, that there are now thirteen large ware kilns besides those used for decorating. The products from these works include sanitary

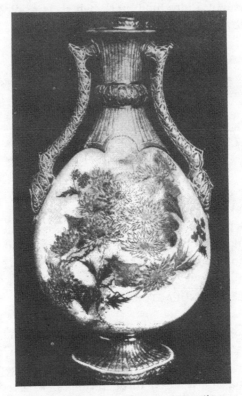

Large vase, chrysanthemum decoration.

earthenware, plumbers' specialties, white and decorated pottery, opaque china, white granite, and art porcelain. A specialty in dinner and toilet services is underglazed decoration on white bodies.

After the Ott & Brewer Company had perfected the body and glaze of their Belleek ware and got it well under way, William Bromley, Sr., went with the Willets Manufacturing Company and instructed them in the process. The manufacture of white egg-shell ware, to which they are constantly adding new designs, is another specialty of these works, and the company is now competing successfully with the Dresden, Limoges, and other foreign factories in supplying white art porcelain to decorators. In form their pieces are graceful and artistic, one of which is represented here. Some small picture frames, in Belleek body, decorated with delicately modelled flowers, are especially noteworthy.

They also employ a number of competent artists to decorate their art goods, many of which are reproductions of the characteristic shell and coral forms of the Irish works. The illustration represents a large Belleek vase with open-work handles and chrysanthemum decoration in delicate tints on an ivory, gold-stippled ground.

THE CERAMIC ART COMPANY, of which Mr. Jonathan Coxon, Sr., was president and Mr. Walter S. Lenox, secretary and treasurer, was established in Trenton in 1889. The first named gentleman became superintendent at the Ott & Bewer Company's works after Bromley left, and the latter was formerly in charge of their decorating department. Here they learned the processes of manufacturing Belleek. They are rapidly making a name by their constantly increasing patterns, many of which are exquisitely conceived and show the touch of thorough artists. Their specialties are Belleek ware and "Indian china," many of their best pieces having been designed by Mr. William W. Gallimore. They have procured the best designers

Left: Egg-shell porcelain, the "Engagement" cup and saucer. *Below:* A carved vase. Both of the Ceramic Art Company.

and painters that can be found and employ both the overglaze and underglaze processes in decorating. Their egg-shell ware is also furnished in the white to decorators. One of these undecorated pieces, a gracefully lily-shaped cup, is here shown. In addition to vases and table pieces, they make many fancy patterns, such as thimbles, inkstands, parasol handles, menu slabs, and candelabra.

Among the most recent productions of the Ceramic Art Company are some beautiful pieces of carved ware, in Belleek body, which possess a high order of artistic merit. The decoration is entirely in relief, and is executed by carving the designs in the clay before burning, the only tool used being an ordinary jack-knife. This work is done by Miss Kate B. Sears, a young lady artist employed by the company. A spherical vase of this character, exhibited at the World's Columbian Exposition, is shown. The interior is galzed, while the outside is porcelain bisque, entirely devoid of coloring in the decoration, which consists of elaborate designs of lilies and child figures extending around a central zone. The soft, white surface of the ware is admirably suited to the subject selected for decorative treatment.

THE TRENTON CHINA COMPANY was incorporated in 1859, "to manufacture and sell procelain, china, chemicals, drugs, and other articles of which clay, sand, and other earthy substances form the basis or principal ingredients." Of late years a specialty of this company has been vitrified china, white and decorated, for table uses. These works were closed in 1891. After undergoing a very troublesome experience before perfecting the quality of their china— which was at last accomplished under the management of Mr. Duggan— the money and patience of its backers became exhausted, and the company went into the hands of a receiver.

At the Arsenal Pottery of the Mayer Pottery Manufacturing Company, of which Mr. Joseph S. Mayer is president, decorated porcelain, underglazed and majolica wares are made. This is, probably, at the present time, the only concern in the United States which manufactures the so-called majoica ware. Their exhibit at the Chicago Fair included some finely modelled Toby pitchers or jugs, which are excellent imitations in form and color of the old English design so familiar to collectors.

The Union Pottery Company, which was closed in 1889, made for the political campaign of the previous year a quantity of six-inch tiles, dinner plates, etc., decorated with printed portraits of the Presidential candidates. This company was incorporated in 1869, the incorporators being Baltes Pickel, William White, Henry Smith, Joshua Jones, and Elias Cook.

The American Art China Works were established December 1, 1891, in what was formerly known as the Washington Pottery, by Messrs. Rittenhouse, Evans, & Co. The ware made here is distinctively an American production, and is placed upon the market as American china. The body is thin, translucent, and strong, and resembles the Belleek ware made at other Trenton factories. The shapes are new, and the decorations artistic. The proprietors of these works are actuated by the laudable determination to demonstrate to the American public that it is possible to produce home goods fully equal in every respect to any that can be made abroad. White china, in all the shapes produced at these works, is sold for decorating.

In the latter part of 1892, Messrs. W. T. Morris and F. R. Willmore commenced the erection of a pottery in Trenton for the manufacture of art wares. The former was at one time connected with the Belleek works, Ireland, and the Royal Worcester Porcelain works, England, and recently with the Ott & Brewer Pottery of Trenton. Mr. Willmore was also for many years empolyed as decorator at the two last-named establishments. Their new works, which they have named the Columbian Art Pottery, were finished in the early part of 1893. Thin Belleek china and ivory ware, of a fine quality, are made here in original forms and decorations, and include articles of utility and ornamental pieces, such as candle-sticks, umbrella holders, *jardinières,* tea-pots, and specialties.

In addition to the Trenton establishments already mentioned are the East Trenton Pottery Co., which, during the Presidential campaign of 1888, produced plates with engraved portraits of the candidates; the Anchor Pottery; Enterprise Pottery Co.; Egyptian Pottery Co.; Equitable Pottery Co.; Warren Kimble; Imperial Porcelain Works of F. A. Duggan; C. W. Donaghue, potters' supplies; and a number of decorating establishments— Pope & Lee, Jesse Dean Decorating Co., W. C. Hendrickson, Tatler Decorating Co., and Poole & Stockton.

Other parties have also been engaged in the pottery industry since 1860 with varying success, some twenty establishments having discontinued business, with an aggregate loss of two million dollars.

Recently the Trenton Potteries Company has been incorporated, to acquire and continue the business heretofore conducted by the Empire, Enterprise, Delaware, Equitable, and Cresent potteries, with a capital stock of $3,000,000. Sanitary plumbing, toilet, and table wares will continue to be the staple productions.

The constant changes which are taking place in the pottery business in Trenton, through the closing of factories and the establishment of new ones every year, render it impossible to present a complete history of the industry to date, for even as these lines are being written word comes to us that new enterprises are being started; and the wonderfully rapid advances in the art furnish evidence that no chronicler can keep pace with the progress of the American potter.

OTHER TRENTON POTTERIES.

BY an Act approved February 9, 1865, the Trenton Pottery Company was incorporated for the manufacture of earthenware and crockery of various descriptions, the incorporators being Appollinaire Husson, James Taylor, John F. Houdayer, and Edmund Husson.

The Empire Pottery of Messrs. Alpaugh & Magowan was established in 1863, and was formerly owned by Messrs. Coxon & Thompson. In 1883 the business passed into the hands of the present proprietors. They manufacture thin porcelain, dinner, tea, and toilet, and decorated wares, principally in white granite body. They make a specialty of sanitary and plumbers' eartheware.

The Mercer Pottery Company was organized in 1868, and at the present time Mr. James Moses is the sole proprietor. The products of this potter consist of a fine line of semi-porcelain dinner and toilet ware, both white and decorated; also white granite wares of the same kind. This firm was the first to produce what is now known as semi-porcelain earthenware in this country. Mr. Moses, we think, is fairly entitled to that credit. He has made a great success of it, and represents one of the leading firms in the United States today.

The New Jersey Pottery Company was organized in 1869, the incorporators being Elias Cook, John Woolverton, Caleb S. Green, Barker Gummere, and Nathaniel E. Britton.

The Fell & Thropp Company, known as the Trenton Pottery, was the old Taylor & Speeler pottery. It is now owned by Samuel E. Thropp and J. Hart Brewer. They manufacture a full line of white granite and C. C. wares. This pottery is the oldest white granite pottery in Trenton.

Messrs. Dale & Davis built the Prospect Hill Pottery in 1880, the latter having formerly been manager for Mr. John Moses at the Glasgow Pottery. They produce a large line of decorated semi-porcelain and white granite dinner and toilet wares.

The Crescent Pottery Company, composed of W. S. Hancock and Chas. H. Cook, was established in 1881. They manufacture sanitary earthenware and a full line of C.C. wares.

At the present time they are one of the leading firms of Trenton.

The Crown Porcelain Works of Messrs. Barlow and Marsh were started in 1890. They produce a fine line of decorated *faience* specialties. Mr. Marsh was formerly connected with Messrs. Robertson & Company of England, and is a practical potter and an artist of no mean ability.

The Trenton Terra-Cotta Company, of which Mr. Joseph McPherson is president, and Mr. O. O. Bowman is treasurer, manufacture an extensive line of fire-brick, vitrified salt-glazed sewer pipe, terra-cotta chimney tops and flues, and garden vases. The latter are particularly elaborate and deservedly popular.

The American China Company of Trenton produced to a limited extent stone china decorated by the chromo-lithographic process, which has been employed in Europe for perhaps forty years. This process consists in the application of vitrifiable decalcomanie designs to the surface of the ware, either under or over the glaze, usually the latter. On a plate in my possession, made by the above-named company, is a central design of a crab, with marginal fronds of sea-weed in colors,—green, brown, black, and red. The effect is that of the ordinary decalcomanie transfer work, but, having been fired, the designs are permanently affixed, as in the other overglaze decorations. This process has been carried to great perfection, especially by the Doulton factory of Lambeth, England, and by some of the French potters, intricate and artistic designs being produced in delicate coloring which resemble fine hand-painted work, but the transfer printing can be distinguised by the dots and lines of the engraving, which can readily be detected on close inspection.

THE JERSEY CITY POTTERY.

THE JERSEY PORCELAIN AND EARTHENWARE COMPANY was incorporated in "the town of Jersey, County of Bergen," on

Above: Semi-porcelain table ware of the International Pottery Company.

December 10, 1825, under an act of the New Jersey Legislature, in which George Dummer, Timothy Dewey, Henry Post, Jr., William W. Shirley, and Robert Abbatt, Jr., were named as incorporators. In the following year the products of the factory were awarded a silver medal at the exhibition of the Franklin Institute, Philadelphia, as being the "best china from American materials." In the Trumbull-Prime collection is a small porcelain bowl, with heavy gold band, which was made at this pottery, of good body and excellent glaze. The manufacture of porcelain, however, does not seem to have been continued there for more than about three years.

The works were purchased by Messrs. D. & J. Henderson about 1829, and a year later they exhibited "flint stoneware" of a superior quality at the Franklin Institute. Mr. A. G. Richmond, of Canajoharie, N.Y., possesses a mottled Toby jug made at that period and marked "D & J. Henderson, Jersey City," in a circle, impressed in the paste (Ill. 50). In 1833, David Henderson organized *The American Pottery Manufacture Company,* "for the purpose of manufacturing the various kinds of pottery, at the works already erected." By an act of Assembly passed January 18th in that year, Messrs. David Henderson, John V. B. Varick, Robert Gilchrist, John Cassedy, and J. Dickinson Miller, of Jersey City, and Edward Cook, George Tingle, and John Steele, of New York, were appointed commissioners to receive subscriptions to the stock, which was to be limited to $150,000. We know little about the ware produced here during the next seven years, excepting the fact that a buff or cream-colored body, of excellent quality, was used extensively. For the first time in America the English method of transfer printing in decoration was adopted by these works. During the exciting Presidential campaign of 1840, or shortly after the election, a large eight-sided water-pitcher of cream-colored ware was produced, bearing on each of the four front panels black underglaze prints, consisting of an engraving of a log cabin at the top, over the legend, "The Ohio Farmer," a

Below: A Belleek shell and cupid pitcher of the Willets Manufacturing Company.

portrait bust of W. H. Harrison in the centre, and the American eagle below. This piece was marked on the bottom, in black, under the glaze, with a flag bearing the inscription "Am. Pottery Manufg. Co. Jersey City." During this period of manufacture, Daniel Greatbach, who came from a family of noted English potters, and is said to have been at one time a modeller for the Ridgways of Cauldon Place, England, was employed at this factory, and designed a large number of ornate pieces, some of which were produced until the factory was closed. An earthen water-pitcher, embellished with hunting-scenes in relief, and handle in the form of a deer-hound, continued to be a popular design for nearly half a century.

In 1842, an exhibit of goods produced by this company was made at the Franklin Institute, consisting of embossed ware, jugs, tea-ware, etc., which took a silver medal. A glazed white-ware spittoon, evidently one of this series, is still preserved in the cabinet of the Institute, which is decorated with raised, conventional designs in white, on a dark-blue ground, the upper surface being fluted and in solid blue. A cream-colored pottery pan or nappie, of fine body and glaze, in the same collection, with the impressed mark, American Potty. Co. Jersey City, is another example at that time.

The name of the establishment was changed to *The Jersey City Pottery* during this period, and many of the best potters of the old school in the United States learned their trade at this factory. In 1848 large quantities of druggists' jars were being made. After several alterations in the firm name, Messrs. Rouse and Turner became proprietors. The former, Mr. John Owen Rouse, came from the Derby Works, England, around this same period. Nathaniel Turner was born and reared among the Staffordshire potteries at Tunstall, and after his death in 1884, the business was carried out by Mr. Rouse alone. The products of the factory for some years were mainly ornamental forms in white bisquit and glazed ivory white for decorators, and porous cups for telegraphic purposes, of which some 5,000 were produced weekly. Of the plain shapes in ivory white ware, one of the most graceful is the "Worcester" vase, so-called because it is a reproduction of an old pattern produced at the Worcester Works in England. It is said that George Washington was presented with a vase of this shape by Mr. Samuel Vaughan of London, in conjunction with a pair of vases of different design, which have been identified as Worcester pieces. One example measures two feet in height and was decorated by Mr. Edward Lycett. On a turquoise blue, mottled ground are artistically painted flowers, poppies on one side, and on the other hollyhocks in natural colors. A graceful wreath of convolvulus ornaments the cover. The handles are gilded and bands of gold encircle the top and bottom.

Another effective form was called the "King" vase. The example here figured was decorated by Mr. W. Lycett, now of Atlanta, Georgia. The subject on the side shown in the engraving is "The Tired Dancing Girl." The painting is applied to the ivory tint of the ware, the borders and handles being of dead gold, heightened with black. On the reverse side is a floral group. This piece measures sixteen and a half inches in height.

When Mr. Rose first became connected with the works he found a large quantity of the old stock of undecorated porcelain in the warerooms, which has since been sold. A large number of engraved copper plates on hand at that time, since stolen or lost, showed to what extent transfer printing had formerly been practised. Hundreds of the old moulds were, until recently, stored in the loft of the building, among which were four different varieties and sizes of Toby jugs, a pitcher with rope and anchor decoration in relief, and another with raised designs of tulips, a figure of Christ, an Apostle jug with raised representations of apostles in panels, hunting pictures, etc., some, if not all, being the work of Greatbach. We have seen examples of the largest Toby pitcher made here (about 1840), nearly a foot in height, with excellent brown glaze outside and lined with white. Pitchers and other pieces were also decorated with medallion

"Worcester" vase decorated by Mr. Edward Lycett, of the Jersey City Pottery Company.

portraits of prominent men, modelled in relief, a likeness of Daniel O'Connell being among the best.

In the summer of 1892 the old pottery property passed into other hands, and the old buildings, which had stood in almost their original condition for more than sixty-five years, were torn down to make way for a new manufacturing establishment. Both wings of the original structure were standing, in good state of preservation until November of that year, when the work of demolition commenced, and at the same time wagon loads of old moulds, which had cost thousands of dollars, the accumulation of over half a century, were hauled away and ruthlessly dumped on the meadows. Thus has disappeared one of the oldest ceramic landmarks, dear to the memory of many an old potter still living, as the cradle of the pottery industry in the United States. All of the moulds of vessels were destroyed, but from this wreck a small series of ornamental designs, believed to have been, for the most part, made by Greatbach during the earlier years of the pottery's existence, were rescued by Mr. Rouse and, at the solicitation of the writer, placed in the collection of the Pennsylvania Museum of Art. These consist of finely modelled leaves, animals in hunting scenes, floral designs, and other decorative details.

In 1878 Messrs. Rouse and Turner presented to the Metropolitan Museum of Art, New York, a pottery barrel, with relief ornaments, made about 1830, at this pottery, by David Henderson. A many-sided pottery pitcher, surmounted with Toby head, is owned by Rev. F. E. Snow, of Guilford, Conn., on which is the mark, "American Pottery Co., Jersey City, N.J." impressed in a circle.

THE principal modeller and mould maker employed at the Jersey City works, as has been previously stated, was Daniel Greatbach, who is said to have come from Harley, England, about the year 1838. Many evidences of Greatbach's proficiency in the art of ceramic modelling are preserved, and it

The "King" vase decorated by Mr. W. Lycett, of the Jersey City Pottery Company.

may be confidently stated that almost all of the designs of an ornamental nature which were produced at these works between the years 1838 and 1848 were originated by him. In 1852, Mr. Greatbach entered into partnership with James Carr and commenced the manufacture of pottery at South Amboy, N.J., but this connection only lasted about a year. Greatbach went to Peoria, Ill., where Mr. George Wolfe, who was then connected with the Peoria Pottery Co., found him in 1861. Shortly afterwards Greatbach moved to Trenton. As a manufacturer he was unfortunate, but as a modeller he was remarkably successful. His designs were meritorious and possessed an individuality of their own by which they may generally be recognized. He originated the hound-handle jugs and hunting pitchers which were so common in this country between 1840 and 1860, and the majority of those found to-day may, with a reasonable degree of certainity, be attributed to him. Mr. James Carr, his former partner, possesses a jug with grape-vine handle and decorations which was made at South Amboy in 1852. The same pattern, or a modification of it, was subsequently produced at the Bennington establishment, with which Greatbach was for a time connected, and it is said that the moulds were taken to Burlington, Vt., by some of the workmen of the Bennington pottery, after the closing of the latter, and used there.

Mr. Greatbach is described, by some of the older potters who are still living and who at one time were associated with him, as of courteous manner and gentlemanly deportment, large and handsome in appearance, always going to the factory well dressed and wearing a silk hat. Before beginning his work he was accustomed to don a white duck suit. Although a man of refinement and education, possessing marked talent and ability, he died in poverty at Trenton, after a varied career. In his declining years he was visited by a former co-worker, who was so touched by the old modeller's destitute condition that he sent the latter a check for a comfortable sum. In return for this act of generosity, Greatbach sent to the donor a box of small figure moulds made by him at various times, which were his only remaining possessions. This is one of the pathetic incidents which abound in the unwritten history of pottery.

Among the modelled designs of Greatbach, produced at Jersey City, was a cream-ware tea set with relief floral decorations, of which the teapot here figured is an example.

About 1840, when transfer printing was first introduced in this country, table-ware was made at the Jersey City Pottery with engraved designs printed in various colors. One of these patterns, in light blue underglaze, was known as the "Canova" which was copied from a design produced a few months earlier by John Ridgway of Hanley, England. Examples of dinner plates belonging to the "Canova" set, bearing the printed mark of the "American Pottery Manufacturing Co., Jersey City," have recently been found.

Mr. John Owen Rouse, the last proprietor of the Jersey City Pottery, died at Bayonne, N.J. on Nov. 14, 1896.

THE ETRURIA POTTERY, TRENTON, N.J.

THE *pâte-sur-pâte* method of decorating was practised, to some extent, at the Etruria Pottery of Messrs. Ott & Brewer, many years ago. The paintings were done in white china clay on a tinted body or colored ground, being built up, step by step, by the application of numerous coatings of slip to form the higher parts. This work was done by Mr. Harry Saunders, a Trenton decorator, among whose best pieces is an octagonal tray with white figures of a female and boys, representing "The Singing Lesson," on a dark blue ground. Over all is a transparent glaze, in the style of the celebrated Solon *pâte-sur-pâte* paintings of the Minton factory. A series of well-modelled, urn-shaped vases was also produced in light blue unglazed body, with white slip designs of birds and flowers, closely resembling

Above: The Old Pottery of Jersey City.

A hunting pitcher designed by Daniel Greatbach.

in coloring and general appearance the moulded "Jasper" ware of the Wedgwood Works at Etruria England.

Soon after the close of the Chicago Exhibition, the firm of Ott & Brewer was dissolved, and the Cook Pottery Co., of which Mr. Charles H. Cook is president, was organized on February 14, 1894, to manufacture white granite and cream-colored wares. The recent demand for so-called Delft ware and blue effects in china stimulated some of the American potters to join the ranks of foreign manufacturers who were competing for public favor. The Cook Pottery Co. began making Delft in 1897 and produced some of the best decorations which have appeared in this country, after the style of the old blue Delft ware of Holland. The original has not only been closely simulated in the appearance of the body itself, and the opaque, bluish-white tone of the glaze, but in the peculiar blue coloring of the decorations and the adaptation of subject, as well. While this work is, to some extent, imitative, it posses elements of originality which entitle it to recognition as an American product. A large vase, of the Etruria "Bourne" pattern, in the Pennsylvania Museum, Philadelphia, is probably the finest example of this kind of underglaze painting which has been done in the United States. It is the work of Mr. P. Paul Gasper, a Trenton decorator, who has caught the spirit of the old Dutch potters in his treatment of the subject, while adapting it to our own time and conditions. There are wind-mills and sailing boats, almost inseparable from the old Dutch tin-enamelled ware, and on the opposite side a charming rural scene—a group of peaceful cattle in a brook-bordered meadow. The irregularly scrolled panels are framed by graceful floral work, sufficiently original in conception and execution to protect the design from the charge of plagiarism.

In 1898 this company introduced a fine variety of underglaze ware with six and eight colors in flower work, mainly in *jardinières,* a notable acheivement being the production of distinct shades of carmine and pink beneath the glaze.

THE CERAMIC ART COMPANY, TRENTON, N.J.

BELLEEK or egg -shell china has been brought to the highest state of perfection in this country by the Ceramic Art Company of Trenton. During the past seven years this ware in its white condition has come into general use among professional and amateur decorators, largely supplanting the French china, which possesses a harder body and softer glaze. This company has also produced, during the same period, a great variety of blue underglaze decorations, of much artistic merit. Among the more elaborate pieces is one painted by Mr. Richard Hicks,—a large vase entirely covered with a bold and spirited representation of the mythological descent of Orpheus into Hades in search of his wife. Orpheus with his lute is depicted in the palace of Pluto surrounded by demons, while the fair Eurydice stands before him in the clutches of the archfiend. The stairway descending from the entrance, guarded by Cerberus, the three-headed dog, is shown, while flames and smoke ascend on every side, fanned by the subterraneous currents. Orpheus stands at the right, in the attitude of playing his charmed instrument.

Another fine example of underglaze painting in blue is a view of Napoleon and his generals, on a tall vase of graceful proportions. The drawing and grouping of the figures are admirable. It is the work of Mr. Sturgis Laurence of Trenton.

A series of finely modelled loving cups, tankards, and jugs, with copied and original subjects in brown overglaze coloring, have met with well-merited popularity during the past few years. The decorative subjects are convivial monks, smoking, bicycling, sporting, and drinking scenes. One of these, which is perhaps, more appropriately American in the spirit than the others, presents a picture of Rip Van Winkle after he has awakened from his long sleep.

Among the later developments of this company is overglaze flower-painting on large pieces of attractive form. A striking

Bust of Cleopatra, *circa* 1876, by Isaac Broome for Ott and Brewer Co., of Trenton, New Jersey.

example of this character is a vase bearing festoons of daintily colored roses in natural tints, the work of Mr. W. H. Morley. The use of gold-plated metal mountings for vases and lamps is a recent innovation. The combination of soft colorings and creamy ground with the bright gold of the metal base and handles is exceedingly rich in effect.

No less attractive is a syle of flower-painting in which closely related tones of color, such as brown and orange, are employed exclusively.

HADDONFIELD, N.J.

A SMALL stoneware pottery, operated by Charles Wingender & Bro., is situated at Haddonfield, N.J. about six miles from Philadelphia. The senior member of the firm learned his trade in the stoneware potteries of Hoehr bei Coblenz, Germany, and his brother, William, studied at the Ceramic School in the same place, where much of the finer ware which finds its way to the United States is produced, particularly the gray and blue beer "steins" with elaborately modelled relief designs of domestic scenes, battles, beer drinkers, and dwarfs. In this country the brothers secured employment for some years at the stoneware pottery of Mr. Richard C. Remmey, Philadelphia. They found little opportunity there for the excercise of their artistic talents and finally decided to embark in business for themselves. Accordingly, about 1894, they secured the old pottery at Haddonfield and here, surrounded by the more congenial atmosphere of an independent establishment, they have been devoting themselves to the manufacture of ornamental stoneware, in addition to the usual lines of common, utilitarian goods. While the capacity of their present plant is limited, they have already turned out some of the best work in the ordinary stoneware body, if not the most original in design, that has been produced by regular manufacturers in this country. While their methods are essentially those of the

German school, and while they have brought over with them many of the patterns and elaborate examples of modelling which they are utilizing in the ornamentation of mugs, *jardinières,* pedestals, and pitchers, they are also producing original work of considerable merit, designed by William Wingender. In quality the ware resembles the German body, although made entirely from American clays. Having overcome the difficulties encountered in the use of new and unfamiliar materials, they have recently been making a specialty of water coolers and large ice jugs, which have met with a ready sale because they are superior to anything of the same character produced in this country.

Among more common wares made here are Toby ale jugs, in several sizes, colored in brown and cobalt blue. The beer mugs are carefully modelled and quite elaborate in design. While some of these are reproductions of German patterns, they are such as are not now imported, and represent the best work of the foremost modellers of the German potteries, executed before the demand for cheap wares had caused the degeneration of decorative designing, so often observed in much of the ware lately sent to this country. Many of these designs, however, are not wholly copies, but are modified and executed by Mr. Wingender in the spirit of the older German work. In the group of beer mugs shown, the central figure represents an enormous example, with a capacity of two litres, entirely covered with a relief design representing the battle of Teutoburg Forest, which took place in September of the year 9 A.D. when Quintilius Varus led the Roman troops against the Germans. In this engagement, which lasted three days, the Roman forces were entirely destroyed, and Varus killed himself in despair by falling on his sword. This spirited design was originally used at the Hoehr works, but has been remodelled for use at the Haddonfield pottery.

Among the larger stoneware designs made here are *jardinières* and pedestals in several sizes, which are usually

"Ivory" vase of the
Royal Worcester Style,
of the Greenwood Pottery
Company.

Willets Manufacturing Company.

decorated with relief medallions of heads of warriors of Greek or Roman type, of animals, and carved ornamentation on a solid blue ground. Such pieces admit of greater freedom of treatment than do the smaller drinking vessels, and are, therefore, more characteristic of Mr. Wingender's peculiar style. They rank in point of workmanship with the best imported wares of the same class, and, indeed, are often mistaken for German productions by those who are not aware that such work is now being done in the United States.

The Haddonfield pottery is one of the few in this country which still continues to make the old-time salt-glazed ware. In a large majority of potteries it has been supplanted, in recent years, by an inferior product, of lighter color and softer body, while the delicate surface film produced by the vaporization of the salt in the kiln has been replaced by a thick and heavy dipped glaze, which obliterates the fine markings of the mould. Even if the day for salt-glazed stoneware has gone by, we must confess to a weakness for it, which the advent of the new so-called stoneware has only served to increase.   —E. A. BARBER

Henderson of Jersey City and His Pitchers

T HE modern American, surrounded by endless variety of manufactured goods, has difficulty in picturing an era when this country produced almost nothing on a large scale and when it was dependent upon England for nearly all decorative household articles. Such manufacture as we had in the first quarter of the nineteenth century was a series of beginnings—a struggle to establish permanent production for the country's needs.

The attempts to make satisfactory glass, china, and pottery were particularly numerous after the War of 1812 had checked importations. Up to that time few potters had even tried to manufacture porcelain or fine earthenware, and the makers of household stoneware, which was gradually replacing the coarse redware of the early country craftsmen, were still working in the same small way as had their forebears. The decade of the 1820's was one of trials and new departures. It was no mere accident that caused this sudden flowering of American industry just before 1830. The levying of a protective tariff in 1824, coupled with an aroused interest in mechanics and inventions, swept the country rapidly towards production that would make it independent of Europe. Tucker porcelain, Sandwich, Cambridge, and Pittsburg pressed glass, and the molded pottery of Jersey City made an almost simultaneous appearance.

We are here concerned with the successful introduction to America of English-style pottery by David Henderson and his brother. Their output from the very beginning was so different from other native wares and so much more sophisticated that we may well call Henderson the Wedgwood of America. Although not endowed with the fine artistic sense of his great predecessor, Henderson turned the course of potting in America, as did Wedgwood in England, away from the primitive traditional wares fashioned by individual craftsmen to ceramic forms that were created by designers and carried to completion by professional workmen. This event spelled the doom of the naive work of our country potters, but it was an inevitable development in a democratic country. The only way in which decorative art could be sold cheaply to the masses of people was by producing it in some labor-saving fashion. In the case of both glass and pottery this was accomplished by the use of molds.

Henderson started his pottery in the works of the defunct Jersey Porcelain and Earthenware Company. His predecessors were allied with the Jersey City Glass Company: George Dummer was an incorporator in both concerns. The glass company was established first—in 1824; the porcelain works was incorporated in December 1825. June 20 of the following year, the glass company conveyed to the porcelain company the property fronting Essex, Warren, and Morris Streets. After the failure of the porcelain business, George Dummer, who then had title to the property, sold it, September 29, 1828, to David Henderson. Two years later (May 11, 1830) Henderson acquired from the glass company two other adjoining lots on Morris and Essex Streets. By this time the new venture was well under way.

David Henderson was the owner of the buildings and

Figure 1: Flint stoneware with the familiar hunting scenes applied in relief. The color is light tan or buff. Height, 7 inches.

Figure 2: A duplicate of Figure 1 with ivory or pale yellow color.

manager of the pottery until his death in 1845. (Administration of his estate was granted October 13, 1845.) During the first five years, and possibly longer, J. Henderson, said to be David's brother, was his associate. The several firm styles, *D & J. Henderson, Henderson Flint Stoneware Manufactory,* and *Henderson's Stone and Earthenware Manufactory,* used as marks, belong to this period. On January 18, 1833, the company was incorporated as *The American Pottery Manufacturing Company.* David Henderson, John B. V. Varick, Robert Gilchrist, John Cassedy, and J. Dickinson Miller, of Jersey City, and Edward Cook, George Tingle, and John Steele, of New York, were appointed commissioners to sell stock to the value of $150,000. In *Early American Pottery and China* John Spargo says that there was a reorganization of the company in 1840, at which time the name was changed to *American Pottery Company.* There seems to be no basis for this statement. In the list of premiums awarded at the American Institute in New York, October 1842, is the note: "American Pottery Manufacturing Co. for best specimen of crockery ware—a silver medal." Mr. Spargo puzzles over the fact that he finds no mark of the period 1833-1840. The probability is that the concern was always known as the "American Pottery Company," the lengthy word "Manufacturing" having been dropped in ordinary use as it was with the Boston Crown Glass Manufacturing Company. Transfer-printed ware alone, which was first made in the late thirties, is marked *AM Pottery Manufg. Co.*

Again, Mr. Spargo says that the style was changed to *Jersey City Pottery* in 1845. This does not agree with Barber's statement that this name was adopted about 1852: *i.e.,* about forty years before the time when he was writing. The *Jersey City Directory* of 1849/50 contains a reading notice that should settle this question. It refers to the company as "The American Pottery Manufactory." We may therefore conclude that the firm, although under different management, kept its name

Figure 3: Flint stoneware having the upper portion glazed brown while the body is light buff. The interior is left unglazed. Height, 10 inches.

Figure 4: Flint stoneware with applied vine motifs smear glazed with a warm buff color. Height, 8¼ inches.

unchanged until the fifties, and that the mark *American Pottery Company* could have been used at any time between 1833 and 1850. In 1849 Oliver S. Strong was president of the company and Thomas McGurran (also spelled McGauran or McGeron) its secretary and superintendent. Its history under this management and later under Rouse and Turner does not here concern us.

The early products of the Henderson pottery are naturally of the greatest interest to the student of American ceramics. A fine quality of stone pottery was the first ware made. This attracted the attention of the editor of *Niles' Register,* who, following his policy of giving new American manufactures a boost, said of it, August 1, 1829:

"The manufacture of a very superior ware called 'flint stone ware' is extensively carried on by Mr. Henderson at Jersey City, opposite of New York. It is equal to the best English and Scotch stone ware, and will be supplied in quantities 33⅓ pc less than like foreign articles will cost, if imported. We have a pair of very handsome and much admired pitchers from this factory; at which a considerable variety of articles is made."

Again on October 31, in describing the exhibition at the American Institute in New York, he says:

"The stone-ware of Henderson which we hope will be successfully introduced, has several times been mentioned by us in terms of approbation. The pitchers of this material, at the fair, are from classical models, and very elegant."

He also refers to "flint ware pitchers on the model of those found in the ruins of Herculaneum."

The Hendersons appear once more in the *Register,* October 30, 1830, when their names were included in the list of those receiving awards at the annual exhibition of the Institute. The item reads:

"First Premium to D. & J. Henderson of Jersey City for specimens of superior stone, flint and cane colored earthenware, a great variety, John Tingle, agent, 78 Maiden Lane."

Even in these brief notices it is evident that the Hendersons in their output had gone a long way beyond the coarse and crudely-fired stoneware of their contemporaries. They used local materials—yellow clay from Long Island, stoneware clay from Amboy, and feldspar from Connecticut—but these were prepared and refined with care to produce pottery quite as good as the Staffordshire wares they were intended to imitate. The 1849 description and notice of the works previously referred to says that English ground flint has been added to the clays up to that time, although they were planning to use Berkshire sand in its place. Either of these ingredients would insure a hard, vitreous body.

A price list of articles made at Jersey City in 1830 was reproduced in *Antiques,* September 1934 (p. 109). It is headed "Fine Flint Ware Embossed and Plain." One of its most important items is a "Toby Philipot." Such a toby pitcher, formerly in the George Horace Lorimer collection *(Antiques,* January 1933, p. 4), is now owned by the Brooklyn Museum. It has a light buff body and is covered on the upper half with a brown glaze. The seated figure of the toper holds a sizable pitcher and is clothed in a long coat, knee breeches, and cocked hat. It is, in fact, a replica of the well-known English tobies in color. It bears the circular impressed mark *D. & J. Henderson Jersey City.* Present-day collectors will be amused to know that Henderson's toby sold for seventy-five cents!

The list includes coffeepots at fifteen dollars a dozen, teapots of three sizes, besides others, round or oval in shape, of two sizes, mugs to hold one quart, one pint, or one-half pint, small jars with covers, from half-pint to two-quart size, tea tubs, nursery lamps, water coolers, ink stands, and assorted toys. Such utilitarian objects as butter boxes, flower pots, spittoons, and pipkins were also made of this excellent ware.

Of particular interest in connection with the pitchers herewith illustrated are those mentioned in this early document. Only one design—the "Herculaneum Pattern"—is noted by

Figure 5: A pitcher of white glazed earthenware with applied vine motifs.

Figure 6: A buff flint stoneware pitcher with an all-over leaf and acorn design, covered with a thin glaze. Height, 9 inches.

Figure 7: An opaque blue glaze covers this buff body pitcher. Height, 7¾ inches.

name. The largest and most costly pitcher of this type was marked with a letter *A*. A succession of letters from *A* to *M* indicated size and probably also different colors or qualities. (This we deduce from the fact that both *E* and *K* were used for pitchers in two-and-one-half quart sizes, while *L* and *M* were reserved for sizes undesignated.) The smallest jug held a little over one pint. The example in Figure 2 has the *K* mark in relief, and that in Figure 4 an *L*.

"Another Quality of Pitchers" was similarly marked with numerals: a *3* for three-quarter pint and so on to a *9* for one-and-one-half gallons. The numbered pitchers were slightly less expensive than the lettered ones. These little marks should be of assistance in identifying Henderson flint ware.

This list makes no mention of earthenware; neither was it exhibited in October 1829. We may therefore conclude that earthenware was introduced commercially some time during the year 1830, but before the Institute exhibit in October. The mark *Henderson/Flint Stoneware/Manufactory* is therefore the earliest. This was probably followed shortly by the stamp *Henderson's Stone/& Earthenware/Manufactory/Jersey City, N.J.* The D. &.J. Henderson mark appears on both flint stoneware and earthenware. It could have been used at any time when the younger brother was associated with the business. He is said to have left the employ in 1833, although I have been unable to find any proof that he did so. The first two marks are so rare that they have been found only on the pitchers illustrated in Figures 1, 2, and 3.

The most noteworthy feature of the pitchers 1 to 5 is the use of applied molded decoration in the manner of Wedgwood jasper ware. The applications on the Henderson examples shown here are of the same color as the body. The pitchers in the first three illustrations are turned on the wheel, not molded, the handles, spouts, and ornaments having been added after the vessels were formed. The beautiful pitcher in Figure 4 was shaped in one operation in a mold and the grapevine reliefs later applied. It will be noted that the vine on the neck is superimposed over the scrolls under the lip, which were part of the molded design. The white earthenware pitcher in Figure 5 is embellished with the very same vine-leaf motifs.

The buff pitcher from the Pennsylvania Museum of Art *(Fig. 6)* was illustrated in *Old China,* April 1904, and there described by Edwin Atlee Barber. It is a handsome example of Henderson's early work. In my own collection is a similar pitcher slightly larger in size, but of the same design, which has been tinted a light azure blue and given a thin smear glaze. Although it is unmarked, and of a color not hitherto encountered in Henderson's ware, I nevertheless believe it to be of his manufacture.

Another Henderson piece not here illustrated is a cream-colored pitcher with dull glaze that was shown in an exhibition of New Jersey ceramics at the Newark Museum in 1915. It was borrowed from the Pitkin collection, and is described as having a bowl-shaped body with scalloped edge, ornamented with relief decoration of scrolls, acanthus motifs, and masks. This pitcher was 8⅞ inches in height and bore the circular impressed mark *D. & J. Henderson Jersey City.*

The unmarked pitcher with blue glaze in Figure 7 was given to the Metropolitan Museum by Mrs. Ernest H. Fairchild with a history of having been made at Jersey City. Its former owner was an elderly woman whose grandfather had worked in the pottery. She said it was the first piece made in this color. Unfortunately the exact date is not known. Its form, however, suggest an affinity with the other so-called "Grecian" pitchers of the 1830's, and it may be attributed with some degree of certainty to that period.

It is not known whether David Henderson created his own models during the first ten years at the pottery. It may be that he employed a number of workmen to originate his designs. James Bennett, afterwards a successful potter at East Liverpool, Ohio, worked at Jersey City from 1834 to 1837, but probably not in

Figure 8: A hound-handled pitcher of white glazed earthenware. The lettering and the eyes of the dog are bright blue. Height, 12 inches.

Figure 9: A buff stoneware pitcher with chocolate brown glaze displaying body color in relief portions. Light glaze inside. Height, 10¾ inches.

Figure 10: A light buff ware pitcher glazed within and without. Height, 8¾ inches.

the capacity of a moldmaker. The arrival of Daniel Greatbach in 1839, however, gave the company the services of one of the most skillful and prolific modelers in American ceramic history. Greatbach, largely through his later connection with the Bennington pottery, became a figure of romance, but he was a very real person. He had been a designer for Ridgway of Cauldon Place in Staffordshire and had come from a long line of English potters. Barber, in whose pronouncements we may place the utmost confidence, says of him that "almost all of the designs of an ornamental nature which were produced at these works between the years 1838 and 1848 were originated by him." Greatbach is listed in the Jersey City directories from 1849 to 1852 as "modeller," with address "R.R. Ave. near Barrow St. H." (Harsimus). This location is now in the heart of the city near the public library and city hall. In May 1852 Greatbach was in Bennington.

Greatbach's fame rests especially on his pitchers with hound handles and hunting scenes. It is thought, and here again we have Barber's confirmation, that most of the jugs of this type made in America were designed by Greatbach, many apparently having been produced in different versions after he had created the Jersey City pitcher. The examples shown here, with one exception, bear the mark of the American Pottery Company. Although they show variations in design and color, they have one distinguishing characteristic: the hound's head rests directly on his paws. Contrary to the opinion of some writers that Greatbach improved upon the modeling of the hound in the pitchers made for the Bennington pottery or for Harker, Taylor & Company of East Liverpool, I consider his Jersey City dog the most truly artistic, as it has no outstanding or open parts, and is in consequence the most suitable for its purpose as a handle.

Many of the American Pottery pitchers have a plain Rockingham glaze. Just when this was first adopted is not known. In the later period the Jersey City color was rich and lustrous and deeper in tone than the brown of the mottled Bennington wares.

Figure 11: A dark brown Rockingham glaze covers this buff body pitcher. The interior is unglazed. Height, 12⅞ inches.

Figure 12: A pitcher with dark brown Rockingham glaze showing light body color in the reliefs. The inside glazing is cream colored. Height, 9 inches.

Figure 13: White lettering highlights this dark brown Rockingham glazed pitcher. Height, 10½ inches.

It will be noticed that Rockingham pitchers from this pottery almost invariably have a light glaze inside.

While the hunting scene on the hound-handled pitchers in fairly constant, the designs on the neck and shoulder present numerous variations and combinations of pattern. The simplest type appears in the unmarked example in Figure 8. The practice of lettering pitchers with the purchaser's name was a common one in the late forties. The letters were formed in molds and affixed to the jug before it was glazed. This pitcher, of white earthenware, has the letters and the hound's eyes picked out in blue. An unglazed white pitcher of the same design, but without lettering, may be seen in the Jersey City Public Library.

Nearly all Jersey City pitchers were made in more than one size, necessitating and adaptation of pattern to larger or smaller forms. this will be noted particularly in studying those with hound handles. Each size exhibits a change in the mold, rather than a mere enlargement of it. Figures 9 and 10 show a design adpated for two sizes. The difference is most noticeable on the shoulder. A buff earthenware pitcher in my collection, which is midway between these two in size, has a more distinct and less fussy band of arabesques at this point. Its glaze is covered with tiny rust-colored specks. The three pitchers are light in weight, but seemingly strong and well suited for holding heavy liquids.

A similar, but very large, hound-handled pitcher in Figure 11 has a beautifully designed neck with the grape pattern carried down over the shoulder. Its chocolate-colored glaze covers the piece well. A peculiarity of the hound to be noted in this example and also in Figure 12 is the small opening between the body and the tail. I have seen a smaller marked version of this pitcher, also with a rich chocolate-brown glaze.

One of the handsomest Jersey City pitchers may be seen in Figure 12. Its particular charm is its rich dark brown color with the contrasting buff of the body showing through the glaze in the relief portions. The border along the rim offers a slight variation in design. Figure 13 shows a still different combination of motifs, with grapevine neck and plain shoulder. The pitcher bears the name *J. Hollingsworth.* Another, unlettered, but identical in size and color, is in the Brooklyn Museum collection. Doubtless each of these various molds will eventually be discovered in several sizes.

Similar in glaze, but unique in pattern, is an apostle pitcher *(Fig. 14),* also said to be the creation of Daniel Greatbach. In 1842 Charles Meigh of Hanley, Staffordshire, put out a "Minster" jug and at about the same time a much cruder apostle pitcher. A comparison of the Meigh version *(Antiques,* April 1930, p. 366) with Greatbach's model shows the superiority of the latter. The architectural details and the drapery of the figures on the American pitcher are far better executed. Concerning this Barber says that the original molds for it and for various other pieces, such as four different sizes and types of tobies, were found in the loft of the potter many years after J. O. Rouse had assumed its management. Barber attributes some of the molds to Greatbach. There seems to be little doubt that he originated this pitcher and the later twelve-sided toby.

The Rockingham pitcher in Figure 15 so closely resembles the famous tea set modeled by Greatbach and produced by the American Pottery Company in both white ware and Rockingham that we need have no hesitation in attributing it to his hand. The same scheme of all-over decoration and the almost identical flower and leaf forms appear on this unuual jug. Its hexagonal form was a popular one in the early forties, when the Bennington works was making six-sided pitchers and glass companies were pressing six-sided sugar bowls.

The more elaborate pattern of Figure 16 may come within the period of the 1830's. This is most original, bearing no resemblance to other identified specimens.

The American Pottery Company made superior white and cream-colored earthenware during its late period. Following the English tradition, Henderson began about 1839 to do transfer printing. His Canova ware, printed in blue or black, was

Figure 14: A buff stoneware Apostle pitcher with dark brown Rockingham glazing. Light glaze inside. Height, 9¼ inches.

Figure 15: Buff stoneware with dark brown Rockingham glaze. Interior is light glazed. The pitcher has an all-over relief design. Height, 8¼ inches.

Figure 16: Buff stoneware with dark brown Rockingham glaze. Interior is light glazed. Height, 8¾ inches.

Figure 17: Harrison campaign pitcher of creamware with a black transfer-printing decoration.

a deliberate copy of a Ridgway pattern. It was, however, distinguished by a printed mark showing the familiar urn and the words *AM Pottery Manufg. Co./Jersey City.* The transfer-printed pitchers with portraits of Harrison brought out during the presidential campaign of 1840 (or possibly after Harrison's death in 1841) and the unmarked mugs with the same portrait are the only other examples of this type of decoration that have come to light. Unique in having the likeness on all six sides—other pitchers with but four heads are known—is the one in Figure 17, formerly in the Alfred B. Maclay collection. It is said that printing plates were executed by Thomas Pollock, and American engraver.

Another ceramic type made by the American Pottery Company is spatterware. A hot-milk pitcher or chocolate pot minus its cover is illustrated in the article on spatterware by Homer Eaton Keys in *Antiques* (April 1930, p. 337). The pot is described as being of cream earthenware sponged with a "pallid blue," its sole decoration. It has the circular impressed mark of the company.

Undoubtedly new forms and new types of pitchers and other objects from this prolific pottery will be discovered as time goes on. The general excellence of the wares will recommend them to discriminating collectors. As examples of the output of the first really successful commercial pottery in America, they have a historical value beyond their intrinsic worth.

—LURA WOODSIDE WATKINS

Ceramics

NEW JERSEY holds first place in the history of America ceramics for she has pioneered in practically every type of ceramic ware produced in these United States. Potteries are recorded at least as early as 1685; others who were active at that time will never be known to us. Since the beginning of the eighteenth century, far too many potteries have been established in various parts of the state for inclusion in this article. Their names and examples of their work are recorded in the catalogue of an exhibition "The Pottery and Porcelain of New Jersey, 1688-1900," held at the Newark Museum in 1947. Fortunately, a number of collectors in our state cherish examples of the early earthenware and stoneware utensils used in kitchen or dairy, as well as more sophisticated pieces of Belleek and porcelain made by such firms as Ott & Brewer or the Willets Manufacturing Company of Trenton.

The first pottery works of importance recorded in New Jersey was established at Burlington in 1688 by Dr. Daniel Coxe of London. Dr. Coxe was no potter, nor did he ever come to America. He was court physician to Queen Catherine, consort of Charles II, and later of Queen Anne of England. He owned a vast tract of land in our state and was governor of West New Jersey from 1687 to 1692. In 1688 Dr. Coxe and two other gentlemen of London agreed to establish a pottery at Burlington for making "white and painted earthenware and pottery vessells." They engaged two potters from London and nearby Lambeth as manager and assistant at the Burlington works. These works were within a few blocks of the Delaware River and according to Dr. Coxe's own statement large quantities of his pottery were shipped from Burlington to Barbadoes and Jamaica. No doubt sailing vessels returned from the West Indies laden with sugar cane, mollasses and rum.

The "pottery vessells" referred to were undoubtedly crude earthenware utensils for household use. As for the "white and painted earthenware," we can guess that these were from the types of earthenware produced in England in the 1680's. William Gill, assistant at the Burlington works, had come from Lambeth which was then producing some of the finest examples of English delftware—the only kind of "white ware" made in England at that period. The Newark Museum has a fragment of a stove tile made at the Coxe pottery between 1688 and 1692. It is of coarse clay coated with a white tin-enameled glaze. Potters had not yet learned how to produce a white clay, similar to Oriental porcelain, so they coated natural-colored clay with a glaze made white with ashes of tin. This tile is the earliest piece of New Jersey pottery in the Museum's collection.

Each new settlement in the American Colonies was forced to develop its own crafts, such as weaving, pottery, carpentry, or cabinetmaking. Without question, the early Dutch and English settlements at Jersey City, Hoboken, "English neighborhood" in Bergen County, or the Swedish settlements in the southern part of our state, produced their own household wares, but we have no record of the potters. William Crews had a pottery in Burlington about 1685. Four years later, Crews moved to Philadelphia, perhaps because of the more ambitious pottery works established by Dr. Daniel Coxe.

Until the 1730's, coarse earthenware, or redware as it was called over here, was the only form of pottery made in the colonies. Then, the right clay having been located, potters began to make stoneware. The special blue clay used for American stoneware was found only on Staten Island and in the vicinity of South Amboy, New Jersey. This deposit may have extended under Raritan Bay. For many years the potters of New York and New England, as well as those of New Jersey, obtained their supplies of blue clay from this source.

The first stoneware produced in our state came from the village of Cheesequake, about two miles from South Amboy. James Morgan who operated a pottery there between 1775 and 1785 was evidently an officer in the Revolutionary War. Soon other stoneware potteries sprang up in Elizabethtown, Matawan, New Brunswick, Flemington. The Newark Museum owns two mugs made by James Morgan at Cheesequake, as well as a water cooler dated 1788 and made by Morgan's son, Charles, at the same pottery. Thomas Warne, son-in-law of James Morgan, also operated a pottery at Cheesequake. He was joined about 1805 by his own son-in-law, Joshua Letts. Both these men are represented in the Newark Museum's collection. Here, also, is a stoneware oyster bowl, dated May 27, 1805, and made by Josiah Van Schoick of Matawan. Evidently oysters were plentiful and good in this locality for Dr. Alexander Hamilton of Anapolis, Maryland, had earlier reported from Perth Amboy, "They have here the best oysters I have eaten in America."

The Fulper pottery works was established at Flemington about 1805. A stoneware crock in the Museum's collection has the firm name G. W. Fulper & Bros. impressed. It is decorated with a little blue bird, probably painted by John Kunusman.

Stoneware is very hard, durable, and impervious to liquids. Some stoneware has a smooth glaze, with a minutely pitted surface resembling the outer skin of an orange. Pieces were decorated with bands of impressed design or, less often, with

with flowers and birds painted in blue or brown enamel glaze. Stoneware cannot be confused with the porous earthenware used for pie and bacon platters, mugs, and other household utensils, until late in the nineteenth century. Many of these humble pieces were ornamented with slip and scratched—or sgraffito—designs traced in white, yellow, or even green liquid clays, known as slip. Only the more experienced craftsmen could do this slip decoration on pottery. The finer examples were considered quite worthy to serve as gifts at a wedding or christening.

One such craftsman was George Wolfkiel of Bergen County. We associate this type of pottery with the Pennsylvania Germans so it is not surprising to find that Wolfkiel came to Hackensack from Pennsylvania. He was active in Hackensack during the 1830's and 40's, his specialty being slipware pie plates and stoneware crocks. The Newark Museum has a number of pieces made by George Wolfkiel and presented by the Bergen County Historical Society in 1925. In the Steuben House at North Hackensack are some strikingly similar plates that might have been made by Wolfkiel. Unfortunately, the pieces are not labeled. Also at the Steuben House is a crock with orange-brown glaze thumb-splashed with black. It closely resembles a jar in the Museum's collection made by Balthasar Krumeick of Newark about 1845.

The production of ceramics in America found its greatest stimulus in the Revolutionary War. Before then, Great Britain and the Continent had been our chief sources of supply. Once the war was over and we were free, there was a tremendous burst of energy. The potters of New Jersey now built up a fine reputation. In 1829 David Henderson of Jersey City introduced an innovation that was to transform our small pottery workshop into factories, make mass production possible, and bring the price of a good piece of pottery within the range of the ordinary pocketbook. This new method, borrowed by Henderson from England, made it possible to cast clay in molds instead of using

A redware churn made at the Richard Acton
Pottery in Salem in 1836. Its height
measures nine inches, the maximum
diameter is five and one-half inches. *Lent
by Mr. and Mrs. Frank Acton.*

A blue and green cut glass bowl done by
Louis Iorio of the Empire Cut Glass
Company of Flemington *circa* 1910-1915.
The height measures two and one-quarter
inches, the maximum diameter is eight
inches. *Lent anonymously.*

a potter's wheel. Casting in a mold not only speeded up production but also made possible the relief decoration that became so popular during the Victorian era. Henderson employed at the American Pottery Company in Jersey City men who had been trained at the great potteries of England. Among them was Daniel Greatbach, the best known of all ceramic modelers in our country. It was Henderson's pottery works that produced the first transfer-printed ware made in America. This was around 1839-40 when Jersey City came out with the William Henry Harrison campaign pitcher bearing a portrait of Harrison, "The Ohio Farmer," together with the traditional log cabin and hard cider barrel. This historic piece was followed a few years later by a pitcher showing the landing of Lafayette at Castle Garden in 1824.

Among other outstanding potteries of the nineteenth century were the Salamander Works at Woodbridge; the Swan Hill Pottery at South Amboy; the Eagle Pottery at Perth Amboy. In Trenton were several well-known firms. Millington, Astbury & Poulson was established there in 1853. The Trenton Pottery Company was incorporated in 1865. The Etruria Pottery was established by Bloor, Ott and Booth in 1863, but two years later the firm became Ott & Brewer. Until 1875 their output was largely graniteware and cream-colored ware. With the Philadelphia Centennial Exhibition in preparation, Ott & Brewer engaged Isaac Broome, an American sculptor, to design figures and busts in parian ware. The Newark Museum has a bust of General Ulysses S. Grant, designed by Broome, which was exhibited at the Centennial.

Before this, various attempts at making porcelain had been tried in New Jersey without success. In December of 1825 the Jersey Porcelain and Earthenware Company was established at Jersey City. The following October, 1826, te Company received a silver medal for the pieces they exhibited at the Franklin Institute in Philadelphia. Other attempts were made, later, at Gloucester and Trenton. However, real success was

Left: Pie plate with slip and sgraffito decoration, inscribed "Manufactured by Phillip Durell October 27th 1793," the only known example of New Jersey sgraffito pottery. *Right:* Toby Pitcher of stoneware made *circa* 1850 at Salamander Works of Woodbridge.

Belleek porcelain basket, hand-made by James Shelton of Lenox Inc. *circa* 1900.

only achieved in 1882 when Ott & Brewer brought to this country William Bromley of Belleek, Ireland. Bromley had been instrumental in establishing a porcelain works at Belleek. Now, under Bromley's guidance, Ott & Brewer of Trenton produced the first Belleek ware made in the United States. Belleek, by the way, is a very light and thin porcelain.

In 1889, Jonathan Coxon and Walter Lenox organized the Ceramic Art Company at Trenton. In 1896 this firm became Lenox Incorporated and is today the leading manufacturer of porcelain in this country. Many readers doubtless have visited the plant.

About 1900 the Fulper pottery works at Flemington began producing art wares and experimenting with different kinds of glazes, including a mottled or flambe glaze copied from Chinese pottery. This company has now moved to Trenton and operates under the name of Stangl.

Sometimes referred to as the $60,000,000 pottery industry, the ceramics of New Jersey have always set a notable example. Today, the greatest output is no longer in our own state but has shifted to New England, Ohio, and California. Therefore, good pieces formerly made in New Jersey may be expected to increase in historic value.   —MARGARET E. WHITE

Textiles

Weavers of
New Jersey

TEXTILE weaving has always been a major activity in New Jersey since its beginning in the 17th century, when it was a prime necessity in every household. During the early years of the 19th century weaving was to become one of the leading industries of our State. Therefore it is fitting that the New Jersey Historical Society should hold an exhibition of textiles and equipment to suggest the development of the craft.

In pioneer days every housewife did her own spinning and weaving, but few of us realize that before she could spin the wool and flax threads required for her loom she had to sow flax and hemp seeds in her garden along with the crops, and she had to obtain sheep that could be raised on the farm, or homestead.

The housewife who had just landed in this unknown country required not only flax and wool yarn for bedding and clothes but also the equipment for preparing home-grown flax—such as a break, a scutching board and knife, flax hetchel and small spinning wheel. Also essential were "cards" with which to comb out the sheared wool and a "great" wheel on which to spin the yarn. Most important was the floor loom, on which were woven the outer garments, underwear, blankets, bed and table linens required by a household.

Any local carpenter or joiner, aided by a wheelwright, could produce the flax and wool wheels or construct a floor loom. the New Jersey Historical Society has such equipment in its collection, as well as flax raised on the Doremus farm in Parsippany and hand-woven linen made from flax grown and spun on a farm near Rahway.

It took days to prepare flax for spinning, but the men and women who came to New Jersey from Sweden, England and Holland understood the various steps in the preparation of flax and wool, and the dyeing of yarns, including the right selection of barks, nut shells, or flowers for the colors desired.

In the first homes built by early settlers there was a "common room" in which all household activities took place. Here would be found the four-harness loom on which the women of the family did their weaving. In addition to the textiles woven in every home there were professional weavers—trained in the craft before leaving the "old country"—who opened their workshops in the larger towns. John Condit (or Cunditt) was a native of Great Britain, who came to Newark with his son, Peter, about 1678. John purchased land "in the bounds of the town of Newark" in 1689 and 1691. In the second deed for 19 acres, dated 1691, John Condit is recorded as a weaver. His will also states that he was a weaver of Newark. Condit died in 1713.

Benjamin Acton, who landed in Salem in 1677, was a weaver, surveyor, carpenter, innkeeper, tanner and miller. Such versatility on Acton's part helps us to understand the appraisal made by John Fenwick shortly after his arrival in Salem in 1675. In a document now in the archives of the Pennsylvania Historical Society Fenwick wrote of the settlers in his colony:

> They get a Livelihood principally from Corn and Cattle, which will there fetch them any Commoditys; Likewise they Sow store of Flax, which they make every one Cloth, and Linsey-woolsey; and had

Jacquard coverlet woven by C. Van Nortwick for Eleanor Todd of Bedminster in 1839.

they more Tradesmen amongst them, they would in a little time live
without help of any other country for their Cloathing; for Tradesmen
there be none but live happily there, as Carpenters, Blacksmiths,
Masons, Taylors, Weavers, Shoemakers, Tanners, Brickmakers.

Twelve other weavers are listed in Salem, Amwellbury, and
Stow Creek between 1676 and 1704.

The master weavers who set up their own shops helped to
keep households supplied with wool blankets, linen and flannel
sheets, fustian or thicksett, and the blue and white striped
linsey-woolsey used for women's petticoats. To these men a
housewife brought the supplies of flax thread and wool yarn
required to fill her order. When not otherwise busy, the
professional weaver could always weave his own materials and
sell them at the nearest market.

Among the early examples of weaving—the names of the
weavers unknown—the New Jersey Historical Society has a
double-woven coverlet made at Preakness in Wayne Township
by a descendant of Gillis Jensen De Mandeville, who, having
fled from France to Holland to escape religious persecution,
came to New Amsterdam in 1641. The weaver was also
connected with the family of Theunis Dey. This blanket was the
gift of Charles B. Vroom.

A blue and white double-woven coverlet in "rose" pattern
was made from materials raised on the farm of George Apgar in
High Bridge, Hunterdon County. This was the gift of Carola W.
Bogardus.

During the Revolutionary period Josiah Beach was a weaver
and farmer in Newark, with a shop on Broad Street across from
Samuel Conger, whose weaving shop was next door to the
Bruen's cabinetmaking shop. In Paterson James Schoonmaker
was a weaver of carpets as well as coverlets. In 1825 he had a
shop on Ward Street with two looms. Are there any known
examples of work by these men?

Of necessity our early bedspreads were woven in geometric
patterns, for only such could be produced on the floor looms

then in use. When the Frenchman, Jean Marie Jacquard (1725-1834), invented the loom that came to be known by his name, a marked change took place in coverlet designs. The Jacquard loom made possible designs that were free flowing and highly stylized. In 1826 the first Jacquard loom was brought to the United States and set up in Philadelphia. Shortly thereafter professional weavers here in New Jersey began to operate the new looms. At first the designs were imported from France along with the looms and some of these patterns are graceful and pleasing, but others are regrettably stiff.

A number of professional weavers produced Jacquard coverlets, among them being David D. Haring of West Norwood, Bergen County; the itinerant weaver, Nathaniel Young, who traveled around Bergen and Hudson Counties; C. Van Nortwick, "Fancy Weaver and Dyer" of Asbury in Warren County; Theunis (or Teunis?) Cooper of Englewood; the Van Dorens of Millstone.

The New Jersey Historical Society has a coverlet in terracotta yarn and natural linen, woven by Van Nortwick for Eleanor R. Todd of Bedminster at the time of her marriage in 1839 to Barnabas Horton Pickle. As may be noted, the word *Union* forms part of the border design. A coverlet made by Van Nortwick for Margaret Bird in 1840, with the word *Liberty* interwoven in the border, is owned by the Newark Museum. Nothing is known about Van Nortwick, and the writer hopes someone will supply information.

Another Jacquard coverlet in the Historical Society's collection was woven by Theunis Cooper for Eliza Ann Vanderbeek, wife of John Martin DeMott. The spread is dated Nov. 18, 1831, and may have been made at the time of Eliza's marriage. The wool used in the bedspread was taken from sheep raised on the Vanderbeek farm, in what is now South Englewood. The design of this coverlet provides a delightful contrast to that of the coverlet woven by Van Nortwick.

In the same collection is an interesting quilted bedspread of

Jacquard coverlet woven by Theunis Cooper for Eliza Ann De Mott.

the 18th century. It is of hand-spun and hand-woven linen, with a Chinese design in blue produced by means of resist dye and block printing. The spread belonged to Aaron Kitchell, who was born in Hanover, New Jersey, in 1774 and died there in 1820. Probably this spread was woven in New Jersey, but there is little doubt that the small designs scattered over the top of the spread were applied in the New York area. At that period it was customary to send one's linen to an expert—to be given small designs, sometimes in several colors, by means of wood blocks or the wax resist process—before the yard goods were made up into a gown, a counterpane, or curtains for bed or window.

To print designs in one color, such as indigo, was a simple matter, only one wood block being required for each of the motifs. To produce flowers, leaves, fruit or birds in natural colors was an exacting task, for each color or shade of coloring required a different block. Before the art of producing a green dye was discovered in the 19th century, a single leaf necessitated two wood blocks with identical design carved in relief. One block was used for yellow and the other for blue dye. By superimposing one color on the other a leaf green was produced.

An interesting illustration of this process may be seen in a quilted counterpane of pieced work and appliqué, said to have been made by Barbara Heck. (In 1760 Mrs. Heck came to New York from Ireland, and the following year she and Philip Embury founded the first Methodist Society in America.) A counterpane made by Barbara's daughter, Ann Heck, is owned by the Newark Museum, and in both these bedcovers identical leaves may be found appliquéd on the top. Evidently the leaves were cut form the same piece of block-printed goods. The quilt owned by the New Jersey Historical Society was presented by Miss Mabel J. Hamburg, who received it from Mabel H. Brookfield, great-great-granddaughter of Barbara Heck. The bedspread in the Newark Museum's collection came from Mrs. Augustus Baker Brookfield, whose husband's aunt, Sally Brookfield of old New Jersey family, had originally owned the quilt.

The terms "quilt" and "counterpane" are used here inter-changeably to denote a covering for a bed. A quilt might serve as an extra blanket but a counterpane was always the spread used on top of a bedstead. The word quilt is said to have derived from the French *cuilte,* which in turn stemmed from the Latin *culcitra,* meaning a stuffed mattress or cushion. A finished quilt is always composed of a top, a lining, and a wadding or interlining of cotton or lamb's wool. Sometimes a wool blanket that had seen better days was used for the interlining.

At a time when all fabrics except those woven in a household had to be imported from abroad, the snippets of material left over from a newly-made garment were cherished in the scrap bag. These fragments of silk, velvet or printed linen from England or France were deemed quite worthy for a quilt, and the mistress of the house regarded the piecing of a quilt top as recreation to be enjoyed when household tasks were done. Out of bits and pieces some gorgeous counterpanes were impro-vised. Having begun in stern necessity during pioneer days, the pieced or appliquéd quilt remained in more affluent years as a pleasurable creative outlet. By this time figured yard goods were obtainable at the general store, and fashionable fabrics could be imported from abroad without undue expense.

One quilt in the collection of the New Jersey Historical Society has a top consisting of three lengths of English copper-plate print, dating about 1800 and showing "The Apotheosis of Franklin."

One of the most decorative in the Society's collection is an "Album" quilt bearing the dates 1846-1848. The top consists of 25 blocks, 15½ inches square, each designed and made by a different person. Written by hand in most of the blocks are inscriptions from the Bible together with the individual's name and a date. "Baltimore, Maryland" also appears in a number of blocks. The designs are in red and green cotton appliquéd on a white ground, the same red material being used for the binding.

The quilting of a bedspread was a sociable affair. When a

"The Apotheosis of Franklin." Quilt made from lengths of English copper-plate print in red and white, dating about 1800.

quilt top was completed and "ready for the frames", the lining, filling and top were stretched on the quilting frames and neighbors joined in the quilting. That is, the three layers were stitched together at frequent intervals in order to hold them in place. Often close examination will reveal quilting stitches that are equisitely fine. After a busy afternoon of stitching and gossip around the frames, the ladies were joined by their menfolk for dinner and an evening of games.

"Friendship," "Album" and "Freedom" quilts were all expressions of sociability. A Friendship quilt was made by a girl's friends when her engagement was announced, each block being signed with the name of the girl who designed and made it. The Album may be regarded as the twin of the Friendship quilt. Perhaps the Album quilt just described was the gift of a clergyman from his parishioners, which would account for the Bible verses. Out of this idea grew the Freedom quilt made in celebration of a boy's twenty-first birthday.

As living conditions improved in the Colonies, as money became more plentiful and homes more sophisticated, we find white counterpanes coming into use in the best bedrooms. During the first quarter of the 19th century candlewick spreads were very popular. There were two types of these bedcovers, those that were hand loomed and woven in one piece without a seam, and those that were made in several lengths of material decorated by hand. The hand-loomed coverlet has a warp of cotton and weft of roving, or candlewicking. The all-over design, in looped or unsheared candlewick, is produced by picking up the weft over a reed or a piece of bone. Two examples in the possession of the New Jersey Historical Society show designs in looped candlewick on a ribbed ground. Above the swag and tassel border are eight-pointed stars. At the center of each spread is an elaborate and conventional design. These counterpanes were made in 1818 by or for Eliza Curry Lindsley, wife of Zebulon Myers. Judging by the backs of the spreads, the candlewicking would seem to have been done by

"Album" quilt. Each of the appliquéd blocks, designed and made by a different person, is signed and dated.

hand and not on the loom, since threads of roving show.

The so-called Marseilles bedspread appeared in France early in the 19th century. Readers of *Jane Eyre* may recall Charlotte Brontë's description of the red room with its massive mahogany bed "spread with a snowy Marseilles counterpane." During the second and third quarters of the 19th century a Marseilles spread was the pride of every well-to-do housewife in America. These early examples are a form of double weave, with muslin top and a loose fabric, resembling cheesecloth, as a lining. Between the two layers is a weft of roving which never shows on the surface. These layers are attached together with threads passing through the roving with mechanical precision to form a diamond quilting, interrupted only to make the pattern, which appears to be padded because of the roving. The quilting stitched in a bedspread by hand and the effect produced here by machine give much the same effect.

As Mrs. Esther I. Schwartz has stated, Colonel Henry Rutgers was producing white bedspreads at the Rutgers factory in Paterson in 1822 ("Notes form a New Jersey collector", in *Antiques,* October 1958, p. 330). According to the Paterson Census of 1825, Isaac Van Riper was at that time weaving counterpanes on Van Houten Street and used the initials I. V. R. in his spreads. It is recorded that as early as 1833 double-cloth pattern bedspreads were woven in Closter, the date appearing in one corner of the spread.

—MARGARET E. WHITE

"Beautifully Draped"

TODAY the fashion for wearing a shawl is as dead as the dodo. Yet there was a time when a piece of thread lace or a Kashmir shawl was considered as fine a gift as one could present to a bride. The Newark Museum owns a square India shawl given to Charlotte Mercer of Newark when she married Theodore Frelinghuysen in 1809. In the collection of the New Jersey Historical Society there is a long shawl that belonged to a bride of 1790. Evidently such gifts were popular for at least half a century, for in the Newark Museum's collection is a reversible Paisley shawl presented to a bride of 1866—the Paisley reversible having first appeared about 1860.

They were gorgeous, those India shawls that began to appear in Europe and the American Colonies in the late 18th century. In 1784 the *Salem Gazette* advertised the arrival of a shipment of assorted shawls; for the East India trade, which had its American center in New England, was alert to the fact that the Kashmir shawl had caught the eye of European fashion. Stimulus was given both to fashion and to textile manufacturers when French and English soldiers, returning in 1798 from the Napoleonic campaign in Egypt, brought home examples of the

Oriental shawl. Through the years of the Conuslate and First Empire (1799-1814) these imported shawls were the height of fashion.

It is said that the shawl's popularity among well-dressed women was due to the fact that its draping, manner of wearing, and manipulation demanded great personal skill. Hence the expression to be "well draped" or "beautifully draped." According to Lester & Oerke *(Accessories of Dress,* p. 230), "The artistic draping of shawls and scarfs received so much consideration that women were instructed in the art of both draping and posing."

At the time of its introduction a Kashmir shawl cost anywhere from $600 to $1500. Small wonder that Augustin Challomel, a French chronicler, reported that "at solemn family gatherings a Cashmere is indespensible, it proclaims the wealth of the wearer," or that "when an occasion arises in which very grand and imposing attire is required, a woman of fashion buys one of these splendid products of India."

There are two classes of Oriental shawl, loom-woven and embroidered. Of the woven shawls some were worked in the manner of a tapestry. That is, the warp was set up in the loom; then the weft threads, instead of being carried from one side of the loom to the other, were worked in by the weaver in short lengths, each color of the design being carried on a separate bobbin. As in tapestry, the weaver worked from the back of the fabric, following closely and exactly the design previously sketched on paper. Other shawls were composed of small segments woven separately by different weavers and sewed together with such precision that the stitching is quite imperceptible. These are referred to as "pieced" shawls. In embroidered shawls the pattern was worked on a ground of plain-colored woolen fabric *(pasmina)* with a needle. This *pasmina* was the fine, soft underwool of the "shawl goat" inhabiting the high regions of Tibet. Lovely as they were, these needle-worked shawls were much cheaper than those woven on a loom, for the latter might require several years to complete.

Corner of a yellow shawl of Canton crepe embroidered in natural colors. Bought in San Francisco in 1849.

Shawls from the Kashmir region are characterized by the elaborate design, in which the "cone" or "mango" pattern is a prominent feature, and by the harmony, brilliance and lasting qualities of the colors. It has been suggested that the "cone" pattern had its inspiration in the jewelled ornament worn in the turban by Mogul emperors. This graceful pattern, with its flowing curves and minute diaper of flowers, is familiar to all lovers of the Oriental shawl.

Because of the high cost of shawls imported from the East, the textile manufacturers of France and Great Britain began very early in the 19th century to imitate them. In France by 1804-5 the first wool shawls were being produced in four to five colors. The Exposition of 1806 at the Palais-Bourbon showed examples from various textile manufacturers of Paris, Nimes, Geneva and Lyons, including a long shawl with a cone pattern imitating a true Kashmir. In 1823 Jean Rey, a manufacturer of French cashmeres *(cachemires)* wrote in his *Etudes pour Servir à L'histoire des Châles,* published in Paris. In this book Rey discusses their "perfect beauty." The Newark Museum has a number of these French shawls, a few with the original Paris labels but not all of them following Eastern designs. In his book *English Women's Clothing in the Nineteenth Century,* Cunnington refers to the French shawls exported to England during 1815-16 and to the beautiful ultramarine blue that appeared in the new shawls of 1833, a color for which France received high praise. He also mentioned the French printed shawls of barege, which during the depression years sold in England for 9/11.

In Britain the two famous centers for shawls were Norwich and Paisley. The silk and woolen manufactures for which Norwich had long been noted date from the reign of Edward III (1327-77). His queen, Philippa of Hainuault, aware of the advantages her native country derived from its textile industry, encouraged Flemish weavers to settle in the county of Norfolk. Thanks to Queen Philipa's protection, the skill and industry of

Flemish weavers quickly raised Norwich to a place of importance. Toward the close of the 18th century the introduction of the shawl gave a fresh impetus to the textile trade of that city. At first these shawls were of the patterned silk for which Norwich was renowned, but the manufacturers were soon producing figured shawls in silk and wool similar in beauty of design and richness of color to those imported from the East. By the 1840's, however, the shawl trade of Norwich had declined due to competition and in the spring of 1848 Queen Victoria was induced by the Countess Spencer and Lady Cahtherine Boileau to see what could be done for the Norwich weavers. With the stimulus thus given, the production of both printed and "filled-over" shawls supplied the industry for the brief period remaining until 1870, when shawls went out of fashion.

As early as 1685 the poll tax roll of Paisley, Scotland, showed that there were 66 weavers in that little town. Their products were homespun linen and wool until in 1760 the weaving of silk and fine muslin was introduced. By 1766 there were over 1700 looms, and in 1820, after the introduction of the Paisley harness shawl, the number of looms had increased to 7,000. From the opening years of the 19th century until fashion demanded new styles about 1870 the shawl trade was Paisley's chief industry. As Matthew Blair states in his book *The Paisley Shawl,* by the end of the 18th century the weavers of Paisley, who were to some extent their own designers, had acquired the intellectual culture and technical skill required to produce the Paisley harness shawl. For three-quarters of a century these maintained their supremacy against competition from Norwich and France. The gorgeous shawls presented to Queen Victoria by maharajahs of India served as patterns for the weavers of Paisley.

The Paisley shawl was woven on a drawing loom, the warp threads having been dyed the required color. The design in full color was always shown in a minature sketch, which was a work of art in itself, and from this sketch the design was transferred to

Cashmere shawl made in France during early 19th century.

point paper. Then, like a tapestry, the shawl was woven face downwards on the loom. The Jacquard loom invented in France early in the century, was not used at Paisley until after 1850.

For summer wear a Paisley shawl had a plain white or scarlet center, into which the design occasionally strayed with beautiful effects. A winter shawl was "filled-over"; that is, all parts were covered by the design, the most characteristic being based on the graceful, sinuous cone or palmette of the Oriental shawl. But as stated in *Accessories of Dress,* "To consider the Paisley as an imitation of the Cashmere is unfair to the beautiful shawl produced in Scotland. Throwing all comparisons aside, the Paisley shawls are in themselves works of art and are best considered not as imitations but as adaptations of the Cashmere to the demands and fashions of that day," (Lester & Oerke, p. 231). During the depression period of the 1840s Queen Victoria purchased many Paisley shawls, one of which was worn at the royal christening of the Price of Wales, later King Edward VII.

Throughout the period of 1837-57 Paisley shawls and scarfs from Kashmir were much worn with "walking dresses." For evening wear there were black lace shawls, worn cornerwise and sometimes large enough to cover the whole dress. In 1849 *Gody's Lady's Book* reports that a lady of fashion should have a "white cashmere long shawl folded carelessly"—very smart if worn with a green cashmere dress and green velvet bonnet. In 1858 Bismarck wrote that no genuine Kashmir shawl could be bought for less than 1200 to 1500 francs, even though a dangerous rival had appeared in the shawl of *crepe-de-chine.*

In the Historical Society's collection is a crepe shawl of cherry red, richly embroidered in vari-colored silk threads and edged with a heavy knotted fringe. This shawl was brought back from China as a gift in 1849. These bright, soft and durable shawls were a delight to every woman of taste, and for several decades they continued to hold their place as an aristocratic item of toilette. In 1862 a crepe silk shawl in cerise was the mode, but regardless of whether milady's wrap of silk or wool came from China, India, France, Norwich or Paisley, how colorful she must have looked. "Imagine a mid-Victorian garden party with one hundred or so of those gorgeous shawls, white, scarlet, turquoise, green, and orange, gracefully draped over crinoline skirts!" (Lester & Oerke, *Accessories of Dress* p. 232).

Aside from its beauty, there was a very special reason why the shawl was so popular; for the sloping shoulder line of 1821-40, the exuberant sleeves of 1820-30 that reappeared periodically in more restrained form, and the expanded skirts of the crinoline period required the use of a very loose wrap. It is interesting to note that as soon as the bustle came in at the end of the 1860s the large cashmere shawl went out, to be replaced by a smaller, light-weight shawl or a modish wrap such as the "visite."

How was the shawl "draped"? In 1839, fashion notes that "The shawl is now becoming one of the important garments... the large shawl worn with the long corner point at the back." Two years later this point descended "nearly to the ground." During the 1840s the long shawl replaced the square in popularity and was worn as a scarf, but by 1850 everything was changed. The shawl, at least eleven feet long, had a center of red, green or orange and very deep borders. This was supposed to be folded in two to form a square and then a corner folded again. Surely all this was cumbersome to manage, which may explain why the square shawl was back in favor by 1853. The latter was folded in a triangle with a point in the center of the back—as in 1839. Apparently the shawl of canton crepe was folded into a rectangle or a triangle according to the wearer's whim—and how its long fringes must have caught in things! In the early part of the 20th century gay Spanish shawls (made in the Philippines) gave women a chance to drape themselves like the young girls in modern Spanish paintings, but this fad was shortlived. However, for a brief moment women felt that to wrap oneself in such a shawl was "like being enveloped in a picture," as suggested by Benito Perez Galdos. "This beautiful garment is being forgotten...it is like the legends and stories of childhood rich in colour, easy to understand, and contrary to the changes imposed by fashion." (Isabel de Palencia, *The Regional Costumes of Spain,* pp.23-4).

—MARGARET E. WHITE

Wheels, Reels, and Coverlets

IN early days, every thrifty housewife did her own spinning and weaving, on equipment made by local craftsmen. Carefully preserved in museums and private homes throughout New Jersey are the objects used in preparing home-grown flax, in carding and spinning wool yarn, the floor and table looms required, and the garments or bed coverings woven from homespun fibers.

When Phebe Davis married in 1797, her dowry included such items as two slaves, blue china for the dining room, spinning wheels and winding reels. Phebe was born and brought up in the old Davis homestead on Franklin Street, Bloomfield, built by Stephen Davis about 1676. The stone house was constructed with exceptionally thick wall, perhaps to withstand Indian attack. Behind this house were the slave quarters.

After living in a century-old house, the young bride must have been thrilled to move into the new home built for her by Isaac Nichols of Newark. This two-story-and-attic frame house stood on Washington Street, near Newark's Four Corners. The wool wheels brought there by Mistress Phebe were still standing in the house in 1928 when they were given to the Newark Museum by members of the Nichols family. While slaves attended to the housework, Phebe Nichols could do the needed spinning or wind the newly spun yarn on a clock reel, ready for the loom. To spin carded wool on the "great" wheel was a tedious job. To draw out the yarn and wind it on the accelerating wheel head meant pacing back and forth endlessly. Winding the wool yarn into skeins on a reel or swift was pleasanter work, for one could remain seated.

The Museum owns a candlewick bedspread, hand-loomed by or for Phebe Nichols in 1813, her name and date recorded in candlewick. Two rows of loops give variety to the tufting while, at the same time, accenting the central design. This is a stepped square containing the eight-pointed star and the pine tree, design motifs frequently used in pieced quilts and hand-woven coverlets. The tree follows quite closely the design of the Pine-tree shilling first coined in Massachusetts in 1652.

The pine tree forms an effective border in a double-woven coverlet from Hunterdon County, New Jersey. This coverlet, in single snowball pattern, dates from the 1840's. It belonged to Mrs. Sarah Ten Van Eyck Derveer in whose home were spun the wool and cotton used for warp and weft. It is thought that the weaving was done by a professional craftsman at Millstone, for double-woven coverlets such as this one required a loom of at least eight harnesses.

Another coverlet in snowball pattern came from Hacketts-town. This too, required professional skill. Thought to have been made in Revolutionary days, the bed cover had been preserved by four generations of one family prior to its acquisition by the Newark Museum. The colors, shown in reverse on the two sides of the coverlet, combine madder rose of particularly rich and mellow tone with white and indigo.

That there were expert weavers in New Jersey at an early date is not surprising. Somerset County was settled by the Dutch in the seventeenth century. Early settlers of Bergen County were chiefly of Dutch and German origin. After the

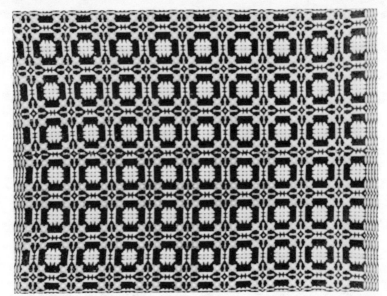

Above: Double woven coverlet, indigo and white, made *circa* 1825 at English Neighborhood, Bergen County.
Below: Winding reel, swift, and flax wheel. Note the pine-tree-bordered coverlet on the wall.

capture of New Amsterdam by the British in 1664, there was an influx of English people between Englewood and Ridgefield, long known as "English Neighborhood." It is but natural that among these people there would have been skilled weavers who had learned their craft in the "old country" and who followed designs long familiar in European textiles.

From English Neighborhood comes a coverlet of unidentified pattern, made for Mrs. Demarest whose husband was minister of the Dutch Reformed Church there in the early nineteenth century. Bergen County is full of such names as Cooper, Demarest, Voorhees, and Zabriskie.

Another coverlet from Bergen County is particularly interesting for its resemblance to old Germanic textiles. It is woven in "Lover's Knot" pattern, but with roses instead of stars. The same design will be found in German reversible hangings of the seventeenth and eighteenth centuries.

Frances Vanole was a Dutch weaver who, in 1836, was living in Newark. He made the "Lover's Knot" coverlet, woven with stars, that belonged to Mary Baldwin. Vanole also wove coverlets for the Peck family, handed down from Margaret (Peck) Jones to daughter and granddaughter.

The Mahlon Johnson homestead stood at the Dover and Parsippany crossroads in Littleton. Susan, daughter of Mahlon and Sarah (Baker) Johnson, was born here in 1806. Two double-woven coverlets made for Susan have been carefully preserved. One of the spreads is a ten-harness twill woven with a tabby. The pattern of the other is "Washington Beauty," a variant of the "Lisbon Star" and an old Germanic pattern. If these coverlets were made at the Johnson homestead they must have been the work of a professional itinerant weaver, perhaps of Germanic origin. The arrival of an itinerant weaver with his pattern book, in which drafts were carefully drawn, presented a lively, diversion in any household. Selecting the design for a coverlet to go in a daughter's "hope chest" must have been even more exciting than selecting a new wallpaper today. Long-established custom dictated the number of quilts and coverlets allotted to each marriageable son and daughter of the family.

Flax was raised on every farm as one of the crops. The New Jersey Historical Society has flax that was raised on the Doremus farm at Parsippany. Here also are shown the flax break, scutching board and knife, flax hetchels, and small spinning wheel, that tell the story of metamorphosis from stalk to woven thread. The wool cards, wool or "great" wheel, clock reels for measuring off the skeins of yarn, and a colonial floor loom are also displayed.

A simple four-harness loom was to be found in every household. On this loom the women of the family would weave the dress goods, sheets, blankets, and table linen needed, as well as coverlets in overshot weave. Coverlets in four-harness weave were the earliest made in the colonies. A lovely example from the Shumway family is "Dogwood Blossoms" or "Dog Tracks," woven in red, blue, and white. The warp is flax thread, the weft is of wool in two colors. No doubt the flax was home-grown and one can picture some housewife of the Shumway family seated at her flax wheel by the big fireplace. New Jersey historians are probably familiar with Mrs. Whitall's flax wheel, now preserved at Whitall house. Whether the wheel or the spinner is more famous is a question, for it is said that while the Battle of Red Bank raged outside the indomitable Mistress Whitall continued to spin. A wool wheel, dating about 1750, stands in the upper hall of the Schuyler-Hamilton house in Morristown. It would be nice to think that Betsy Schuyler used it for spinning some of her yarn.   —MARGARET E. WHITE

A red, white, and blue Jacquard coverlet done by P. S. Van Doren of Millstone *circa* 1848. The length is one hundred inches, the width is eighty inches. *Lent anonymously.*

A needlework picture done by Ann
Elizabeth Brokaw of Bound Brook on
November 14, 1836. The length and width
each measure nineteen inches. *Lent by Mr.
and Mrs. David McGrail.*

Samplers

MANY of us have at least one sampler in our possession, fondly cherished as the work of a beloved great aunt or respected as the fine needlework of some unknown ancestor. The lugubrious verses and little pictures so neatly cross-stitched into canvas are amusing and quaint to our present-day minds, geared as we are to TV and commercials. Seldom do we consider the social mores or child psychology lying back of these examples of embroidery. Nor do we give thought to the instructress who watched over this work, perhaps with a loving heart but certainly stern in her admonitions for neat preciseness, or to the awkward little fingers too often pricked by a seemingly recalcitrant needle.

Take, for instance, poor Ann Elizabeth Bruen of Newark! At the age of ten this serious child stitched into her sampler the following verse:

Jesus permit thy gracious name to stand
As the first effort of an infant hand
And while my fingers o'er this canvas move
Engage my tender heart to seek thy love.
With thy dear children let me share a part
And write thy name thyself upon my heart.

Beneath this is added, "The fear of the Lord is the beginning of wisdom." While these sentiments of 1817 are highly commendable they seem to us of the 20th century rather solemn thought with which to occupy young fingers.

Or take Sally Crane Hays of Newark who, in 1803 at the age of eight, worked into her sampler the following quotation from Thomson and surrounded it with flowers:

> The best preparation for all the uncertainties of futurity consists in a well ordered mind, a good conscience, and a cheerful submission to the will of Heaven.

The beautiful wildflower border is worked in long-stitch with harmoniously blended threads of silk. Both these samplers are owned by the New Jersey Historical Society, but in the Newark Museum's collection is a sampler of 1804 on which Mary Carman, aged seven, worked the same lines from Thomson. Another of the Museum's samplers, worked in 1834, repeats the "child's petition" exactly as given by Ann Elizabeth Bruen. The latter sampler was intended as a memorial to a nine-months-old baby, including in its design the traditional tombstone and willow tree.

As the needle in their little fingers went laboriously in and out of fine homespun canvas, what were these children really thinking about? One cannot but question if many did not secretly agree with the less inhibited Patty who frankly stated in her sampler for all the world to read

> Patty Polk did this and she hated every stitch she did in it. She loves to read much more.

Restive Patty may not have realized that as she worked "every stitch" she was learning not only the gentle art of embroidery but also the rudiments of design and color harmony and, quite obviously, the meaning of words. It would seem that the major purpose of the sampler was to teach simultaneously the alphabet, numerals, and simple stitches. In needlework the sampler corresponded to the hornbook which was the earliest lesson book made for a child's own use. Into the sampler went a girl's first lessons in reading, in Bible history, geography, and pictorial art.

According to Candace Wheeler, samplers were "baby work—a beginning as necessary as being taught to walk or talk." Certainly, little girls were hardly out of babyhood when they commenced these exercises in stitchery, taught at home by mother and, sometimes, at a Dame School as well. The mistress of a Dame School was frequently a widow or some young gentlewoman who wished to eke out an income. Here very young children learned the alphabet, the catechism, and a little reading and writing, before progressing to a grammar school. Even in the latter girls were taught to sew and the Newark Museum has a four-patch for a quilt top made by Eliza Pierson in 1851 under the supervision of Miss Johnson who was then teacher at the Lyons Farms Schoolhouse now re-erected in the Museum Garden.

A choice item in the Newark Museum's collection is a scrapbook showing "Specimens of Needlework Executed in Viscountess Lorton's Model School, Errorona, by Margaret Whiteside 1840," this caption being worked in finest cross-stitch within a leafy border. At this private school in Ireland, Margaret learned not only to work samplers and to "sew a fine seam" but also to make buttonholes, tiny doll clothes as forerunners of what she would later maker for herself and her children, to do fine drawnwork and lace making. The book is an illuminating record of what was expected of young girls in the 1840's.

Just how long ago samplers were first worked is a question. A book of patterns for samplers was published in England by Peter Quentel in 1527 and is referred to in a later book of "borders and corner pieces" published in 1701. John Taylor gives a full list of old-time stitches in his *Praise of the Needle,* 1640. Samplers are even mentioned by those famous bards Shakespeare and John Milton. In these literary references the word sampler is variously spelled sam-cloth, sampleth, saumpler, and exampler, for it was literally a sample or example.

The earliest samplers were long and narrow, the stitches done on a foundation of linen and intended, it would seem, as a record of patterns. The choicest seem to have been made in England, which country has always been noted for its fine embroideries. The elaborately embroidered pictures and the bed hangings of crewelwork done by colonial ladies in their leisure hours had their inspiration in earlier English needlework. In the New Jersey Historical Society is a long, narrow sampler dating from the 18th century and done by a member of John Hart's family in Hopewell. Across the bottom of the sampler a gaily colored shepherd and shepherdess are shown tending their sheep. Judging by the quality of the needlework one feels certain the young maker progressed with ease to the execution of more elaborate pictures worked on silk.

So far as known, the first sampler made in the American Colonies was the work of Lora Standish, born 1623 and the daughter of Miles Standish. It is now preserved at Pilgrim Hall in Plymouth, Massachusetts. During the latter part of the 17th century samplers made in the Colonies changed their shape, becoming shorter and broader, until by 1720 they had assumed a strictly American style.

By the end of the 18th century the variety of American samplers was infinite for each was an expression of the individual designer and maker. Colors used in the needlework were home dyed and therefore, soft and pleasing. It is only as we approach the mid-19th century that we find harsh colors and unimaginative patterns, often worked in wool. Because childish fingers could not attempt complicated designs we find the simple Greek fret used as a border, or else a meander in strawberry or vine pattern. The pious verse first appeared as part of the sampler about 1760 and, as already indicated, we find these verses or variants of them used on many different samplers. Here is a popular verse of which several variants are known:

This is my Sampler
Here you see
What care my Mother
Took of me.

On a sampler made by Mary Ford Alling in 1819 she stitched the following:

This I have done to let you see
What care my parents took of me.

In 1836 Henrietta Elizabeth Baldwin worked this variant,

Remember me when this you see
What care my parents took of me,
When I am dead and in my grave
This piece of work my friends shall have.

Mary Alling's sampler in the Museum's collection, shows the alphabet in three different sizes, but is it possible that Mary could not count beyond six? Henrietta Baldwin's sampler is illustrated. As she was careful to state she "completed work in the ninth year of her age, July 17th 1836." In later years Henrietta became Mrs. Theodore R. Beardsley.

The other sampler illustrated here was worked by Eliza Hendricks, later Mrs. John Christopher Denman, who was born in 1818 and died about 1870. She was buried in Westfield Presbyterian Churchyard. The New Jersey Historical Society owns a water color drawing of Eliza Hendricks Denman as well as her sampler, which is an unusually fine piece. The stanza at the top reads

Full many a gem of purest ray serene
The dark unfathomed caves of ocean bear
Full many a flower is born to blush unseen
And waste its sweetness on the desert air.

It is a bit startling to find that at the age of seven Adelia R. Stiles of Caldwell, New Jersey, was expected to work these lines into a sampler:

A little learning is a dangerous thing.

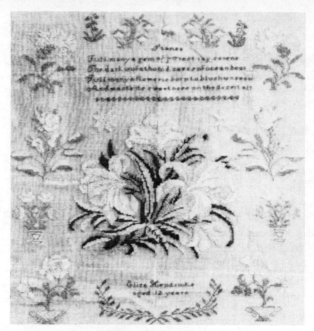

Above: A sampler worked on about 1830 by Eliza Hendricks and later by Mrs. John C. Denman, then aged twelve.
Below: A sampler made by Henrietta Elizabeth on July 17, 1836 when she was nine years of age.

Drink deep or taste not the Pierian spring:
There shallow draughts intoxicate the brain,
And drinking largely sobers us again.

Below a stiff band of flowers Adelia has added,

May I govern my passions with absolute sway,
And grow wiser and better as life wears away.

Mary A. Hice, born December 29, 1819, tried to relieve her depressing verse with a spray of flowers. After all, it's depressing enough to be born only four days after Christmas and thus be deprived of birthday excitements.

How shall the young secure their hearts
And guard their lives from sin.
Thy word the choicest rules imparts
To keep the conscience clean.

Sophia Pope at the age of seven proved herself an expert needlewoman, as did her twin sister, Elizabeth. Sophia's cross-stitched lines are enlivened by a parrot in a tree, cocking its head in saucy fashion at a squirrel and French poodle.

I wish with Martha while I serve below
The lawful things of Time to learn and know
But so to be engaged with things Devine
That Mary's better part it may be Mine.

Surely the parents of Eliza Webb must have smiled with sincere pleasure at her work "finished September 24, 1814."

Behold! the labours of my tender age,
And view this mark which did my hours engage,
With anxious care I did these colours place,
A smile to gain from my dear parents face,
Whose care for me I ever will regard,
And hope that Heaven will give a kind reward.

Though worn in places Eliza's sampler is an excellent illustration of good design, softly blended colors, and careful workmanship.

After reading such thoughtful and depressing sentiments it is refreshing to come across pictorial samplers whose charm is enhanced by the utter lack of perspective and which offer simple views of a red house flanked by trees; a primitive interpretation of the Nativity scene; a boy and girl romping with a puppy.

Samplers in the collections of the New Jersey Historical Society and the Newark Museum represent various types and also serve as historic records of local families. At Marlpit Hall in Middletown may be seen several samplers by young members of the Taylor family and other historical societies of the state own pieces of local interest. It is good to know that these bits of embroidery, so carefully cherished by fond mothers of long ago, are still treasured by men and women who, for the very reason that they could not possibly do such fine needlework, appreciate the samplers as an expression of American folk art.

—MARGARET E. WHITE

Antique Sewing Tools

FOR many years sewing tools have been associated exclusively with women and their charm is supposed to appeal only to the feminine gender. What about tailors who for centuries have made garments for women as well as men? How about the male embroiderers of East Indian shawls, the silk waistcoats worn by the fashionable gentlemen of London and Paris, or the makers of sails before steamboats were invented?

The description of an English tailor's shop of 1659 reveals the variety of garments fashioned there, for in the shop were woolen hats, men's breeches and waistcoats, women's cloaks and petticoats, a lady's doublet and gown. It is interesting to note that among the items always listed on a tailor's bill was the thread used in making an article of any kind.

In her book, *Two Centuries of Costume in America,* Alice Morse Earle refers to a gift sent by Mr. Smith, Tailor of England, to the Winthrop household in Massachusetts, consisting of "scissors and a hundred needles and the like homely gifts." John Winthrop came to the Massachusetts Colony in 1630 and was followed in August of 1631 by the women of his family. One can imagine how very welcome such "homely gifts" must have been to lonely English women stranded in the wilds of New England.

Quilting was the fashion in the 17th and 18th centuries, and although for years after the American Colonies were established, women's garments were made by tailors, many women must have quilted their own hoods and the silk petticoat which formed part of a lady's formal dress. In 1664 Samuel Pepys refers in his *Diary* to his wife's yellow birds-eye hood "very fine, to church, as the fashion now is." Some petticoats were richly embroidered in gold, silver and colored silks, the patterns composed of flowers, shells, or the Spanish plume. Silk aprons, also richly embroidered, were worn to protect these handsome skirts—even Queen Anne wore embroidered aprons.

Lady Mary Wortley Montagu wrote in the 18th century, "It is as scandalous for a woman not to know how to use her needle as for a man not to know how to use his sword." But evidently even lords and kings of olden time knew something of the needle; for when they led into battle, and therefore traveled from place to place, they carried with them needle cases or sheaths. In 1538 the King of Navarre owned a jasper case in which were three needle cases set with rubies.

It was appreciation for the historic background of such small items as sewing accessories, as well as for their fine craftsmanship and artistry in design, that caused Wilbur Macey Stone and his wife, Lillian Newton Stone, to assemble the collection of sewing tools which is now in the Newark Museum. It is said that those who get the most pleasure out of collecting are those who study the subject, learning the history behind the items—when and where they were made, what part they played in the social life of a people. This was definitely true of the Stones. Their home on North Arlington Avenue in East Orange was almost a museum in itself. In addition to the sewing tools, Mrs. Stone's collections included scent boxes, Victorian card cases, valentines. The valentines are said to have been the second largest collection in the world, numbering more than a thousand items and dating back to 1643.

A hand-painted needle case of about 1830 from Salem, Massachusetts.

As well as being a collector, Wilbur Macey Stone was a mechanical engineer and patent attorney with an office at 15 Park Row in New York City. He was born in Winona, Minnesota, the son of the Reverend George Marvin Stone and Abbie Barnum Seeley Stone. During Wilbur's early boyhood the Reverend Mr. Stone was called to a pastorate in Hartford, Conn., and it was here that Wilbur Stone later met and married Lillian Newton. Mr. Stone, a graduate of Stevens Institute of Technology, was a member of the Carteret Book Club of Newark, the New Jersey and Connecticut Historical Societies, the American Antiquarian Society, the Bibliographical Society of America, and he was a trustee of the Newark Museum. Shortly before his death in 1941 Mr. Stone was described by a newspaper reporter as "a striking and patriarchial personality, with abundant white hair, white mustache and white beard." His collections included literature for juveniles, the earliest a book written by Martin Luther and printed at Lübeck, Germany, in 1558; a collection of some 600 to 700 minature books (some of them fitting on a finger nail); prints and broadsides; samplers; and dolls from the 16th to the present century.

Anyone who recalls Mr. and Mrs. Stone will remember how lovingly they would pick up some object to tell you its story, and what pleasure Mr. Stone derived from making protective cases for his tiny books or rare paper dolls. One of their best-loved items in the collection of sewing tools was a white silk needle case of about 1830 from Salem, Massachusetts, with soldiers handpainted on the leaves and each man holding a needle as his weapon. The sheaths or needle cases illustrated are of various materials, one being a bone case in the form of a carrot, another—a sheath from France—a wooden tube covered with a fine network of beads. The latter is said to be quite uncommon.

It was only after the Civil War that needles were made in the United States entirely by machine. With a needle went a "needle pusher" or thimble. Open-ended thimbles of bronze have been found in Herculaneum and in Roman ruins in Britain.

Above: Sheaths or needle cases of silver, bone, and beadwork.
Below: Thread winders used before the days of spools. Made from wood, bone, cardboard, and mother-of-pearl, the last having a delicate ornamentation incised. Note the animal-head carved on one of the stilettos.

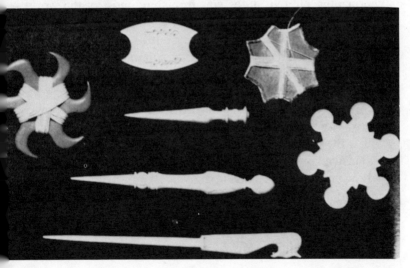

Some early specimens were rings rather than the dome-like thimble we know, some were shield-shaped and held to the finger by means of a leather strap. Another requisite for the needle was the burnishing emery into which needles were thrust several times over to remove rust or dirt. These closely compressed cushions of emery, covered with cotton or velvet, were essential to every needlewoman. Have you one in the form of a red strawberry in your work basket?

Probably the earliest needles and pins were contrived from thorns or fish bones. In the 14th century pins made from precious metal were scarce and expensive and regarded as a fitting gift. The wimples worn by ladies of the 14th and early 15th centuries required many pins to hold them in place. There was a guild of pin makers in 15th century France, and until King Henry VIII permitted the importation of the newer French pins of brass wire, England used pins made of inferior iron wire. Pins with solid heads were first made in 1797 by Timothy Harris of England. In 1824 Lemuel W. Wright, an American, invented a better device, and by the beginning of the present century the United States was furnishing most of the world's supply of pins.

Centimeters were not introduced until 1799 and the French word for tape measure is *mètre en ruban,* deriving from the Renaissance custom of measuring with ribbons on which lines were embroidered at a fixed distance apart. Later came tape measures in cases of mother-of-pearl, carved boxwood, bone or ivory, with a pin passing through the center of the little case on which the tape was wound.

Beeswax, who would use it today? "Sewing wax," pale yellow or white, was made up into small round cakes about one and a half inches in diameter and used to wax thread for bead stringing, for making or mending shoes, and other purposes. The thread, spun on a flax wheel, was placed on little holders or winders before the spool was invented. These old thread holders are found in a charming variety of shapes and materials, such as shell, cardboard, wood or ivory.

The stiletto was an indispensable accessory for tailor or needlewoman. Before hooks and eyes were invented (it's hard to imagine such a time) garments had to be laced with hand-made tapes and the eyes for lacing were made with a stiletto. Darned net with flowers having open centers was popular in the early 19th century for ladies' scarves and dress trimmings. Here again we see a use for the stiletto to form the centers of the embroidered flowers.

Have you a sewing bird to use when hemming? These little clamps of bronze or stamped tin were attached by a vise to a table's edge. If you pinched the bird's tail it opened its beak to grip your sewing and on the bird's back there was often a tiny pincushion covered with velvet. Not all of these clamps were bird-shaped. Some are of olive or other grained wood, sometimes they are gaily painted, but always these are supplied with a stuffed cushion to which the sewing can be attached.

Imagine how important a pincushion must have been in the old days when pins were scarce. The earliest pins were treasured in boxes; then came some form of cushion, and many a work basket is still equipped with one of red flannel shaped like a tomato.

—MARGARET E. WHITE

Printing

Collecting
New Jersey Books

N EW JERSEY books have been collected since the nineteenth
century. William A. Whitehead, an early historian and a
founder of the New Jersey Historical Society, formed the first
significant New Jersey collection. Though considerably
stronger in historic manuscripts than in books, Whitehead's
collection included most of what had been published up to that
time relating to New Jersey. Much of Whitehead's collection is
now in the New Jersey Historical Society. William S. Stryker,
Adjutant General of New Jersey and a leading nineteenth
century historian, built an important collection of New Jersey
books and manuscripts, a part of which was catalogued by Stan
V. Henkels and sold by Davis & Harvey in Philadelphia in
April of 1901.

The outstanding New Jersey collection of the late nineteenth
and early twentieth centuries, and probably the most significant
group of New Jersey books ever assembled by one individual,
belonged to William Nelson. A lawyer, historian, book collector and prolific writer, Nelson gathered a tremendous collection
of New Jersey books, pamphlets and broadsides, some of which
were exceedingly rare. In February of 1902 the great Paterson

fire severely damaged portions of Nelson's library. Nelson died in 1914 and his library was sold by the American Art Association in November of 1915. From time to time books from Nelson's collection re-appear on the market, many tragically burned around the edges. The sale catalogue itself is today a very collectible New Jersey book as well as an important reference work. After Nelson's time there was no private collection of the same magnitude, however, institutions had begun to acquire New Jersey books. The New Jersey Historical Society and Princeton University were the most active early collectors, followed by the New York Historical Society and the Historical Society of Pennsylvania. In later years significant New Jersey collections were formed by other institutions. These collections will be discussed below.

A "New Jersey" book can be many things. It can be a book about New Jersey, or about a particular place, event or time period in New Jersey; it can be a book about a New Jersey resident, or a book written or illustrated by a New Jersey resident; it can be a book printed, published or bound in New Jersey; or it may have nothing at all to do with New Jersey but be a New Jersey book by virtue or its association with some significant New Jersey person, place or event. All of these books are highly collectible and, taken together, comprise what the book collector calls "New Jerseyana". Each is worthy of individual examination.

By far the most numerous New Jersey books are those about the state itself. Within this category the most common, and the most collected, are the histories. There are state, county and local histories, as well as histories of churches, families, organizations, events and practically any other subject of which a history could be written. The first history of New Jersey was Samuel Smith's *The History of the Colony of Nova-Caesaria, or New Jersey,* printed in Burlington in 1765. This book is a cornerstone to any New Jersey collection. Though by no means rare, it is eagerly sought by collectors, and copies in original or

THE

HISTORY

O F

THE COLONY

O F

NOVA-CÆSARIA, or NEW-JERSEY:

CONTAINING,

AN ACCOUNT OF ITS FIRST SETTLEMENT,

PROGRESSIVE IMPROVEMENTS,

THE ORIGINAL AND PRESENT CONSTITUTION,

AND OTHER EVENTS,

TO THE YEAR 1721.

WITH

SOME PARTICULARS SINCE;

AND

A SHORT VIEW OF ITS PRESENT STATE.

By SAMUEL SMITH.

BURLINGTON, in NEW-JERSEY:
Printed and Sold by James Parker: Sold also by
David Hall, in Philadelphia. M,DCC,LXV.

The title page of the first history of New Jersey, Samuel Smith's *The History of the Colony of Nova-Caesaria, or New Jersey,* published in 1765.

contemporary binding have become increasingly difficult to find. Such copies currently bring between $250 and $400. The book was reprinted in 1877 and again in 1890 and even these early reprints have now become collectible. Like most other important New Jersey reference books, Smith's *History* is currently available in reprint. Other collectible state histories are Thomas F. Gordon's *The History of New Jersey* bound with *A Gazeteer of the State of New Jersey* (Trenton 1834), and John W. Barber and Henry Howe's *Historical Collections of the State of New Jersey* (New York 1844 and numerous later editions). Both of these books are plentiful but, again, basic to any New Jersey collection. Numerous other state histories exist, including several multi-volume sets. All are quite common and readily available.

County histories in recent years have exhibited a marked increase in popularity and an even more marked increase in price. In the 1870's and 1880's, histories were compiled for practically every county in America. Often two or more adjoining counties would be represented in the same volume. These books, usually in large two-column format, several hundred pages in length and elegantly bound in gilt-decorated leather, were occasionally compiled by reputable local historians but more often were the products of commercial historians. The content was standard: about half of the book was history, the other half was biographical sketches of the "useful citizens" of the county. Accompanying each biography was a full-page steel engraving of the subject of the sketch. As a result of this format, county histories of this period are often referred to as "mug books" or "head books". Every county in New Jersey is represented by at least one history compiled during this period, though a few are not in the "mug book" format. Despite their dubious accuracy, they are eagerly sought by local historians, genealogists and collectors. Most are available in reprint, but this has had only a slight effect on the prices of the original editions. In general, those that have been reprinted bring between $75 and $100; those not yet reprinted bring as much as $125. Local antique dealers often ask, and occasionally get, substantially higher prices. These large format leather-bound county histories are difficult to find in good condition. The leather is usually dry and the covers are frequently detached.

Around the turn of the century county biographical volumes were very popular in New Jersey. These are similar to the county histories but contain only biographical sketches and portraits, with little or no local history. In the late 1920's the Lewis Historical Publishing Company issued a series of multi-volume county and regional histories of New Jersey. Unattractive in format and generally unscholarly in historical content, these sets are still readily available and generally do not command very high prices.

Local histories, by their very nature, have a smaller market, but demand for some of the scarcer titles, especially within the local area, can be great. The first New Jersey local history is generally considered to be Robert G. Johnson's *An Historical Account of the First Settlement of Salem, in West Jersey, by John Fenwich, Esq.* (Philadelphia 1839). Every city in New Jersey has at least one, usually several, histories. Some are scholarly and accurate accounts, some are attractively illustrated, some are handsomely printed and bound. A few are all of these; many are none. There are town histories, township histories, municipal histories and village histories. Some are more readily available than others, but none are rare.

There are many hundreds of New Jersey church histories. In the nineteenth century ministers frequently delivered "historical discourses," usually on the occasion of an anniversary of the church. Most were subsequently printed and often contain valuable genalogical information on the early families associated with the church. Most church histories are small pamphlets. However some, such as W. Northey Jones's *The History of St. Peter's Church in Perth Amboy* (Perth Amboy

A SKETCH

OF THE

PASSAIC FALLS,

OF PATERSON, N. J.

EMBRACING A HISTORY OF ALL THE RE-
MARKABLE EVENTS THAT HAVE OCCUR-
RED SINCE THE IMMORTAL FATHER OF
HIS COUNTRY WAS ENCAMPED THERE.

ILLUSTRATED WITH FOUR ENGRAVINGS,

Representing the Great Falls; the Heroes of the
Revolution, Washington and Lafayette, in
Council; the Cottage on the Cliffs; and
the Nine Witches of the Rocks.

A GUIDE TO THE FALLS,

Describing each particular scene, with an account
of the various Manufactories, &c. &c.
in its immediate vicinity.

BY PETER ARCHDEACON.

New York:

PRINTED BY MICHAEL T. O'CONNOR,
27 CROSS-STREET.

1845.

A charming and highly collectible local history is Peter Archdeacon's *A Sketch of the Passaic Falls, of Paterson, N.J.* The book mesures 4¾ by 3 inches. Archdeacon was at the time proprietor of the land adjoining the falls and hoped to attract visitors to the area by the publication of this rather overly-dramatized account of the falls.

1924), Hamilton Schuyler's *A History of St. Michael's Church, Trenton* (Princeton 1926), and Frank R. Symme's *History of the Old Tennant Church* (Cranbury 1904), to name a few representative examples, are exhaustive and scholarly compliations.

Family histories, or genealogies of New Jersey families, have been published since the middle of the nineteenth century. Most were privately printed in small editions and many are now quite scarce. They are occasionally found in elaborate presentation bindings of full calf or morocco, richly gilt and hand tooled. A few classic examples are R. Morris Smith's *The Burlington Smiths, a Family History* (Philadelphia 1877), Thomas Coates Stockton's *The Stockton Family of New Jersey and Other Stocktons* (Washington 1911), and William Ogden Wheeler's *The Ogden Family in America, Elizabethtown Branch* (Philadelphia 1907).

Biographies of New Jersey residents, or of persons connected in some way with the state, are also collectible. There are biographies of New Jersey governors, statesmen, military figures, signers of the Declaration of Independence, inventors, industrialists, printers and theologians. Biographies may be full-length books, small pamphlets, memorial addresses of funeral orations.

In addition to books about New Jersey residents are books by New Jersey residents. In the eighteenth and early nineteenth centuries, these frequently were in the form of printed sermons or public orations. Traditionally, sermons and orations have not been in great demand by collectors and they are more often sought for their printer's imprint. However, eighteenth century sermons, and particularly those prior to the Revolution, are now becoming scarce. As a general rule, any non-religious book by a New Jersey author published prior to the Civil War is collectible. As will be discussed below, those printed in New Jersey are even more desirable. If the book is an early contribution to a technical or scholarly field, it may have

SILVIA DUBOIS,

(NOW 116 YERS OLD.)

—•—

A BIOGRAFY

—OF—

The Slav who Whipt her Mistres

—AND—

GAND HER FREDOM.

BY C. W. LARISON, M. D.,

PRINCIPAL OF THE ACADEMY OF SIENC AND ART AT RINGOS, N. J.;
FORMERLY PROF. NATURAL SIENC IN THE UNIVERSITY AT LEWIS-
BURG, PA.; AUTHOR OF ELEMENTS OF ORTHOEPY;
THE TENTING SCHOL, &c., &c.

—•—

RINGOS, N. J.:
C. W. LARISON, PUBLISHER.
1883.

A rare New Jersey biography is Cornelius Larison's *Silvia Dubois*. The indominatable Dr. Larison interviewed the 116 year old former slave in her hut in the Sourland Mountains. The book is printed in phonetic type—Larison's answer to the problem of English orthography.

additional value to a collector. Books by New Jersey authors after about 1890 cease to be considered "New Jerseyana," though they may be collectible nonetheless. The desirablity of first editions of American authors is subject to often-changing trends. Frank R. Stockton was a very collected author in the 1920's and 1930's. Today there is virtually no market for his books. Everett T. Tomlinson, one of New Jersey's most prolific authors of boy's books during the first three decades of this century, is now growing in popularity among collectors. Unfortunately, with often-reprinted popular authors such as Tomlinson, many of the books being sold as first editions are nothing more than standing-type reprints. Distinguishing a true first edition from an almost identical standing-type reprint is a job for an experienced bookman.

Perhaps the truest "New Jersey" books are those actually printed and published in the state. New Jersey's first permanent printer was James Parker, who began printing in Woodbridge in 1754. Prior to that date, practically all printing for New Jersey was done either in New York or Philadelphia. About seventy percent of the products of Parker's press were related to, or printed for, the province of New Jersey. Like most early printers Parker was both a job printer and a publisher. Job printing, and in particular being "Printer to the King's Most Excellent Majesty" (or, later, "Printer to the State"), provided the reasonably reliable income that enable often-impoverished printers to remain in business. However it is the more obscure books and pamphlets published by the printer himself that are of more interest to the collector. Parker printed sermons and religious tracts, orations, histories, an account of the College of New Jersey, and minutes of an Indian treaty, to mention a few examples. Copies of Parkers imprints have now become scarce. Sets of Samuel Nevill's *The Acts of the General Assemble of the Province of New Jersey,* the second volume of which was printed by Parker in 1761, *Conductor Generalis* (1764) and single issues of the *New American Magazine* (1758-1760)

Anti-Paedo-Rantism ;

OR

Mr. SAMUEL FINLEY's

Charitable PLEA for the Speechless

EXAMINED and REFUTED:

The Baptism of Believers

MAINTAIN'D;

AND

The Mode of it, by Immersion,

VINDICATED.

By *ABEL MORGAN*, at *Middletown,*
in East-Jersey.

Isa. 9. 16. *The Leaders of this People cause them to Err.*
Mark 16. 15, 16. *And he said unto them, Go ye into all the World, and preach the Gospel to every Creature. He that* believeth, *and is* baptized, *shall be saved.*
Col. 2. 12. *Buried with him in Baptism.*

PHILADELPHIA:
Printed by B. FRANKLIN, in *Market-Street.*
M,DCC,XLVII.

An early work by a New Jersey theologian is Abel Morgan's *Anti-Paedo-Rantism; or Mr. Samuel Finley's Charitable Plea for the Speechless Examined and Refuted,* published by Benjamin Franklin in 1747. Samuel Finley would later become President of the College of New Jersey, now Princeton University.

appear on the market from time to time, but other Parker imprints are seldom seen.

The next printer in New Jersey, and one whose books are much more readily available to the collector, was Isaac Collins. A Quaker who first printed with Joseph Crukshank in Philadelphia, Collins printed in Burlington from 1770 to 1778 and in Trenton from 1778 until 1796. Of the approximately 260 known New Jersey Collins imprints, about 160 are state documents, the majority of which are acts and proceedings of the legislature. Isaac Collins printed the first almanac in New Jersey, *The Burlington Almanac for the Year of Our Lord, 1771, by Timothy Trueman* (Burlington 1770). He continued to print one, and sometimes two a year for every year he was in the state. Almanacs were the best-selling items in the stock of all eighteenth and early nineteenth century printers, and there was seldom a printer who did not publish at least one almanac a year. Collins almanacs appear on the market occasionally, though those prior to 1780 are now becoming scarce. Almanacs are frequently found in very worn condition or lacking one or more leaves at the end. The standard bibliography in the field is Milton Drake's *Almanacs of the United States* (New York 1962). One of Collins's best-known imprints, and fortunately for collectors also one of the most common, is the 1791 edition of the *Holy Bible*. This was the first Bible printed in New Jersey (preceeded only by editions of the New Testament) and was the second quarto edition of the Bible printed in America. It is a superb specimen of eighteenth century typography. According to tradition, Collins's children read the proof sheets eleven times. Collins Bibles generally begin between $40 and $100 today, depending largely upon the condition of the binding. Naturally, copies in the original binding are most desirable. A good biography of Collins is Richard F. Hixson's *Isaac Collins* (New Brunswick 1968). This work contains a useful, but very incomplete, bibliography of Collins imprints.

Other prolific printers in New Jersey prior to 1800 were

ESSAY

ON THE

CONNECTION

Between the

DOCTRINE of JUSTIFICATION

BY THE

Imputed RIGHTEOUSNESS of CHRIST,

AND

HOLINESS OF LIFE;

With some Reflections upon the Reception which that
Doctrine hath generally met with in the World.

To which is prefix'd,
A LETTER to the Rev. Mr. *JAMES HERVEY*,
Rector of *Weston Favell, Northampton-shire*, Author
of *THERON* and *ASPASIO*.

By *JOHN WITHERSPOON*, M. A.
Minister of the Gospel in *Beith*.

GLASGOW:

Printed by JOHN BRYCE and DAVID PATERSON
M, DCC, L VI.

The first work of John Witherspoon's to bear his name on the title page was his *Essay on the Connection between the Doctrine of Justification by the Imputed Righteousness of Christ, and Holiness of Life.* In 1768 Witherspoon left Scotland to become President of the College of New Jersey, now Princeton University. In 1776 he was one of New Jersey's five signers of the Declaration of Independence.

Shepard Kollock (Chatham 1779-1783; Elizabethtown 1786-after 1800), Abraham Blauvelt (New Brunswick 1789-after 1800) and John Woods (Newark 1791-1798). Imprints of these printers are obtainable without much difficulty, though sermons, religious treatises and almanacs appear much more frequently than do the more unusual items. Other printers who worked in New Jersey prior to the year 1800, and whose imprints are obtainable, are:

Shelly Arnett (New Brunswick)	John Mershon (Trenton)
William Black (Salem)	Isaac Neale (Burlington)
Elijah Cooper (Morristown)	Samuel F. Parker (Woodbridge)
Gershom Craft (Trenton)	Aaron Pennington (Newark)
Matthias Day (Trenton and Newark)	Samuel Pennington (Newark)
Daniel Dodge (Newark)	Frederick Quequelle (Trenton)
Phillip Freneau (Mount Pleasant)	George Sherman (Trenton)
Jacob Halsey (Newark)	Isaiah Thomas (Trenton)
Heinrich Kammerer (Burlington)	James Tod (Princeton)
Jacob Mann (Morristown)	Stephen C. Ustick (Mount Holly)
	John H. Williams (Newark)

Pamphlets were usually issued with a cover of the same paper as the text. Occasionally the cover was plain or bore a shortened version of the title; more frequently it was an exact duplicate of the titlepage. The pages, or "signatures," were generally stitched together with linen thread about one-quarter of an inch in from the edge. In later years collections of pamplets were often sewn together, trimmed at the edges and bound into a volume. While the most desirable state of a pamplet is uncut, with the original cover, today most pamplets that appear on the market have been removed from bound volumes.

Eighteent century books are found in two different styles of original binding. One is generally termed "original boards" and is nothing more than front and rear binder's boards covered in blue-gray or off-white paper, with a paper or linen-covered spine, sometimes lettered by hand and sometimes with a paper label. This was the least expensive eighteenth century binding

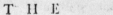

THE
ACTS

Of the GENERAL ASSEMBLY

Of the PROVINCE of

NEW-JERSEY,

From the Time of the Surrender of the Government of the faid Province, to the Fourth Year of the Reign of KING *GEORGE* the Second.

Collected and Published by Order of the faid ASSEMBLY.

With a **TABLE** of the Principal Matters therein contained.

PHILADELPHIA: Printed and Sold by *William* and *Andrew Bradford,* Printers to the King's Moft Excellent Majefty, for the Province of *New-Jerfey,* MDCCXXXII.

Prior to the establishment of the first permanent printer in the colony in 1754, New Jersey's printing was done in Philadelphia and New York. This compilation of *The Acts of the General Assembly of the Province of New Jersey* contained all of the laws of New Jersey from 1703 to 1732 then in force. It was compiled by John Kinsey, Speaker of the Assembly.

and was actually not a true binding but merely a way to hold the book together until its owner could have it bound in leather. A book in the original boards, in good condition, is almost always more desirable than the same book in a contemporary leather binding. The other method of binding books in the eighteenth century, and the binding found today on most books of that period, was calf skin. Often the binding was treated with acid to give it a decorative speckled or mottled effect. Full calf binding, with a red leather spine label, was the most popular eighteenth century binding. Early in the nineteenth century, as full leather became more and more expensive, half and three-quarter leather bindings were frequently used. Brightly-colored "marbled" paper was often used to cover the boards. By the 1840's cloth had superseded leather as the most common binding style.

Many eighteenth and early-to-mid nineteenth century books contain tiny brown spots throughout the book. This condition, known as "foxing," is caused by impurities within the paper and often has been aggravated by storage in a damp area. Foxing, for practical purposes, cannot be removed, and unless it is unusually severe, it does not significantly alter the value of most non-illustrated books. Waterstaining, on the other hand, can greatly effect the desirability of a book, as can torn pages, old library stamps or broken bindings.

Nineteenth century New Jersey imprints are also collectible, but because of the great number of printers, most collectors prefer to acquire books printed in a certain town rather than those printed by a particular individual. After about 1820 the majority of New Jersey imprints were pamphlets. Most books were printed in New York or Philadelphia, where the work could be done cheaper and faster by larger, more modern firms. Frequently a book would be printed by one individual and published by another. With the advent of "sterotyping" and other faster methods of printing, more and more of New Jersey's printing was being done in New York. While there was always

THE

HISTORY

OF THE

REVOLUTION

OF

SOUTH-CAROLINA,

FROM A BRITISH PROVINCE

TO AN INDEPENDENT STATE.

By DAVID RAMSAY, M. D.
MEMBER OF THE AMERICAN CONGRESS.

IN TWO VOLUMES.

VOL. I.

TRENTON:
PRINTED BY ISAAC COLLINS.
M.DCC.LXXXV.

A copy of David Ramsay's *The History of the Revolution of South Carolina* was in George Washington's personal library.

job printing to be done by local printers, by the post-Civil War period very few books were being printed in New Jersey.

Occasionally the New Jersey collector has to compete with non-New Jersey collectors. This occurs when a New Jersey book has more value in another collecting field than it has as New Jerseyana. For example, Walter Minto's *An Inaugural Oration, on the Progress and Importance of the Mathematical Sciences* (Trenton 1788), the first mathematical oration delivered in America, has more value to a collector of mathematical books than it has to a collector of Isaac Collins imprints. William Coxe's *A View of the Cultivation of Fruit Trees and the Management of Orchards and Cider* (Philadelphia 1817), the first American book on fruit and fruit culture, was written by a Burlington resident and printed by a Burlington printer (David Allinson). However, its value as the cornerstone to a collection on American pomology far exceeds its value as a New Jersey book.

Book collecting is subject to trends just like any other field of collecting. For the past several years, children's books have been eagerly collected, and prices are rising rapidly. There are now antiquarian booksellers who deal exclusively in children's books. The first children's book printed in New Jersey was James Janeway's *A Token for Children* (Burlington 1772). Only two complete copies are known to exist. Between 1772 and 1820 approximately twenty-two children's books were printed in New Jersey. Shortly after this period, Benjamin Olds, in Newark, printed several children's books, including a very charming series of small toy books. An even more current collecting trend is in early photography. Prices have reached astounding highs and show no signs of tapering off. In the book field, collectors of "photographica" are interested in books illustrated with original photographs. In general, this method of illustrating was used between 1850 and 1900. As a rule, earlier photographs are more desirable than later ones, and those which identify the photographer are especially sought after.

A

TOKEN

FOR

CHILDREN.

BEING

An Exact Account of the Conver-
fion, Holy and Exemplary Lives,
and Joyful Deaths of feveral
Young Children.

In TWO PARTS.

By JAMES JANEWAY,
MINISTER OF THE GOSPEL.

—————*Suffer little Children to come unto me,
and forbid them not ; for of fuch is the King-
dom of God.* Luke x. 14.

BURLINGTON,

Re-printed by ISAAC COLLINS, MDCCLXXII.

The title page of the first children's book printed in New Jersey, James
Janeway's *A Token for Children*, published in 1772.

Here again, the New Jersey collector is at the mercy of a highly-inflated photography market. The first edition of L. W. Brodhead's *The Delaware Water Gap* (Philadelphia 1867) is illustrated with original tipped-in photographs. A few years ago this relatively common book sold for about $15 in New Jersey. At recent major auctions of photographica it has brought between $50 and $100. In the past there was practically no market for annual pictorial albums of the College of New Jersey (now Princeton University). Today those earlier editions containing actual mounted photographs of the faculty and students are considered collectible examples of nineteenth century photography.

One final catetgory of New Jersey books that should be mentioned briefly is association copies. These are non-New Jersey books that have become New Jersey books by virtue of their association with a significant New Jersey person, place or event. Usually these are books from the libraries of prominent state figures, such as signers of the Declaration of Independence, governors, statesmen or early settlers. Occasionally they may contain inscriptions or bookplates.

The fine New Jersey books must be purchased at book auctions or from book dealers or from other collectors. Antique dealers generally know very little about books and often tend to grossly overprice many relatively common books. The worst place to by a local or county history or atlas is in an antique shop in or near that county. It will almost always be overpriced. While there are occasionally "sleepers" to be found in boxed lots of books purchased at house auctions, desirable local histories never seem to be in those boxes. When these books are sold at local auctions, they frequently bring twice the price for which they could be bought from a rare book dealer.

While book auction houses are important sources for fine and rare books, the small number of New Jersey books that appear at auction in a given year would not offset the relatively high annual subscription costs for the sale catalogues. Without

COBB'S TOYS,

SECOND SERIES,

No. 8.

STORIES

ABOUT THE

WATCH, CLOCK, GLOBE, INKSTAND,
PEN, SLATE, CRADLE, AND
ANCHOR,

IN WORDS OF

ONE AND TWO SYLLABLES.

NEWARK, (N. J.)

BENJAMIN OLDS

1835.

PRICE TWO CENTS.

One of a series of tiny (4 by 2½ inches) and charmingly illustrated toy books printed in Newark by Benjamin Olds.

doubt the best source of better New Jersey books is a knowledgeable antiquarian book dealer. Most used or rare bookshops in the New Jersey-New York City-Philadelphia area will have a section of New Jerseyana. Unfortunately, the same book from different dealers may vary in price as much as two or three hundred percent. In general, New York City and Philadelphia dealers will overprice New Jersey books, and the collector would be wise to purchase from a New Jersey dealer when possible. As in any collecting field, an active and knowlegeable collector can often provide a reliable and candid appraisal of the various dealers within the field. In addition to bookshops, there are numerous booksellers and book "scouts" who deal out of their homes, by appointment. The majority do not advertise in the media buy most are well-known among collectors. Private booksellers are probably the collector's best source of New Jersey books. As they have little or no overhead or expenses, their prices are often substantially lower than large dealers. In addition, they will usually accept collector's "want lists" and search for books that they do not have in stock. Some private booksellers issue periodic lists and catalogues, as do many of the larger dealers. Names of those private booksellers who deal in New Jersey books can be obtained from any New Jersey collector or from a member of the staff of any of the leading New Jersey collections.

The two most comprehensive collections of New Jersey books are in the New Jersey Historical Society in Newark and the Special Collections Department of the Rutgers University Library in New Brunswick. Librarians in both of these institutions are authorities on New Jersey books. Somewhat smaller collections are in the New Jersey State Library in Trenton, Fairleigh Dickinson University in Rutherford and Princeton University in Princeton. Public libraries in the larger cities, Newark in particular, contain substantial New Jersey collections, as do a few of the state colleges. Some of the great rarities, particularly very early New Jersey books, can be found in the

Wil: Livingston —

A NEW SYSTEM
OF
HUSBANDRY.
From many Years Experience,

WITH TABLES SHEWING THE

Expence and Profit of each Crop.

That a Farm of a 150 Acres will clear 402*l*. 4*s*. sterl. a Year
How to stock FARMS to the best Advantage. How the
CROPS are to follow each other by Way of Rotation.
Of Trench-Ploughing, shewing how to raise good Crops

WITHOUT MANURE

On REARING, BREEDING, and a new discovered

CHEAP FOOD FOR CATTLE.

Of CABBAGE and TURNIP Husbandry
Of the NAKED WHEAT, with many other new discovered

Grains and Grasses suitable for the Land
and Climate of America.

Also shewing the great profit of RABBIT WARRENS, and
how to stock them,
A FARMER's and KITCHEN GARDEN CALENDAR
Of all Sorts of MANURES, MARLS, CLAYS, SANDS, &c.
A NEW INVENTED THRASHING FLOOR
Also many chosen RECEIPTS in *Physic* and *Surgery*,

For the Human Species,

AND OTHERS

For the Cure of all sorts of Cattle.

To which are annexed a few *Hints* humbly offered for the
perusal of the Legislators of America, shewing

How to put a stop to runaway Servants

By C. VARLO, Esq.

VOLUME I.

PHILADELPHIA: Printed for the AUTHOR. 1785.
[*Price 3 dollars in boards or 3 and a half bound.*]

An interesting New Jersey association is William Livingston's copy of Charles Varlo's *A New System of Husbandry*. Varlo, an Englishman, had come to America in 1784 to pursue a claim to much of New Jersey, based upon a seventeenth century land grant. Unsuccesful in his claim, he returned to England the following year. Livingston at the time was the Governor of New Jersey.

more venerable institutions such as the New York Historical Society and the Historical Society of Pennsylvania. The largest collection of pre-1800 New Jersey imprints is in the American Antiquarian Society in Worcester, Massachusetts. Rutgers University and the New Jersey Historical Society also own substantial collections of New Jersey imprints.

As libraries and institutions continue to acquire New Jersey books, fewer and fewer choice items appear on the market. Like any other collectible, books are rapidly increasing in price as supply diminishes and demand increases. Yet the New Jersey book collector still has a comparatively large field from which to choose, and with some well-spent time and effort, a fine New Jersey collection can be assemled.   —JOSEPH J. FELCONE

Money of New Jersey

A FREQUENT and continuing source of irritation between England and its North American Colonies was its limitation on currency. England wished to monopolize trade, hence developed a gigantic barter system, generally swapping manufactured goods for raw materials. Colonial trade with others was frowned on, but carried on surreptitiously to some extent by barter and any available currency. Wampum was used for internal trade with the Indians and other colonists.

Quarrels between England and France were extended to America and the settlers of both nations fought with the help of their Indian allies. Payment of the troops sent against French Canada became a real problem and in 1690 Massachusetts solved it by issuing the first paper money in what is now the United States. Following its example, New Jersey became the fourth colonial issuer in 1709. Its first notes totaled 3000 pounds, in denominations five shillings to five pounds. Other issues followed.

These notes were generally redeemed by succeeding issues, frequently on terms unfavorable to the original holders. Gold, silver and copper coins of any description were preferred but were hard to come by. Fortunately, the twenty-three paper money issues prior to the Revolutionary War were not huge, so inflation was kept within bounds. New Jersey itself was a battleground during that war, largely restricting normal activities and requiring maintenance of many troops. As a consequence, the issue of March 1776 was by far the largest (125,000) up to that point and acutally was exceeded later only by the 225,000 pounds issue of 1780.

Collectors of New Jersey Colonial notes prize the issues of 1737 and 1746 since they were printed by Benjamin Franklin (his name appears on their reverses) and some notes of February and March 1776 issues which were hand signed by John Hart, signer of the Declaration of Independence for New Jersey. Unfortunately, Mr. Hart did not live to see the happy ending of the revolution. The final issues of New Jersey Colonial notes came in 1781, 1784 and 1786. In all there were twenty nine issues. Many bore the inscription "To Counterfeit is Death." Actually, few offenders were executed, but punishments included imprisonment, pillory and dismemberment.

The Revolutionary War was largely financed by eleven issues of Continental Currency authorized by the Continental Congress. These notes were issued from 1775 to 1779 in denominations ranging from one-sixth dollar to eighty dollars. They were printed by Hall and Sellers, successor firm to the partnership of Benjamin Franklin and David Hall. Because of inflation this money was in a continuous state of depreciation, so much so that by the end of the War it was practically worthless and thence came the expression "Not Worth a Continental."

Before 1790 the money circulated in New Jersey included New Jersey Colonial paper money, Continental Currency, foreign coins and New Jersey Cents. New Jersey issued copper cents in the period 1786 to 1788 inclusive. Minted in several places in the general New York area, they were of one basic design but with forty-one striking variations. The obverse

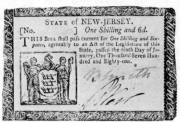

Colonial notes of 1763, 1776, 1780 and 1781. The 1776 note was signed by John Hart, one of the signers of the Declaration of Independence.

pictured a plow and horse's head from the New Jersey Shield, with the words "Nova Caesarea", latin for "New Jersey". The reverse had a shield with date below. Under the United States Constitution, adopted in 1789, the right of coinage was reserved by the Federal Government.

The foreign coins were mostly of Spanish, French and English origin. Of these the most important was the Spanish-American eight reales silver coin (piece of eight) called the Spanish Milled Dollar. Continental Currency was issued in denominations of that coin. In addition to the dollar, there were minor coins of 4 reales, 2 reales, 1 real and ½ real. They were spoken of as "bits" and since the 2 real piece was about the size of our twenty-five cents, our present day quarter is still called "Two-bits." In recent years thousands of Spanish-American coins have been recovered from galleons sunk off Florida and the West Indies.

Except for a minor issue of paper money in 1815, no circulating notes were issued by the United States Government until the Civil War. This void was filled by notes of chartered banks and scrip. Two banks were of special significance. The Bank of North America was chartered by the Continental Congress in 1781. This was expected to be of country-wide significance, but by 1791 it was apparent that a stronger bank was required, hence the Bank of the United States was chartered by Congress for a period of twenty years. It lost its charter in 1811, but a second Bank of the United States was authorized in 1816, again for a twenty year period. Both banks had numerous branches, but none in New Jersey, although their notes circulated freely throughout the state.

The first bank chartered by the State of New Jersey was the Newark Banking and Insurance Company. Founded in 1804, it exists today as the Midlantic Bank. The second bank, the Trenton Banking Company, founded later that same year is today the First Trenton National Bank. Other banks sprang up rapidly and by 1861 the banks in New Jersey numbered fifty

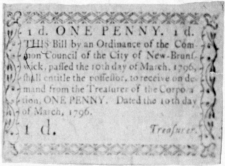

Early scrip notes of New Brunswick. Note the English denominations.

one, and many others had closed. Subject to state regulations, banks issued paper money, secured only by their own assests. The first bills were rather crude, but as the art of engraving progressed, they became more elaborate and colorful. In fact, by the time of the Civil War the quality of paper money engraving had peaked and has never been excelled. These notes were produced by numerous engraving firms, mostly antecedents of the present day American Bank Note Company. New Jersey also had its own engravers, Peter Maverick and the Durands, Cyrus and Asher B., both of whom were important around 1830.

By the time of the Civil War it is probable that 50,000 or more kinds of paper money (bank bills and scrip) circulated in this country. New Jersey had at least its share, being exceeded only by New York, Ohio and Pennsylvania. A large percentage of the circulating bank notes were counterfeit. These fraudulent notes were of four kinds: (1) Imitation of the genuine, (2) Denomination raised on the genuine (3) Spurious, designed to circulate as money of a certain bank, with no resemblance to the genuine notes, and (4) Altered—notes of failed banks with name, location and signatures changed so that they purported to be notes of going concerns. Some alterations were made by changes in the original plate, but generally the worthless individual notes of a failed bank were changed by judicious use of an eraser and stencil. Sometimes the counterfeiters did not even bother to change the signature of the failed bank's cashier and president. In other cases the state seal of the original note was left intact although processed for use in another state. Widespread illiteracy of the times facilitated illegal tampering with the currency. Collecting fraudulent notes can really be fascinating! The bad currency problem became so acute that counterfeit detectors came into existence around 1830. Usually these were of magazine size, issued monthly or even more often. They listed all operating banks, not only describing their fraudulent notes, but listing the discount applicable to "good" notes. This discount was an indication of the credit rating of each bank. Banknotes were accepted by exchange brokers anywhere from par to 20% or so of face value. In some instances there was a designation of "worthless". Exchange brokers acted as a sort of clearing house for paper money in the fashion of checks today. Banks and merchants lived dangerously if the did not own the latest counterfeit detector. Imagine the poor storekeeper—besides accepting French, English and Spanish Coins (legal tender in the U.S. until 1857) he was forced to evaluate all of this paper money of varying value.

Everyone knew that the money situation was intolerable. The coin situation was easily straightened out when the Government decreed that foreign coins must be turned in for redemption and that henceforth only U.S. mintages would be acceptable in commerce. This left the problem of good and bad paper money of so many kinds and so many values. This was brought to a head in 1861 when the U.S. Government had difficulty financing the Civil War. With insufficient specie (gold and silver) it was forced to issue its own paper money. This provided a good example of Gresham's Law—the premise that good money drives out bad. Our dollar dropped to forty cents in foreign exchange and all coins disappeared from circulation. In 1863 the National Banking Act was passed under which banks could be given Federal charters. If such banks deposited adequate security with the Federal Government, they were permitted to issue National Bank Notes backed by the United States Treasury. For a time U.S. paper money and notes of state chartered banks circulated together, but in 1865 Congress imposed a tax of 10% on non-government paper money, effectively destroying such issues. This gave the U.S. Government a monopoly on paper money used in this country.

In the cutover from local to national currency, the state chartered banks redeemed their currency as presented, but with a time limit. Some banks still in operation today will redeem their old notes as a matter of courtesy and pride—but unless the

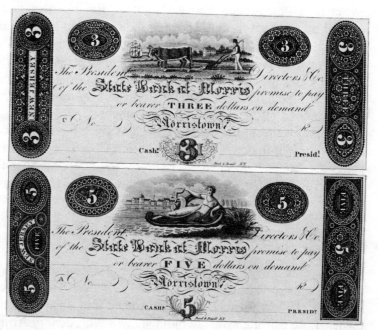

Bank notes were usually printed in sheets of four, so this two-note sheet (c. 1820) is a rarity.

notes are just rags or of very high denomination, they are worth more to collectors.

Many banks which elected to become Natinal Banks issued currency as mentioned above. National Bank Notes were printed in standard format, showing the name and location of the local bank and its charter number. They were printed in sheets of four bearing the signatures of the Register of the Treasury and the Treasurer of the United States. Upon their receipt, the local bank cut them into individual notes and added the signatures of their cashier and president.

As time went on, the standard designs were modified, and there were four major revisions. The First Charter notes, very elaborate, were succeeded in 1882 by those of the Second Charter, and again in 1902 by Third Charter notes. The designs became simpler at each stage, culminating with the 1929 small sized series in which the notes, except for the wording, resemble our currency of today. No National Bank Notes were issued after 1935.

Scrip notes were usually issued for the convenience of making change in trade. The earliest New Jersey scrip was issued in 1774 by the Hibernia Furnace and signed by its owner, Lord Stirling, who later joined the Revolutionary Army and became a general. Other early scrip notes were issued by the cities of Elizabeth, New Brunswick and Perth Amboy and by churches, idividuals (generally storekeepers) and organizations, mostly around 1790. Many scrip notes were issued around the end of the War of 1812, again during the depression of the 1830s and the early 1840s, but the greatest number were of the Civil War era, when coins were not available due to hoarding. The cities of Newark and Jersey City were very prolific issuers in 1862. While there were minor issues of scrip notes in the post Civil War era, cheifly by companies for use of their employees in company stores, no widespread issues of scrip appeared again until the great depression of the 1930s.

Notes of unusual denominations. Above, one and a half dollars, issued by the Belvidere bank, and below, a nine-dollar note from the People's Bank of Paterson.

How a one-dollar note was changed to a ten.

Then the scrip notes were chiefly of two types:

(1) Temporary substitutes for money (such as Clearing House Certificates) when the banks were closed by Presidential decree, and (2) Promissory notes of counties or municipalities. The latter were generally issued to pay police, firemen, contractors, teachers, etc., as a temporary measure until tax receipts were sufficient to provide for their redemption. In the meantime they were accepted locally as money. In fact, a limiting characteristic of all scrip notes, of whatever era, was that they were accepted only locally and strictly on the basis of the credit of the issuer.

Coin collecting has been a hobby for centuries, but it is only in the last twenty years that paper money has become really popular. Its current popularity may be attributed to the many books on the subject now available to collectors.

Because of its broad scope, and the impossibility of collecting everything, there is a tendency to specialize. Some collectors like Colonial coins and paper money. Others like old scrip or notes with pretty vignettes. Proof (sample) notes are rare, beautiful and valuable and make an exotic collection. Some collecting interests cut across general categories because of special denominations or special vignettes. For example, there are collectors of notes depicting coins, trains, animals, birds, ships, etc. Aside from scrip notes which have some unusual denominations. New Jersey collectors will find $1.25 and $1.50 bank notes and several varieties of $6, $7, $8, and $9. Because of the extensive glass industry in New Jersey there are many collectors of glass company scrip.

Serious collectors will meet with similar interests in coin clubs. Meetings, usually mentioned in the local newspapers, present opportunities for learning more about the subject and for acquisitions or disposals. Memberships in these national organizations are also very worth while:

American Numismatic Association. P.O. Box 2366, Colorado Springs, Colorado 80901. Dues are $12 per year and include a subscription to its monthly magazine *The Numismatist.*

Society of Paper Money Collectors, P.O. Box 4082, Harrisburg, Pennsylvania 17111. Dues are $10 per year and include a subscription to its bi-monthly magazine *Paper Money.*

It should be understood that neither of the publications mentioned above give special treatment to New Jersey money, but many of the subjects covered are related, and of interest. Other publications in the numismatic field having a wide circulation include *Coin World, Numismatic News, Bank Note Reporter,* and *Coins.*

The advertisements in all of the above publications are good sources for new acquisitions. It is also a good idea to get on the mailing list of those dealers who run auctions of numismatic material. Usually attendance is not required, bids being accepted by mail. The most important collections are disposed of by auction. Some auction catalogs furnish estimates of the expected selling price, but the actual price may be much higher or lower. Usually, but not always, the estimates are on the high side. However, as in all auctions, an estimate is apt to be greatly exceeded if two or more bidders have a keen desire for the same item!

These are estimated values for some types of money used in New Jersey:

```
Colonial notes  .....................................  $ 25.00
The same, signed by John Hart .......................    60.00
New Jersey Cents  ...................................    40.00
Notes of state chartered banks ......................    20.00
Proof notes of state chartered banks  ...............   125.00
Scrip:
      1790 period  ..................................   150.00
      1840 period ...................................    35.00
      1862 period ...................................    10.00
      1933 period ...................................     8.00
```

The above prices are for items usually encountered and in average condition. Generally speaking, the rarity and condition

When the Waubeek Bank of Nebraska failed, one of its three dollar notes was altered to the Belvidere Bank, a going concern in New Jersey.

of a numismatic item determines its price. For example, a very rare Colonial note in excellent condition will probably bring many hundreds, perhaps even thousands. The above values will more nearly apply to the March 1776 issue available in all conditions and probably worth five dollars in only fair condition but a hundred dollars uncirculated. The same reasoning applies to the other items listed. Although most recently issued, the pricing of the 1933 scrip is perhaps more complex. Most items are scarce, but recently hoards of several 1933 varieties were released and a buyer should exercise caution. Numismatists usually find their hobby enjoyable, educational and financially rewarding.   —GEORGE W. WAIT

Political Campaign Memorabilia of New Jersey

WITHIN the last decade, Americans have become increasingly interested in collecting memorabilia of our country's recent as well as distant past. In contrast with the fine furniture, paintings, and jewelry which have long been sought, public attention has focused on ephemeral items which were often given away or purchased at a nominal price. They were rarely meant to have any lasting significance or even survive more than a few months. Yet, today those items which somehow did survive are often more revealing of their period's social, political and economic life than the society's formal monuments. They are colorful and fascinating mementos of a bygone era. Consequently, their value has rapidly increased to what would have been their original owner's weekly or monthly salary.

Perhaps the most popular attraction in this growing field of interest is the study and collection of political memorabilia. Although the hobby can be traced back to the last century, it has only been within the past ten years that both public interest and prices have soared. State political material (including those used in New Jersey) is still available and reasonably priced but it is also attracting greater attention and prices. Such an enormous variety of items have been made since the early 1800's that the political collector soon finds his hobby overlapping with almost all other collecting fields. In addition to medals, ribbons and buttons there are political post cards, watch fobs, jewelry, glass, pottery, items of clothing, paintings, lithographs, photographs, lighting devices, tin containers, advertising cards, dolls, games, writing implements, tapestries, embroidered pillows, quilts, books, signed documents, statues, and clocks. The political collector soon finds that his hobby demands an awareness and appreciation of many objects and different levels of craftsmanship. He also develops a greater knowledge and interest in the history of his country and state.

The New Jersey collector can approach his hobby from many directions. He may specialize in presidential candidates who were identified in some way with the state of New Jersey. He may collect any presidential item which also includes reference to New Jersey and its candidates for state offices. Finally, he may collect New Jersey gubernatorial and senatorial campaign material.

References made to the "selling price" or "value" of the items described are, of course, only estimates as the cost of buying campaign material (especially the rarer buttons) has increased considerably during the last two years. Even so, the lucky collector still has the opportunity to purchase rare pieces for only a dollar or two. Despite increased publicity, many antique dealers still have not made any attempt to familiarize themselves with the field.

The value of campaign material varies considerably. It is based upon the presidential candidate portrayed, the rarity or attractiveness of the design, and the condition of the item. Although there are many exceptions, pictorial items are more valuable than just words or names. Buttons picturing both the presidential and vice presidential candidates (called jugates) are more valuable than those only portraying the presidential candidate. Also, picture buttons and badges are more valuable than medals and tokens. Naturally, as with all collectibles, the value of political material is considerably reduced by fading, foxing, scratches, dents, rust and other such damages. The extimates given are for very fine condition or better.

The collector must be particularly wary of reproduced campaign buttons. Usually, the poor coloring and inappropriate type or style of metal backing make it reasonably easy to identify most of the phony pre-1920 buttons. Post-1920 items may also be authenticated but it becomes increasingly difficult once you get into the 1940's. Reproductions are occasionally purposely rusted in an attempt to acquire an aged look. It is usually brighter and more pronounced than the subtle toning, foxing and dark pitting of original items. Members of the American Political Items Collectors Association can purchase an extensive and up to date listing of known reproductions and learn how to distinguish them from authentic pieces.

New Jersey's favorite sons have rarely been selected as major party candidates for president or vice president. The list, of course, could be increased if it included candidates who lived a number of years in the state or who died here. New Jersey collectors, for example, could seek articles concerning such men as: 1820 Democratic-Republican candidate for Vice President Richard Stockton; 1844 Whig Vice Presidential candidate Theodore Frelinghuysen; 1856 Republican Vice Presidential candidate William Dayton; 1864 Democratic Presidential candidate George McClellan (Governor of N.J. from 1878-1881); 1868 Republican candidate for President Ulysses S. Grant (lived in Long Branch N.J.); 1880 Republican candidate for President James Garfield (died in Elberon N.J. while attempting to recover from an assassin's bullet); 1884 Democratic Presidential candidate Grover Cleveland (born in Caldwell, N.J.); 1896 Republican Vice Presidential candidate Garret Hobart; and 1912 Democratic Presidential candidate Woodrow Wilson (Governor of N.J.).

The following is an examination of the small campaign memorabilia of Cleveland, Hobart, and Wilson.

Grover Cleveland was born in Caldwell, New Jersey. His home there is still maintained and opened for viewing. Clevelands political career, however, developed in New York State before it culminated in his election to the Presidency. Nevertheless, the New Jersey collector may forgive Cleveland for his early wanderings, especially since he lived his post-Presidential years in Princeton, N.J.

Cleveland ran for President on three different occasions and with a different running mate each time. He won with Thomas Hendricks in 1884, lost with Allen Thurman in 1888 and won with Adlai Stevenson in 1892 (grandfather of the 1952 candidate). During the course of Cleveland's three elections, many new as well as traditional campaign items were sold and distributed.

Before the 1860 presidential election, most campaign items were holed medals (brass, copper, white metal or silver), brass clothing buttons, printed ribbons, and occasionally lithographic prints under glass. Campaign medals were usually holed at the top to facilitate wearing it on clothing. Unlike the defacing of U.S. coins, holes do not detract from the value of campaign medals. With the 1860 election, photographic processes that were discovered and commercialized during the 1850's were now used to revolutionize campaigning. Brass-enclosed photographs on paper or japanned iron sheets (erroneously called tintypes) were issued for all the leading candidates.

As illustrated, many of the Cleveland campaign pieces were the traditional holed medal. Sometimes they are found hanging from pin back eagles as in *#30* and *#31*. Often, a ribbon would pass through the hole and then the ribbon was pinned directly to clothing as in *#38*. New materials were now being used. In addition to the common brass and white metal, items were

Examples of Grover Cleveland campaign pieces.

pressed out of wood, as in the wooden checker #*29*. This was part of a regular checker game in which the reddish wood checkers were struck with Cleveland's image while the black wood checkers revealed the bust of his 1884 opponent James Blaine. With the commercial development of celluloid during the mid 1880's, this material was soon applied to the manufacturing of campaign items such as item #*1*, #*12*, #*22*. Celluloid was often purposely produced to simulate an opaque "ivory" look. The picture and name were usually printed on top of the "ivory." It was not until the 1896 Presidential election that clear transparent celluloid was used to cover and protect the photograph and the printed message of the campaign button.

By 1892, the cheap commercial processing of aluminum made it possible for this remarkably light and strong metal to be used to make campaign medals. Being unusual, campaign items made out of wood, celluloid, hard rubber or aluminum were eagerly sought. They were kept and shown off to the wonderment of others who had never seen pressed "picture wood", fake "ivory", or aluminum, the metal that was once more valuable than gold.

Today, the #*1* celluloid ribbon would probably sell for three times the $15.00 one would pay for ordinary printed ribbon #*5*, printed flag ribbon #*2* or oil cloth ribbon #*23*. Similarly, item #*22* (which advertises the Plymouth Rock Pants Company on the reverse) would probably sell for two or three times the $10.00 to $15.00 you would pay for each of the other medals pictured. On the other hand, aluminum medals would not particularly be worth a premium. The size, relative rarity and beauty of Democratic Convention Medal #*41* would place it in the $25.00 to $35.00 price range. In contrast with the more common medals. pin back badges including #*3*, #*13* and #*20* would sell for about $20.00 each.

Cleveland supporters could display their partisanship by the real buttons they used as actual fasteners. Brass shank button #*21* could actually be used as a clothing button. With the appropriate leather belts, a Cleveland activist could also wear C & T (Cleveland and Thurman) belt buckle #43 and C & S (Cleveland and Stevenson) belt buckle #44. Without being quite as ostentatious, he could hold his tie in place with the popular style tie pins of the day: items #25 and #27. Being fairly common, #21 and #25 sell for about $10.00 each; #27, #43, and #44 would each cost from $15.00 to $20.00.

Among most political collectors today, pictorial campaign items tend to be more popular than medals. By the 1884 election, ferrotype (tintype) campaign pins had definitely given way to the mass-produced paper photographs. The more intricate the metal frame enclosing the photograph, the more desirable the piece becomes (especially when both the presidential candidate and his running mate are pictured). Hence, a simple Cleveland single picture stud #16 would sell for only about one fourth the $45.00 to $65.00 price of embellished #35.

Not all photographic campaign items are obvious to the naked eye. Items #18 and #42 enclose micro-photographs called stanhopes. Although micro-photography goes back to the 1850's, it was not extensively used for political campaigning until the 1880's. Instead of having to use a microscope, the photograph was attached directly to a small cylindrical lens for close enlarged viewing. Item #18 is a brass pig with a lens enclosed within a hole extending through the pig's rear end and out its mouth. By looking through the pig's rear, one can see a handsome photograph of Grover Cleveland. Although the photograph itself is not an unpleasant picture, the pig was undoubtedly worn by an 1884 supporter of Republican Presidential candidate James Blaine. These pigs currently sell for about $60.00 each. Selling for about one half that price, item #42 is a drilled and intricately designed handle for what was probably a letter opener. The stanhope may be viewed through the top hole. It is a picture of Cleveland and his beautiful young wife Frances Folsom. Starting as a White House bride, Frances

Cleveland soon became one of the most popular First Ladies in American history. Items #*13,* #*38* and #*40* all feature Cleveland with his popular wife.

Perhaps the most sought after campaign items are those which display a mechanical movement. Item #*34* is a brass nose-thumber. Closed, it appears to be simply a small brass caricature of the formally dressed Grover Cleveland. By pressing the heel of his shoe, his arm and hand move out in a gesture of ridicule. Some of these mechanical models also have a devil's tail that emerges from the rear. Being rather rare, nose thumbers usually sell for $150.00 to $200.00. Very similar but much more common versions were made for Warren Harding's 1920 election campaign. Although it is not as interesting and only about one fourth as valuable, item #*36* also has a mechanical feature. The portrait of Cleveland slides up and down under the multi colored, lithographic, tin shield.

Garret Hobart was born in Long Branch, N.J. and was a resident of the state when he was selected to be William McKinley's running mate for the 1896 election. Since Hobart died in Office (1899) McKinley had to select a new Vice Presidential candidate (Theodore Roosevelt) for his 1900 effort to win re-election.

1896 was the first year for the famous celluloid campaign button. The Whitehead and Hoag Company of Newark, N.J. was one of the earliest and most famous button manufacturers. With their 1896 patent on the celluloid button process there was a clear movement away from the much more expensive medals and tokens. The Company identifies their buttons by enclosing a paper insert within the button's metal back. Modern political buttons are not comparable to the beautifully colored, cleverly designed celluloids of the 1896-1916 period.

Ordinarily, William McKinley buttons from the 1896 election are neither rare nor particularly valuable (especially those which only portray McKinley). The items pictured would be of

Examples of McKinley-Hobart campaign pieces.

special interest to New Jersey collectors because they all include the picture or name of Vice Presidential candidate Garrett Hobart. In general, this collection is a fair but by no means complete sample of the various small campaign items distributed at the time. Thousands of different McKinley buttons were manufactured for the 1896 and 1900 elections. As opposed to a $5.00 to $10.00 price for common single picture buttons of McKinley, the jugate picture buttons of McKinley and Hobart shown would sell for from $10.00 to $20.00 each with the larger ones being somewhat more valuable. Item #2 would also fit into this price category since it is rare to find vice presidential buttons. Colorful button-ribbon #19 would fetch three times the $10.00 to $15.00 price of the plain ribbon #9.

With the introduction of campaign buttons, campaign medals were issued with much less frequency after the 1896 election. Although most medals would sell in the $10.00 to $35.00 range, item #12 is an exception. Within the past half a dozen years, the Dusterberg Book *The Official Inaugural Medals of the Presidents of the United States* has encouraged an enormous increase in the value of inaugural medals. Consequently, the beautifully designed 1896 inaugural medal #12 would be worth several hundred dollars. In contrast, medal #15 and the impressive brass shell #6 could probably be purchased for only $10.00 to $15.00 each. Since item #6 is a hollow shell and not a solid metal, it has a safety pin attachment on the back for wearing on one's clothing.

Item #14 is also not an ordinary medal. By twisting it, the eagle lowers its wings. The reverse warns of the devaluation of the dollar unless McKinley-Hobart are elected. Although this medal is not particularly rare, its mechanical qualities place it within the $30.00 to $40.00 range. Two other desirable mechanical items are #11 and #13. The gold bug was a symbol for those who favored the gold standard and sound money. The wings folded within the bug under spring pressure. Depressing the end tip released the catch and permitted the wings to spring open again. In #*13* folding closed, a McKinley picture covers the Republican elephant with a "metallic blanket" until the catch is released. Each of these pictorial mechanicals would sell for a minimum of $50.00.

Most of the items pictured were attached to clothing with the pin back arrangements still commonly used today. Items #*7,* #*10,* and #*18* used a stud backing for the lapel button holes which were popular for many years but are no longer in style.

Undoubtedly the most famous New Jerseyan to succeed in national politics was Woodrow Wilson. Wilson was actually born in Staunton, Virginia. However, his years as a Princeton student, professor, and college president and his term as New Jersey's Governor all entitle him to be a New Jersey favorite son. Furthermore, Wilson's summer White House was located on the grounds of what is now Monmouth College, West Long Branch, New Jersey.

The Wilsonian memorabilia displayed are a good general selection of items issued during the period 1911-1920. Most of the buttons are from the 1912 or 1916 Presidential election, but some may be 1911 Gubernatorial items whereas others were probably World War I patriotics. Slogan buttons which refer to Peace, the 8 Hour Day, America First, Progressive Policies, Become Law, and His Pen is Mightier Than the Sword, are in all likelihood 1916 campaign pins.

Although it is difficult to date the buttons with complete certainty, at least two of the items pictured were definitely New Jersey campaign material: item #*1* "For Governor" and item #*6* "Governor Wilson Inaugural Ribbon". Both are rare, eagerly sought and worth at least $50.00 each.

In general, the non-pictorial name and slogan buttons are worth $5.00 to $10.00 respectively. Most of the small (7/8th inch) single picture buttons sell for $10.00 to $15.00 with the picture-slogan usually being the more valuable. Because of its rarity and beautiful color, #*27* would be about three times more

Examples of Woodrow Wilson campaign pieces.

valuable than any one of the other small buttons.

Items #8, #9, #10, #15, #16 are jugate buttons. Small (7/8th inch) Wilson jugates, picturing both Woodrow Wilson and his running mate Thomas Marshall, usually sell for $20.00 to $25.00 each. Item #9, however, would be at least twice as valuable. Its attractive, uncommon design is much closer in style to the buttons manufactured during the previous decade.

In contrast with earlier decades, larger (1¼ inches or more) pins were not as common during the Wilson elections. Large jugates (none shown) are especially rare and would sell for a minimum of $75.00. Item #3 is not a Wilson-Marshall jugate but it is an excellent example of the slogan and coat tail politics of the day. It would sell for $35.00 to $45.00. Although item #5 is an interesting piece of Wilsonian it is more World War I patriotic than political. Its price would also be somewhat reduced because it was manufactured off center. As it is, it is worth about $10.00 to $15.00. Similarly, item #46 is an interesting historic piece manufactured by Tiffany & Co. Although it is pro-Wilson it is not a presidential campaign medal. The reverse publicizes the 1914 American Red Cross Bazaar held in New York.

Items #2, and #4 are large but they are both fairly common and would only sell for about $15.00 each. On the other hand, #7 (perhaps a convention item) and #26 are large, uncommon, and attractive display pieces, each valued at about $35.00 and $75.00 respectively. Other than the 1913 inaugural medal #48, the most valuable item here is #39. Its size, unusual and attractive design, and its rare reference to Wilson's home state would all make it a desirable $125.00 item. Its value also increases because it is a campaign mirror. There are numerous collectors who specialize in advertisement and political mirrors. After ratification of the 19th Amendment that gave women the constitutional right to vote, the distribution of political mirrors and thimbles became popular during the 1920's.

In the pocket watch era which preceeded the overwhelming

switch to wrist watches, the watch fob was also often used for advertising and campaign purposes. Item *#49,* copper *#50,* and silver *#51* are all examples of Wilson political watch fobs. Although some fobs are very rare, these particular ones are not that uncommon and would sell for about $10.00 each. Item *#52* is a much more interesting and desirable $35 piece. The knife and file fold within the medal. The reverse depicts the White House.

Wilson Inaugural Medals *#48* and *#47* are respectively from the 1913 and 1917 Inaugurations. The value of these two pieces, however, are wide apart. Item *#48* (made by the Whitehead and Hoag Co.) is the official 1913 Wilson Inaugural Medal. As a result of the increased awareness and interest in such items, this beautifully conditioned rarity would sell for several hundred dollars. A similar medal in poorer condition would sell for considerably less. Care must be taken not to confuse these "official" privately minted pieces from the presidential medals made every four years by the United States Mint. Their reverse also refers to the inauguration date. Copies of the government medals may still be reasonably purchased directly from the mint. Item *#47* is also a handsome (especially the reverse eagle) privately minted inaugural medal but it was not the "official" medal. Furthermore the piece was obviously originally hung as part of a larger badge. Consequently, it would probably only be worth $10.00 to $15.00.

The most valuable New Jersey campaign buttons are those which also picture the party's presidential candidate. These buttons combine the desirability of presidential items with the relative rarity of state material. They usually sell for significantly more than items which only picture the presidential candidate. Many are also excellent examples of coattail politics. Local office seekers eagerly identify with popular presidential candidates running at the top of their part's ticket.

Pictured are an assortment of presidential New Jersey items

Examples of New Jersey presidential campaign pieces.

issued from the 1880's to the 1960's. Item #*1* and #*2* are handsome Newark ribbon-celluloids issued by local clubs: the 1888 Banking, Insurance and Real Estate Club and the 1896 Frelinghuysen Lancers. Attached to #*1* is a thin oval celluloid sheet with the picture of Benjamin Harrison printed on top of it. Item #*2* uses the "modern technique" of covering the candidate's picture with clear celluloid. Each would sell for about $35.00.

The three most valuable items shown here would probably be #*8,* #*6* and #*13.* Badge #*8* pictures the 1904 Democratic candidate Alton Parker and his elderly running mate Henry Davis. The back of this badge is also a celluloid which reveals that the badge was issued by the City Executive Committee of Elizabeth, New Jersey, for its 1904 Annual Outing. Although Parker 1¼ inch jugates generally sell for only $25.00, this large and uncommon badge would be two or three times more valuable. Item #*6* is also an unusual piece since it depicts four candidates in a clover leaf design: 1916 Republican contender Charles E. Hughes, Vice Presidential candidate Charles Fairbanks, and New Jersey's candidates for Senator and Governor. With the Seventeenth Amendment, U.S. Senators were no longer selected by their state legislatures, they were elected by their state's voters. This stimulated the production of presidential-state buttons. As one of the most desirable, Hughes' items #*6* would sell for $100.00 to $150.00. Item #*4* is also from that election, but Vice Presidential candidate Fairbanks has been omitted, thereby dropping the button's value by about two thirds. Campaign mirror #*13* requests the newly franchised woman voter to support Hoover and all of New Jersey's 1928 Republican candidates for governor and senator. The $150.00 price tag on this item could have filled the housewife's cooking pot with over 100 chickens.

Three of the buttons are actually not presidential, but they are highly collectible. Items #*5* and #*7* were issued as part of the New Jersey Women's Suffrage Movement which successfully culminated with the 19th Amendment. They would sell for $5.00 to $10.00 each. Item #*10* is a magnificently colored piece issued by the Anti-Saloon League at its 1915 Atlantic City Convention. Prohibition collectors would probably pay $15.00 to $20.00 for this piece.

The 1888 cloth covered Harrison stud #*11* (Frederick Potts was an unsuccessful Republican candidate for Governor), the 1908 Shirley Taft Club button #*12* (Shirley presumably refers to the N.J. City of that name), and the 1928 Coolidge New Jersey Women's Club Button (a great post 19th Amendment item) would each be worth $10.00 to $15.00.

Al Smith's campaign button #*9* and ribbon #*27* would be about $25.00 each but for different reasons. The Al Smith button would be $15.00 to $20.00 even without the Camden County Ribbon. Ribbon #*27* lists Smith's name with New Jersey Democratic candidates for Senator and Governor. Its most interesting feature, however, is the inked autograph of Maryland's Presidential hopeful Governor Albert Ritchie. Personalized campaign items (assuming the signature is authentic) are exceptionally rare.

Also pictured here are five Franklin D. Roosevelt pins including two (#*14* and #*15*) issued by the New Jersey Labor Non Partisan League, and three, (#*16,* #*17,* and #*18*) that also name the Democratic Senatorial Candidates. Metal pin back #*16* is also an anti-prohibition item. Item #*14* would be worth about $15.00, the others would have about half that value. Of the remaining New Jersey Presidential pieces, all but three would fall into the $2.00-$6.00 price range. Large buttons #*19,* #*21,* and #*23* are relatively rare. With the enormous number and variety of Wilkie buttons manufactured in 1940, relatively few Stevenson buttons were issued. Consequently, extremely rare #*21* would sell for at least three times #*19*'s selling price of $5.00 to $10.00.

Although Johnson button #*23* was distributed not too long ago, the recent upsurge in the price of 1964 campaign items has increased the value of this button to a minimum of $15.00. A Johnson specialist might pay considerably more.

There is one final problem which must be noted. In categorizing non-picture, last-name-only buttons which refer to Gubernatorial or Senatorial candidates, there is always the possibility that the items were issued for another state's candidate with the same last name. Hence, for example, #25 could be referring to Michigan's Soapy Williams. Hopefully, the increasing national interest in state campaign memorabilia will eventually reduce this confusion.

Until the early 1970's the demand for state campaign material was so low that Governor and Senator buttons usually only sold for a dime or a quarter. Ironically, most of the pre-1950 local pins were probably far rarer than presidential items but the demand was still exceeded by the supply. The major exceptions were local button for candidates who later ran for president, as exemplified by the Woodrow Wilson for Governor button described above.

With the decreasing availability of presidential items, collectors are now avidly seeking state campaign pins. Auction and sales lists now have governor and U.S. senator buttons in the $2.00 to $5.00 price range.   —ENOCH L. NAPPEN

Scarce New Jersey Postmarks

S OME of the most interesting varieties of postmarks used in New Jersey during the second half of the nineteenth century are known as the "county-postmaster" types. They are also extremely scarce since only single examples on envelopes, mailed from some of the few post offices that used them, are known to exist.

These postmarks, as the name implies, included the name of the county, or that of the current postmaster, or sometimes both. This information, in addition to the names of the post office and the state and the date, was never required procedure at any time; it was given voluntarily by the postmaster and at his own expense.

A postmaster in Georgia may have started this trend about a quarter of the way through the nineteenth century. He used a fancy style of rectangular marking which contained the information that this was a postmark from "WATSON'S STORE, COLUMBIA CO. GA." and the date was 1824. This is the first recorded example.

This post office must have been in a general store, a frequent location at that time and for many years afterwards, kept by a

Mr. Watson. Perhaps business had not been so good that year, or perhaps some competitive store by the same name had been opened a few miles away in a neighboring county. So, as postmaster, he not only publicized his store in the official post office name, but also, the fact that it was located in Columbia County.

This county-naming idea, for which no official authorization was needed, spread very slowly for the next thirty-five years, by which time some of the postmasters had begun to include their own names in the postmarking devices. This could have been based on personal pride, particularly if they had a "presidential" class of post office and their appointments came from the President of the United States—or it might announce in this subtle way that they were of the same political party!

Then came the rugged individualist type of postmaster who included both his own name and that of the county in the postmark and this brought into use some larger and fancier styles.

The only way of learning where and when these types of postmarks were used has been through compiling a checklist of known examples. This was done by H. K. Thompson, M.D., in 1949 and published as "Billig's Handbook on Postmarks, Volume 8" and your author collaborated with him in the preparation of this data.

It chronicled all the known United States county and postmaster postmarks by place, style, date, quantity and color of marking. The use of capital and lower-case letters and slantmarks indicated the arrangement of the data as well. In the meanwhile, there have been many additions to this original list.

New Jersey's marking sources in that list totalled only 19— but two have been added recently. The entire group so far recorded consists of the following:

Post Office (by county)	Year	Style
Oceanville, N.J./Atlantic Co.	1887	CD
Hasbrouck Heights/Bergen Co. N.J.	1890	SL

D	Lewistown, N.J./ ?	1885	CD
	(balance of legend is undecipherable:		
	place known located in Burlington Co.)		
	Tuckahoe/Cape May Co. N.J.*	1891-1893	CP
	Newark, N.J./Correct/William Ward, P.M.*	1882	CP
	Vailsburgh/Essex Co. N.J.	1884	CP
D	Greensbury/Mercer Co. N.J.	1857?	CP
	Plainsborough/Middlesex Co./New Jersey*	1887	F
D	Key East, Monmouth Co./N.J.	1885, 1886	CDI
D	Middletown Point/Monmouth Co./N.J.	1848	CD
	Barnegat, N.J./Jeremiah S. Storms, P.M.	1881	CD
	Bay Head/Ocean Co. N.J.	1883, 1886	OvDF
D	Collier's Mill/Ocean Co. N.J.	1887	CDID
D	C.C. Bristol/Post Master/Manchester	1869	OvP
	Ocean Co. New Jersey		
	Bloomingdale/New Jersey/E.K. Ball, P.M.	1885	CD
	Hewitt/Passaic Co. N.J.*	1880	CI
D	Midvale Passaic Co. N.J.*	1878	?
D	Mountain View/Passaic Co. N.J.	1882-1895	OvDF
	Asbury, N.J./C.R. Carpenter, P.M.	1884	CP
	Blairstown, N.J./J.D. Vail, Postmaster	18?9	C?
	Broadway/Warren Co. N.J.	1886	OvDF

Legend: *—marking struck in colored ink, other than black
D—post office no longer in existence
C—circle   P—plain   D—double   I—inner circle
F—fancy   Ov—oval   SL—straight line
?—some data missing in reported item

Most of these were third and fourth class post offices. Newark was the chief exception and that marking also contains the word "Correct." (Incidentally, that post-marking stamp was used in error on a piece of first-class mail but was required on a registry list bill when a corresponding package of registered letters had been received.)

Nearly one-third of these post offices have been discontinued (D), due to changes in population centers, industries, transportation and communication in the meanwhile.

Up to the present time the item from Middletown Point with its 1848 date is the earliest known from New Jersey. That reported from Mountain View for 1895 appears to be the latest. The most items so far recorded are from Middletown Point,

Miss Grace R. Allen.
31 — 127th St.
Harlem.
N. Y.

POSTAL CARD.

NOTHING BUT THE ADDRESS CAN BE PLACED ON THIS SIDE.

Mrs. J. R. Hunter.
St. Catharines.
Ontario

Mountain View and Tuckahoe—yet the number is only four from each place.

However, the matter of quantity is an uncertain one. For instance, letters from Greensbury may show up from descendents of friends in New York or Florida, whereas mail from Key East may have followed members of a family to the west and eventually appear in Arizona or Oregon.

Then too, if the community had a well-known industry at that time, such as a charcoal furnace at Collier's Mill, this should result in a larger amount of business correspondence which could still be recovered in many places.

Some comparative statistics may be of interest. As of June 30, 1890, Delaware, with only 13 post offices, had but one recorded county-post master marking: Pennsylvania, with 4,570 offices, had about 350 such markings or 8% of the total; New Jersey, with 831 offices, had 21 known markings or only about 2½% of its total.

In fact, varieties of these types of markings are known from every state and most territories in existence during their period of use, the most prolific of which was between 1880-90. The great majority of New Jersey's markings are during that decade, too.

This is undoubtedly due to the several manufacturers of these devices, called "daters" in post office parlance, who advertised their individual designs in the annual Post Office Guides and monthly Supplements between 1879 and 1890. Their prices were from $1.08 to $3.00, the latter in combination with other stamping equipment.

That many postmasters yielded to these attractive offers is confirmed by the large number of county-postmaster dater markings known used during that period particularly. The idea might be considered as a sales gimmick that appealed to a postmaster's vanity to see his name in the dater and he was willing to pay a small price to own and use it. Why the number in

After............days, return to

Rural Free Delivery Route No............
MOORESTOWN, Burlington Co., N. J.

R. F. D.
Moorestown,
FEB 19 1904
N. J.

Mary B Palmer,
4957 Religious Ave.,
Germantown,
Pa.

New Jersey is so small is just one of those mysteries that leads to even further research.

The canceller—a marking device to "cancel" a stamp so it could not be re-used if soaked off the envelope or wrapper and thus "defraud the government of legitimate revenue"—was sometimes attached to the postmarking section and sometimes separate from it. This accounts for its variable location in relation to the dater section.

The very earliest of these county-postmaster daters required no cancellers because, although adhesive stamps had been issued in 1847, their use for prepayment of postage was optional until 1856. Therefore, the stampless 1848 Middletown Point item cited above has no cancellation, only the "Paid" and "V" to show the 5c. rate prepaid for the distance covered.

From 1856 on the cancellations have shown up in a large variety too, following the permissive practices of the period. A popular favorite was the star, solid, outlined or intaglio, large and small, with and without a circle and even with another stamp inside. Another favorite was the target with concentric circles.

The Broadway postmark shows the also popular series of black cancelling bars which took the form of circles, rectangles and ovals.

Another design, used much less frequently, is the graceful maltese cross which can be distinguished on the stamp to the right of the faint CP dater for Asbury.

Other county-postmaster markings from New Jersey post offices can be expected to be found as quantities of personal and business correspondence and unreported items held by postal historians come onto the philatelic market and as other people, perhaps reading an article like this on the subject for the first time, are motivated to search their own stored and forgotten family papers. It is to aid such research as this that those who settle estates or dispose of old personal papers are urged to contact some authority who could first record the data and have the benefit of the information before it is lost completely through trash disposal or burning.   —EDITH R. DOANE

SECTION EIGHT
Potpourri

Collecting Antique New Jersey Tools

THERE are many facets to collecting New Jersey tools. One can collect tools made in a certain town or county, or tools used in a particular craft, or those made by a specific craftsman or company. There are collectors who prefer fine tools manufactured by large companies, and others who would rather collect what are known as primitives made in small home shops. Of the latter group there are those who collect only tools made from files, rasps, bolts, and other pieces of scrap metal a blacksmith might fine lying around his shop. Miniature tools are also collected. These consist of salesman's samples, advertising promotions, toys, and actual small tools used by craftsmen. Whatever form it takes, a collection of New Jersey tools should contain examples identifiable as having been made within the state. There are few if any types of tools which are unique to New Jersey, but many of the tools which were made by New Jersey toolmakers were considered of the highest quality.

Though tool making was discouraged in the colonies by the government in England, the cost of those tools exported to America was often prohibitive. For this reason, from the time this state was first settled, New Jersey blacksmiths were kept busy supplying farmers and craftsmen with the tools they needed. Besides those tools wrought at the local blacksmith's forge, there were many made of wood by others of the citizenry. Farmers made their own hayforks, rakes, and flails, as well as handles for the metal tools they bought from the blacksmith. Craftsmen who lacked the knowledge to perform the intricacies of working metal were usually able to make any wooden tool parts they needed. Few of these early tools dating prior to 1700 still exist, and of those that do even fewer could be identified as having a New Jersey origin. The colonists had little time to embellish their tools with names, dates, and places of manufacture. It goes without saying that any tool so marked as to give proof of having been made in colonial New Jersey would be of great value and worth many times that of a similar tool without such authentication.

The greatest opportunity to identify New Jersey tools lies in those manufactured after 1802, the year that the U.S. Patent Office was established. After that date manufacturers often stamped their tools not only with patent dates but also with their names and places of business.

By 1800 most populated areas of New Jersey had tool makers. However, large cities such as Newark and Trenton produced the bulk of the tools made within the state. In 1847 Mark Fisher, who made the first anvil manufactured in America, opened his anvil works in Trenton with the help of a partner named Norris. Their trademark was an eagle cast into the sides of their anvils. Fisher & Norris anvils were made with cast iron bodies to which steel faces were welded and were superior to the anvils imported from Europe. Between 1847 and 1961, when the business was sold, Fisher & Norris produced anvils ranging in weight from 2½ lb. salesman samples to the largest one ever cast which weighed 1,600 lbs. and was shown at the Centennial Exposition of 1876.

The first anvils made by Fisher & Norris had short, heavy horns. In later years the horns became longer and slimmer. The shape of an anvil is one way to determine its age. The eagle trademark also changed through the years being larger at one time and smaller at another and disappearing altogether on later types. Once in a while one of these early "Eagle" anvils will sell at auction usually bringing about $60, which is a small price to pay for such an historically significant tool. Fisher & Norris also manufactured leg vises for use in blacksmith shops. At today's sales they bring from $20 to $30.

Another New Jersey manufacturer of blacksmith tools was Heller Bros., started in Newark in 1836 by Elias Heller. Also of Newark was the firm of Benjamin Atha & Co. started in 1875. Heller Bros. produced a large variety of blacksmith and farrier tools. Their name and horse trademark can be found on hammers, tongs, pincers, hot and cold chisels, hoof knives, swages, fullers, and hardies, as well as other tools. Benjamin Atha's trademark of a capital A within a horseshoe is stamped or cast in hammers, chisels, hardies, and tongs. Besides these large manufacturers of blacksmith and farrier tools there were numerous blacksmiths who made their own tools, and occasionally one of these tools can be identified as made in New Jersey. Hand wrought tools made by local blacksmiths are treasured items and are worth the detective work it takes to discover them.

Quite a few manufacturers of carpenter tools can be identified as being in business in Newark prior to 1850. Planemakers A. Mockridge and Elias Francis are listed as working at 143 Washington St. in the 1836 Newark Directory. Planes can be found today bearing their names both singly and together. In the same 1836 directory is listed Parkhurst & Co. who were turners and planemakers. Also listed is a George Williams, toolmaker. Two other early Newark planemakers were G. W. Andruss and S. E. Farrand. By searching through antique shops and flea markets or attending auctions, it is possible to find planes bearing any of these names. They usually sell for from $8 to $10. W. Johnson of Newark made a variety of fine tools including some of the most graceful saws and spoke shaves ever

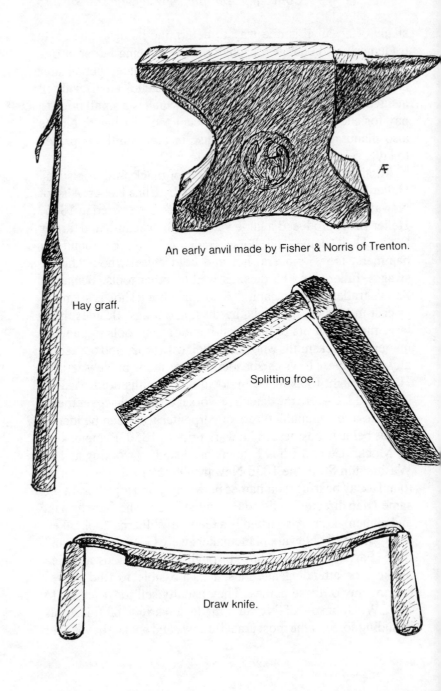

An early anvil made by Fisher & Norris of Trenton.

Hay graff.

Splitting froe.

Draw knife.

produced. Others working in that city as carpentry tool makers were J. Garside who made spirit levels, L. A. Sayre, maker of edged tools, and P. Quigly who made a variety of tools including spoke shaves. A maker of planes from another part of the state was S. C. Cook of New Brunswick.

Kirk Bride's *New Jersey Business Directory* published in Trenton in 1850 mentions William Knott of Essex County who made drawknives and A. Bunnel of Plainfield who made files. The same publication lists as makers of farm tools a man by the name of Applegate who made grain cradles in Salem County; H. Weston maker of shovels, hoes, and forks at Weston's Mill, Middlesex County; and John Young of Rocksbury who manufactured plows. Early Newark plowmakers were J. and E. Meeker who were in business prior to 1836. Another early manufacturer of plows was Hiram Deats who started making them near Quakertown in 1831. His father, John Deats, a blacksmith near Stockton, had taken out a patent in 1828 on an improved plow mold board which scoured better than any previous one. Hiram Deats, Jr., nephew of Hiram, took charge of his uncle's firm in Pittstown in 1879 and became very successful in manufacturing plows and other agricultural equipment. Early Deats plows are occasionally sold at farm auctions, and because of their sculptural beauty they bring from $40 to $60, depending on their condition.

Whenever New Jersey tools are mentioned, the city of Newark is bound to come up. Not only was it a center for the manufacture of carpenter and blacksmith tools but many other forms of tools were made there. It was the home of C. S. Osborn & Co., the largest saddle and harness tool maker in the world. This firm was established in 1826, and by 1880 the four story building which housed it took up a good part of a city block. They made every conceivable type of harness and saddle tool including awls, checking tools, ticklers, creasers, cutters, round knives, draw guages, and punches. They also made stitching horses, horse collar measures, and such non-harness tools as screw drivers, parallel vises, spoke shaves, and hoof hooks. It is still possible to find some of the numerous early harness tools made by this firm, and many of them can be bought for less than a dollar each.

Collecting these early tools manufactured in large New Jersey cities such as Newark can be very rewarding. The fact that the tool companies often identified their wares by stamping their names and sometimes addresses on them simplifies the search. It is far more difficult to be sure of the origin of tools made in small town shops since they seldom have identifying marks. To find one of which the maker was so proud that he stamped his name and address and perhaps even a date is like discovering buried gold. Just such a tool is a fish gig in the author's collection. It was hand wrought around the turn of the century by George F. Green, the son of a blacksmith whose shop was in Sergeantsville. The gig, which was probably used in the nearby Delaware River to spear shad, is stamped G. F. Green on both the lower end of the handle and on the head. Without the identifying name stamped on it the gig would still be a fine example of the blacksmiting art, but with the mark it becomes a very important tool. George Green died in 1975 at age 88. He grew up on a farm in Sergeantsville. His father, Jim Green, had a blacksmith shop which still stands in the center of town. George was a self taught machinist who at age 14 built a gasoline engine now in the collection of the Ford Museum in Dearborn, Michigan. In 1914 George established a machine shop in Lambertville. The author knows of no other tool stamped with his name but considers it possible that others exist. To put a value on such a tool as this gig would be difficult. There were very few fish gigs which were signed by the maker and even fewer made in New Jersey.

Half the fun of collecting early tools is the detective work necessary to discover some of the history behind them. One fascinating tool owned by the Pascack Historical Society and housed at their Museum is the world's only wampum-drilling machine. It was the invention of the Campbell brothers of Park Ridge who manufactured wampum for the U.S. Government and fur traders for use as barter with the Indians. This machine enabled six shell pipes to be drilled simultaneously.

There are many such interesting early New Jersey tools just waiting to be discovered in some old barn or house attic. Searching flea markets, antique shops, various garage, barn and lawn sales will reap many rewards for the knowledgeable collector.

The marks on a tool can be far more important to a collector than its rarity or condition. A scarce bowl adze, for instance, is far more sought after than a common drawknife. However, should the drawknife be stamped with an historically important name, address, or date a collector might prefer it over the bowl adze. For this reason it is not inconceivable that some unscrupulous dealer or collector might try marking an old tool in an attempt to make it more desirable. This would be a very difficult deceit to get away with since the mark would look too sharp to be old, but an expert forger might fool an unsuspecting neophyte tool collector.

In this country faking most antique tools would involve too much work and thus would not be profitable. However, imported tools of recent vintage are often sold as American antiques. They come from such countries as Mexico and Spain where labor costs are low and there are plenty of craftsmen able to do hand work. There are also some simple hand-wrought tools turned out in this country that are passed off as antiques. Since antique tool collecting has become more popular it has become a practice of some to alter tools to make them look older and more unique. Axes and other edged tools have had their shapes changed through grinding; wooden and metal surfaces have been stained to make them appear older; and parts have been added or subtracted to improve a tool's image.

A good example of tool alteration can be noted in what has recently happened to splitting froes. The prices paid for common straight, shingle splitting froes today is between $18 and $30, whereas coopers' curved froes bring around $60. Those wishing to cash in on the difference have been heating straight froes in a forge and curving them over an anvil horn. This deception can be easily spotted by noting the surface of the blade. However, collectors have been fooled into buying them. Of course some tools have been changed without any intention to defraud. They were simply modified to fit a job which had to be done. These tools, if altered eighty or more years ago, are still antiques and worth collecting. If there is evidence of recent tampering it is best to avoid them.

One way to prevent being sold tools which are not as represented is to study examples which are known to be authentic. Learn what clues to look for to determine the age of a tool. Steel cutting edges welded onto wrought iron axe heads was a practice not done in America until the late 18th century. The steel used was blister steel, and it was not until the 19th century that cast steel was employed. Thus, any tool marked cast steel was not made in America until well after the beginning of the 19th century. There are numerous other clues which indicate when a tool was produced such as shapes of heads and handles, styles of letters used in maker's marks, and the patina formed on wood and metal parts.

There are many fine museums within New Jersey which have collections of antique tools which may be studied. A general knowledge of tools can be gained by visiting several of these museums as well as private collections. The large majority of tools on display can not be attributed to New Jersey makers. In fact, one will find few documented New Jersey tools exhibited, though chances are there will be many which are undocumented. Also one may find tools mislabelled as to maker, date, or function. Tools are a new field of collectibles for many museums, so they occasionally make mistakes. Also they sometimes accept heresay when cataloging their exhibits. Without marks, patent papers, or contemporary letters or drawings to document that a tool was made in New Jersey it should always be considered suspect. For this reason the more collections seen the truer is the knowledge of New Jersey tools. Another way to learn about tools without having to leave home is through the many books published on the subject. Until a short while ago there was very little written about tools and crafts, but in the past few years a number of fine books have come out which have dealt with the subject. For those who wish to pursue further the collecting of New Jersey tools, the following list gives some average prices one could expect to pay for early New Jersey tools. These prices will vary somewhat depending on the condition, age, and rate of inflation, but all tools should be marked "N.J." or have the name of a known New Jersey tool-maker:

Bow Saws by W. Johnson	$30
Spoke Shaves by W. Johnson	$12
Hewing Broad Axe, 10″ to 12″ wide blade	$50
Felling Axe	$12
Post Mortising Axe	$45
Shingle Splitting Froe	$45
Cooper's Froe	$85
Carpenter's Adze	$35
Cooper's Chamfer Knife	$85
Bowl Adze	$85
Cooper's Side Axe	$85
Cooper's Hand Adze	$30
Draw Knife	$15
Molding Planes by A. Mockridge, Elias Francis, G. W. Andruss, and others	$8 to $10
Leather Awls and Punches by C. S. Osborn & Co.	$1 or less
Round Knives by C. S. Osborn & Co.	$10
Wheelright's Traveler, wrought iron	$45

Fisher and Norris "Eagle" Anvil, 150 lbs.	$60
Hoof Knife by Heller Bros., bone handle	$8
Blacksmith Hammer by Atha	$5
Hay Fork, wooden	$50
Hay Rake	$10
Reaping Hook, 24″ long blade	$18
Hay Gaff	$20
Butter Paddle	$18
Butter Mold with design	$85 up
Dough Scraper	$125
Yarn Winder	$60
Spinning Wheel	$300
Hetchel	$45
Fish or Eel Gig	$60

New Jersey Museums with displays of tools are as follows:

Camden County Historical Society
Park Blvd. & Euclid Ave., Camden
Craft Shops with Tools

Clinton Historical Museum
Main St., Clinton
Good collection of tools

Liberty Village Ltd.
2 Church St., Flemington
Craft Shops—Tool Collection
Palmer Collection of Carpenter Tools

Batsto Historic Site
Batsto R. D., Hammonton
Tools

Rutherford Museum
91 Crane Ave., Rutherford
Tools

Salem County Historical Society
79-83 Market St., Salem
Agricultural Tools

Space Farms Zoological Park and Museum
Beemerville Rd., Beemerville
Tools

New Jersey State Museum
205 W. State St., Trenton
Tools

Gloucester County Historical Society
17 Hunter St., Woodbury
Farm implements

The Museum of Early Trades and Crafts
Madison
Tools including goose-wing axe said to have been made by
  Major Luke Miller, 1759-1851

Hopewell Museum
28 E. Broad St., Hopewell
Agricultural Tools

Ralston Historical Assoc.
Rte. 24, Mendham
Agricultural tools before 1814

Montville Historical Museum
84 Main Rd., Montville
Agricultural tools

Rutgers University, College of Agriculture
Nichol Ave., New Brunswick
Agricultural Tools

Pascack Historical Society
19 Ridge Ave., Park Ridge
Wampum drilling machine

—ALEXANDER FARNHAM

Button
Collecting

DURING the American Revolution, many of the men of the armed forces of New Jersey wore buttons made of pewter with the designation "New Jersey" in script letters. While some of the other state's forces wore buttons with the initials or abbreviation of the state's name, New Jersey was the only state with the entire name on the button. Several of these buttons have been found at Fort Ticonderoga, where members of the First New Jersey Battalion were located during the summer and early fall of 1776. The buttons have also been found at Valley Forge, where troops suffered during the winter of 1777. It should be noted here that several present day colonial companies wore replicas of these buttons during participation in skirmishes as a part of the nation's Bicentennial celebration.

During the early part of the nineteenth century and particularly after the War of 1812, thousands of independent military companies were organized throughout the country. New Jersey was included, but no distinctive buttons of this period are known. According to the Adjutant-General's report for 1860, the militia of New Jersey included about one hundred companies with a total of forty-four hundred active members. The buttons worn by many of the New Jersey troops during the Civil War period bore the device similar to the State seal.

In March 1864, the Legislature organized the New Jersey Rifle Corps. Shortly thereafter, buttons bearing a horse's head and a plowshare with the initials "N. J. R. C." appeared on the uniforms. This Corps consisted of one brigade of thirty two companies. Summer encampments were held at Somerville in 1864, at Jamesburg in 1865 and at Long Branch in 1866.

In March, 1869, the Legislature organized the National Guard of New Jersey into two brigades. The Rifle Corps was transferred to the National Guard. This organization included about three thousand men. The authorized buttons show an eagle in flight with a shield suspended from a cord held in its beak, the inscription "N. J. M." and "National Guard" encircle the device.

In 1879, the National Guard consisted of forty seven infantry companies, one artillery battery and two Gatling gun companies. The Adjutant-General's report contained the following orders: "General and General Staff Officers will wear the United States Staff buttons. All Regimental Officers and Enlisted Men will wear the regulation buttons as herein described: quality fire gilt, convex, device:—Infantry: crossed rifles; Artillery: crossed cannons, with the letters 'N. G. N. J.' in spaces." Later, the cavalry was organized and their uniforms had buttons bearing crossed sabers and the initials. Then the hospital corps was added and their buttons had the raised outline of the Geneva cross with the initials.

Among the many independent military companies in New Jersey, only three are known to have worn buttons with distinctive devices. They are the Essex Troop, the Sewell Guards and the Morris Guards.

The Essex Troop of Newark was formally organized in 1890, although its roots go back to Colonial days. It was New Jersey's crack cavalry company for many years. The device on their button is an upturned saber and a spur, with "Essex" above and

"Troop" below.

The Sewell Guards, a well-known artillery company of Camden, was organized in 1864. It was named in honor of William J. Sewell, a famous general of the Civil War. Their button shows crossed cannons encircled by "Sewell Guards 1864".

The Morris Guard of Atlantic City was organized in 1887 and named in honor of its benefactor Colonel Daniel Morris. It is interesting to note here that former Governor Walter E. Edge was a lieutenant in this company during the Spanish-American War in 1898. This button shows the old English initials "M. G." within a wreath.

There is one distinguished military company worthy of being mentioned here, although it did not wear a special button. It is the Phil Kearney Guard, organized in Elizabeth in 1868, named in honor of General Phil Kearny, who was killed at Chantilly in 1862. It was quite fitting that this company was selected to represent New Jersey in the Centennial Legion which was made up of thirteen famous regiments, one from each of the original states. This Legion, together with troops from other states, took part in a distinguished military parade on Independence Day 1876, in connection with the Centennial Exposition in Philadelphia. Here, this company was referred to as "the most perfectly drilled military company in the United States." So far as is known, the Phil Kearny Guard wore the "N. J. M. National Guard" button.

Today, the National Guard is a part of the federal armed forces and its members wear the general service button bearing a device similar to the Great Seal of the United States. The State seal button is worn by uniformed employees and officers of the State, and by some uniformed municipality employees.

The present-day hobby of button collecting began with the organization of the National Button Society in 1938, in connection with the Chicago Antique Exposition and Collector's Fair. This event was sponsored by Otto C. Lightner, the

Revolutionary War
1776

Civil War
1861

Rifle Corps
1863

Militia N.G.
1869

New Jersey National Guard

Artillery

Cavalry

Infantry

Ambulance

Essex Troop
Newark

Sewell Guards
Camden

Morris Guards
Atlantic City

publisher of *Hobbies Magazine.* Today this Society has more than two thousand members, most of whom have uniform buttons in their collections.

It is interesting to note that uniform button collecting began with the close of the Civil War, when the veterans returned home with Confederate buttons. It is generally recognized that Luis Fenollosa Emilio was the pioneer collector of uniform buttons. Mr. Emilio, a Captain of the 54th (colored) Infantry Regiment Massachusetts Volunteers, began his collecting when he brought home a number of Confederate buttons which he found on the battlefields. He continued gathering specimens both in the United States and on his trips to Europe. He also traded with other collectors. In 1902, when the American Buttonists Society was formed, Captain Emilio was elected Historian.

With the passing of the years, Captain Emilio gave thought to the disposition of his collection. Finally, he decided to offer it to the Essex Institute, a historical society in his native city of Salem, Massachusetts. The collection was formally accepted by the Essex Institute in 1908, with the understanding that the collection would always be kept in view apart by itself and labeled "The Emilio Collection of Military Buttons, Gift of Captain Luis F. Emilio". At the time of the transfer it was understood that the donor would arrange, classify, and if possible, publish a catalog of the collection at his own expense. This catalog, a hard-bound book of 286 pages was published in 1911, with a reprint in 1947. It lists 1569 buttons from the United States, Great Britain, France, Spain and several other countries. Each button is listed according to size, metal, type and description of device. Historical notes are also included. Two hundred and forty of the most interesting and rarest buttons are illustrated on ten plates. Both editions of this book are out of print and are rare collectors' items.

This collection is contained in eye-level glass cases. Each button is mounted on a card with identification. Other major collections may be seen at the New York (City) Historical Society; the Lightner Museum in St. Augustine, Florida; the Ertell Memorial Button Museum in Liberty Village, Flemington, N.J.; Just Button Museum in Southington, Conn.; the Smithsonian Institution, Washington, D.C.; and the Confederate White House in Richmond, Virginia. Other museums and historical societies throughout the country have limited collections of these buttons.

At the present time, there is great interest in several areas of collecting. Some of this interest has been generated by the use of metal detectors. Many of these instruments are utilized at the battlefields and campsites of the Civil War. Many valuable buttons and other artifacts of both sides are being discovered. Some are in unbelievably good condition. In a recent excavation for the Delaware Expressway through the Queens Village section of Philadelphia, a pewter button of the Continental 5th Battalion was retrieved. It was found to be in good condition after having been in the ground for 200 years.

In recent years, the scarcity of some of these specimens has been realized and the values have gone into the three-figure area. Compared to coins and stamps of comparable rarity, the present advanced prices are still in a reasonable range. Of course, there are hundreds of the more plentiful but interesting buttons available for the nominal figure of a dollar or two. The New Jersey pewter button of the Revolutionary War is so rare that no price has been established. As only six or seven of these pieces are known to exist, their value would in all likelihood be set at several hundred dollars each. Of the other pictured buttons, the New Jersey National Guard Cavalry button is valued next highest at $15.00. The 1861 Civil War button would sell for $10.00. Valued at $5.00 are the Rifle Corps, Militia N.G., National Guard Ambulance, Sewell Guards, and Morris Guards buttons. The National Guard Artillery button is valued at $3.00. Finally, the National Guard Infantry and the Essex Troop buttons are valued at $2.00.

General button collecting in New Jersey is quite active. The New Jersey State Button Society was organized in 1941, one of the first in the country. Today there are about 200 members. Two regular meetings are held annually, at the Stanton Grange on Route 31, on the second Saturday in May and September. All collectors and the public are welcome to attend these meetings in order to meet other collectors and dealers. Persons interested may join the Society by writing to the Secretary, Miss Ann B. Wilson, 54 Maple Ave., Maplewood, N.J. The annual dues are $2.00, and entitles the members to recieve the New Jersey Button Society New Bulletin.

—ALPHAEUS H. ALBERT

Collecting
New Jersey Decoys

NO one knows who used the first decoy to lure ducks out of the sky and into his stomach. There were probably many different men who "invented" decoys independently. American Indian Decoys—made of bull rush stems bound together—have been found which are thousands of years old. However, the great age of the decoy covers the era from the close of the Civil War through 1920. During this time "Market Gunning" was at its zenith. Professional hunters made their livelihood providing game for sale in markets and restaurants of the cities. The success of market hunters depended on their ability to withstand the rigors of nature, their shooting, knowledge of their quarry and their decoys.

During this era, almost every coastal town had its baymen; those men who lived on what the coastal waters had to provide. Far from wealthy, these men made the tools they needed: boats, oars, blinds and decoys. This is a far cry from today's duck hunter who goes to his local sporting goods store, and buys a couple of plastic factory-made decoys, piles them into his aluminum boat and motors to his prepared blind for a few hours once or twice per week.

The professional hunter spent seven days per week hunting; days that began long before dawn and ended after his day's take had been sold, long after dark. There were literally thousands of professionals. They spent the off-season repairing and adding to their equipment—the most important of which were their decoys.

All along the coast localized wind, water, and weather conditions led to the development of regional styles in decoys. The very light "Barnegat Sneakbox" led to the type of "dugout decoy" that is synonymous with "Jersey Decoy". The more decoys a hunter could set out with, the greater his chances of decoying flying ducks. With his small sneakbox, weight and space limited the number of decoys a New Jersey hunter could rig.

Thus the general shape of the Jersey Decoy evolved into a generally smaller than life size body rounded on all sides. There were no square edges to take up space. Even the weight pads on New Jersey Decoys were carefully flattened to conform to the body outline. Generally a flat two inch by three inch lead pad was nailed or screwed to the bottom so that it didn't stick out more than one-eighth of an inch from the belly. Some makers even inserted the weight into the bottom of the decoy. The decoys could be stacked on their tails around the racks along the sides of the sneakbox.

To compensate for the smallish bodies, heads were made slightly larger than the real heads of ducks and geese they represented. The Barnegat decoy had reached this stage by 1870. However, it wasn't until about a decade later that the evolution was complete. The problem of weight still remained to be solved. The solution came by hollowing out the decoys. Two pieces of cedar were gouged out and joined together for the body. That basic, hollowed, rounded shape is found in all New Jersey Decoys made after 1880. Rigs of several hundred of these round, hollow decoys were the order of the day.

The making of a dugout decoy involved many steps. First a

piece of pine was selected for the head. This was roughed out with a hatchet and then finished with a knife and sandpaper. Then the body pieces were selected. White cedar was the first choice of most carvers. Two pieces, about two inches thick, were cut to length and width, hollowed out, and then joined temporarily while the body shaping was done. Then the two pieces were caulked for water tightness, and joined permanently. The head was then dowelled to the body. A lead weight was then added where needed to stabilize the decoy in the water and balance it so that it sat naturally. Final sanding led to a primer sealing coat of paint, followed by painting the decoy to resemble the species intended. If this sounds simple, try it!

The principle lure which makes decoy collecting so fascinating is the endless diversity of styles which originated in the minds and hands of those who carved decoys. A decoy is really a caricature of a living bird. It is a craftsman's conception of what the bird looks like and an exaggeration of its characteristics. Each carver saw something unique in the ducks he copied and each put some unique thing of himself into his work.

Hundreds of carvers lived along Barnegat Bay in New Jersey. For every name that has come down to us, many are lost to time. None of those hard working carvers, who sold their decoys for six dollars per dozen, ever dreamed they were creating lasting sculptures that would endure. How were they to know that their creations would please collectors years after they were long forgotten. Yet, today there is an ever increasing population of collectors seeking a diminishing supply of old decoys.

Why do people collect? The reasons are many. Some collect for investment; others for the esthetic beauty they see in the wooden art form; others as a link with hunters of another age. Being a hunter, I view decoys as a tool to a trade. Yet, I am constantly amazed at the endless variety of stylization different men put into wooden blocks depicting living ducks, Brant, and geese. At present, I have scaup decoys by ten different carvers. None of the works are alike, yet each truly represents a scaup

Three Brant decoys. Left, by an unknown carver; center, by Lloyd Parker, circa 1920; right, by Capt. Jess Birdsall, circa 1890.

(or blue-bill or broad-bill as they are also known). A glance at the accompanying picture shows three New Jersey Brant decoys—by three different carvers. The three are very different in style, yet when set afloat, each definitely looks like a real Brant.

So individualistic was each man's work that seldom did the carver affix his name to his decoys. Names, initials, brands, or other identifying marks are almost always the owner of that decoy and not its maker. How then, does a prospective seller or buyer determine who carved a particular decoy? Only by studying known decoys. There are several books that will give a basic knowledge of who worked, when he worked, and what he carved, however, only by handling, talking about, and viewing decoys will the words and photos in these books begin to merge into knowledge. Once you have actually held a Harry Shourdes, a Taylor Johnson, or a Roland Horner decoy, all your study of the literature will galvanize and you will be able to recognize their work again, even in a different species. Take the opportunity to talk about decoys whenever you can. Tap those who know more than you do. Visit museums, antique shops, collectors , and increase your knowledge of decoys.

It is easy and rewarding if you are interested enough to take the time. However, there are some flies in the ointment. Some men's work changed over the years that they carved. Lloyd Parker's early and late works are very different. Not surprising! Remember, these men made their living fooling birds into coming to their guns. When they came up with a better idea, they were quick to change.

Another draw-back to "knowing it all" in the decoy world is the innumerable dugouts still to be found which were made by unknown carvers. Some of these unknowns may, someday, become known as more information is unearthed. Most will not. It is not the name we are collecting, but the work. The goldeneye is by an unknown hunter, long gone. Certainly knowing the name of the carver would not make the decoy any

Discovering the carvers of old decoys is often possible only by comparison. Here, at left is a Redhead, and at right, an American Goldeneye.

better. It is truly a gem all by itself. The same can be said for the redhead in the same picture. That is what collecting is all about anyhow; if you like the article more than the money being asked for it, it's yours. Don't be afraid of decoys by unknowns. You don't have to justify liking a good decoy by tacking on someone's name.

The temptation to make some quick money is not lost in the decoy world. There are fakes. New decoys made to look old and old decoys remodelled to appear like that of a known carver are on the market. Be wary of any "old" decoy with new paint. This doesn't mean decoys that have been repainted are frauds. In order to keep their rigs in their most seductive condition, all the old timers had to repaint their decoys every year. In fact, several layers of old paint showing means the decoy is old. Water has a wearing effect unlike any other. A decoy that has been afloat many years feels different than one that has been sanded. If there is a worn area around the underside of the bill and tail, it is a pretty safe bet it has ridden the waves.

The term "old" is different when applied to decoys than when applied to furniture. There are very few hundred-plus year old decoys to be collected. There are many that are from fifty to one hundred years old. A decoy made in 1920 can be very collectible and "old" while a sofa may not be.

The best way to avoid being sold a fake is to buy from a reputable dealer in decoys. I have seen junk being offered as "New Jersey Decoys". An old bayman using them would have been laughed off the water in a hurry; or he would have starved. Don't buy from anyone who says he "doesn't know anything about it, but it is old, unless you know more than he does! I have found some good buys that way, but I have found more often these decoys to be over-priced rather than under-priced.

Ah, price!! What is a good decoy worth? Basically, New Jersey Decoys sell for less than comparable decoys from other states. I don't know why, but I'm happy about it. Condition, naturally, has much to do with price. Bad splits, broken necks and/or bills detract from a decoy's value. New paint jobs do the same.

Availability also has much to do with price. Shourdes made thousands of scaup decoys and, therefore, they bring less than his mergansers, of which few were made. More scaup decoys were made than any species. Black ducks and Brant were the next most made species. New Jersey geese and Brant decoys are generally recognized as the best made anywhere, and there are too few geese left to go around. Relatively few mallards were made.

Redhead duck decoys were once plentiful, but the redhead declined in numbers after the opening of the Point Pleasant Canal let in salt water and killed off the wild celery. Since the basic shape of the redhead and scaup was the same, the former was repainted and used as scaup decoys. A New Jersey redhead in original paint is rare. Goldeneyes, pintails, old squaws, American mergansers and red-breasted mergansers were made, though not in larger numbers. They are therefore much sought but seldom found. New Jersey Canvasbacks are almost unheard of. Wood ducks, blue-wing and green-wing teal, also, were seldom made and almost impossible to find.

Generally, prices range from $45.00 to $250.00 with most in the $65.00 to $125.00 bracket. If that sounds like a lot, wait until next year! Prices will continue to climb. Do not discount the old bartering system. Most dealers and collectors of decoys enjoy trading. It is fun and can be mutually beneficial to both parties. Sometimes a trade will get you a decoy that money would not.

Market gunners did not live on ducks alone. Shorebirds were on the menus of every restaurant near tidal waters. Decoys were carved to lure sanderlings, sandpipers, knots, dowitches, yellowlegs, plovers and curlews. Unlike duck decoys, there is no basic Barnegat shorebird decoy. Bodies were not hollowed, as there was necessity for handling them off shore. A rig of stand-up decoys was set at the water's edge and hunters took cover in a blind near-by.

Many duck decoy carvers also made shorebirds. Some carvers made shorebirds only. Each had his own style of carving. Variation between carvers is greater than that among those who carved duck decoys. Compared to decoys for ducks, Brant and geese, shorebirds seemed to be of minor importance and relatively few were made to be sold.

Unlike duck hunting, which still continues, all gunning of shorebirds was outlawed in 1918. Therefore, there was no need for decoys after that date. The result is that fewer shorebird decoys remain today. They are highly collectible and prices are higher than for floating decoys of the same age. Many collectors seek only shorebirds. They require much less room on a display floor.

For variety in a collection, there are the "confidence" decoys. These were usually a non-game species, but were added to some rigs to lend a sense of atmosphere to the total rig. For example, swans are very wary birds. A swan decoy set near a spread of ducks lent an "all's safe" atmosphere to the rig and encouraged flyers-by to stop in and join the meal. Great blue heron and Herring gull decoys were made to serve the same purpose. Confidence decoys were made infrequently and are rare items. If you find a good one, buy it.

So far I have dealt with decoys from salt water. New Jersey, however, has another side. Market hunting took place along the Delaware River as well. Most hunting took place where the river widens out from Trenton south to Delaware Bay. Gunning on this side took a slightly different form. Instead of large spreads of hundreds of blocks luring ducks to hunters in blinds, smaller rigs were used. Perhaps forty decoys of mixed species were used to pull ducks. When they alighted, the hunters, who were upstream in a boat, would then "scull" down on them.

For this reason, the decoys had to continue to fool their real brethren even when viewed a wing's length! Hollow bodies were used, but more detailed carving went into them. Wing and tail feathers were carved into the body. Eyes also were included. (Most of the Barnegat decoys, if they had any eyes at all, merely had them painted on.) More restful head poses are also typical of river ducks. Since river decoys didn't have to contend with waves, they didn't have to be as broad as their salt water counterparts.

Delaware River decoys were never carved in such vast numbers as coastal blocks, so even though the water was not as corrosive, fewer of them remain to be collected. Therefore, you can expect to pay more for them than for comparable decoys in the same condition from Barnegat. If you can find them at all! Shown here is the added attention to restful pose and detail that typefies our decoys from the Delaware. With the possible exception of those decoys from Stratford, Connecticut area, no decoys were more carefully made or more beautifully carved anywhere in the world.

Locating good New Jersey decoys is usually by chance. Looking is part of the fun and made worth-while when you discover one in an unusual place. Begin with people who know decoys. The more knowledge you gain of decoys, the more you learn the names of people who deal in them. One contact can lead to others. Friendships may result as a special side benefit.

A few shops which always have good New Jersey decoys are the following:

Michael and Vernice Lyons
Point Pleasant, New Jersey

Ray Davies
The 1807 House
Farmingdale, New Jersey

Oliver Orvis Shop
Clinton, New Jersey

A black duck from the Delaware River. Note the detailed carving of the eyes, wings and tail, and the restful position of the head.

Nicholas A. Calcese
Yardville, New Jersey

Antiques At The What-Da-Ya-Want? Shop
Lebanon, New Jersey

There are others, of course. Stop in any one of these shops. We
are all willing to talk decoys!   —DALE DALRYMPLE

Old Dolls and Toys of New Jersey

THERE were and are presently many doll and toy makers in the state of New Jersey. It is impossible to write about all of them. Instead, we will cover a few of the outstanding doll and toy makers of New Jersey from different periods in our history.

The Fulper doll made in Flemington, New Jersey is a bisque-headed doll made during World War I when we could not import dolls from Germany and France. It is the first bisque-headed doll made in this country and was made at the Fulper Potteries which were founded in 1805. Such illustrious doll firms from New York as Amberg, Colonial, and Horseman contracted for the heads which were then mounted on the doll bodies by the manufacturers who purchased them. The heads were impressed with the Fulper Trade Mark and "Made in U.S.A." They carried in addition to the Fulper mark, the name of the company they were made for, i.e. Colonial, Amberg, Horseman. Finally the heads were cast in the molds of the Armand Marseille Company of Germany.

Fulper made "Peterkin," an all bisque doll designed by Helen Trowbridge in 1919. Peterkin was eleven inches tall, had molded features, was jointed at the shoulders with stationary

362 *Collecting New Jersey Antiques*

legs set wide apart. The doll resembles the illustrations of Peterkin in the 1915 edition of *Peterkin and the Little Gray Hare* that was first published in 1887. An all bisque Kewpie was also made by Fulper Pottery in 1920 and had painted features. These two dolls were the most rare of the Fulper dolls, since so few of them were made. The more popular Fulper dolls fall into one of two categories, either a shoulder and head piece with a cloth body, or a ball-jointed head with a composition body. The one outstanding feature of the Fulper heads was that they all had protruding or "buck teeth." The doll is a much desired collector's item and in spite of the unattractive mouth, most collectors who own a Fulper doll are enthusiastic over its beauty. The period of making Fulper dolls was very short and only lasted from 1918 to 1921. Their manufacture was discontinued after World War I when German dolls were again available.

The Fulper dolls sell from $300 to $400. The head can also be found on certain bent-limb, baby bodies. Only Peterkin and the Kewpie have molded heads, while the other heads have a top opening and wear wigs. The Fulper doll is difficult to locate. One might try antique shops. The largest collection is located at the Raggedy Ann Antique Doll and Toy Museum in Flemington, where the doll was originally manufactured.

In 1928 a patent was taken out for "Kampkins—A Dolly To Love." The doll was created by Louise R. Kampes of Atlantic City, and was a rag doll with a molded mask face. It was first made in 1920 and the hair was sewed in concentric circles on the head. "Kampkins" was sold at a shop on the boardwalk and cost between $10 and $15.00 each, depending on the clothing. Both boy and girl dolls were made, and new outfits were designed for each season. If one can locate this doll, its value ranges from $150-$250 depending on condition. In 1948 Ruth Gibbs of Flemington, created Godey's Little Lady Dolls which are very much sought after by today's doll collector. The dolls were copied after certain Victorian dolls that had not been made in this country or in Europe since 1910. The Ruth Gibbs factory started with fourteen employees and made only a 12 inch doll appearing to be china, but with a secret formula that made it unbreakable. The business flourished and many new employees were hired. A 7 inch doll was then made to sell in greater quantity. Ballerinas, Scotch Lassies, Irish Colleens, and dolls in just about any other costume you can imagine were made during this period. In 1950 the famous March family from Louisa Alcott's "Little Women" was made, and soon the Ruth Gibbs dolls were known all over the United States and Europe. The McCall Pattern Company became so intrigued that in 1949 it designed outfits for the larger dolls—25,000 patterns in all were sold by the McCall Pattern Company that year. Ruth Gibbs stopped making the dolls in 1955 because of competition from Japan. She was no longer able to afford the fine quality work at the same price as her Japanese competitors, and so she chose to stop making the dolls. Occasionally, one will see these dolls turning up at antique shows or shops throughout the country. However, most people lucky enough to have one of these dolls cherish them and will not give them up. The value ranges from $35.00 to $75.00.

There are several well known doll artists in New Jersey at the present time who are involved with the National Institute of American Doll Artists. This group of dedicated men and women artists was organized in 1963 with the purpose of gaining recognition for artists' dolls as works of art. Astry Campbell of Short Hills served as President of this fine organization from 1971-1973. He has made and is still making outstanding dolls. Another famous New Jersey doll artist was Dorothy Heiser, deceased, of Madison. Her fine collection is part of the permanent display of the Morristown Museum. There is also Eunice Tuttle of Lakewood, a fine artist, and Beverly Cerepak of Saddle Brook. Their original dolls range in price from $250-$300.

An excellent reference for present day manufacturers of

commercial dolls and toys is a magazine named *Playthings* which consists of doll and toy merchandising. It has been published since 1877. The address of *Playthings* is 51 Madison Ave., New York, N.Y. 10010.

What little girl or boy from age 8 to age 80 hasn't loved or cherished a Raggedy Ann or Andy? There is a poignant and true story about Raggedy Ann. It concerns the daughter of famed cartoonist Johnny Gruelle. The incident occurred in 1912 when daughter Marcella went up into the attic of her Silvermine, Connecticut home and found an old rag doll with its legs sticking out of a barrel. Upon pulling the doll out, Marcella found that the old doll did not have a face. She ran down to her Daddy who immediately painted a face on the beloved doll and called her Raggedy Ann. He selected the name from two popular childrens stories of that era "Racketty Packetty" and "Orphan Annie," and from those two names derived the name Raggedy Ann. In 1914 Marcella died and the grieving father started to write the Raggedy Ann stories in memory of his only child Marcella. They are still published by the Bobbs-Merrill Company.

The original Raggedy Ann had a candy heart but the children were tempted by the candy, and later Raggedy Ann Dolls had a heart drawn on the body with the words "I Love You." There is very little value in the old Raggedy Ann. They are usually so faded, worn, and dirty that they would not make a nice addition to a collection. The hand made and commercial dolls range in price from $1.50 to $45.00. Raggedy Ann is known and loved throughout the world, and is manufactured by Knickerbocker Toy Co. Inc. of Middlesex.

We cannot leave a chapter on dolls made in New Jersey without mentioning Thomas Alva Edison of Orange, New Jersey who invented the Edison phonographic doll (which he also manufactured). The bodies and the talking mechanisms were made in New Jersey, while the heads of bisque were imported from Germany. In 1890 about five hundred people were engaged in the manufacture of phonographs and talking dolls at the Edison establishment. It took eighteen women just to recite the nursery rhymes for the cylinders to go with the dolls. The factory had a capacity of about five hundred talking dolls a day or 100,000 per year. Almost every invention of Thomas Edison soon had its toy version or led to toys of many kinds, but Edison himself did little in the toy field other than his talking doll.

There were many toy makers in New Jersey, although most toys in the early nineteenth century came from New England, New York, and Pennsylvania.

One of the most important toy developments of the early 20th century was the coming of the electric train. Lionel Trains, whose manufacturing plant was in Irvington, was founded by Joshua Lionel Cowen. In 1900 Cowen made a small electric motor which he attached to a fan, and then wondered for what else he could use the small motor. That is when the idea for an electric train came to him. He constructed a flat car which carried the motor and battery, put it on a circle of brass track he had built—and it went. After several failures Cowen was able to make a satisfactory transformer and toy trains took a giant step forward. He copied the electric locomotive used by the Baltimore and Ohio Railroad in its Baltimore tunnel, and this started a demand for replicas of real trains. The Baltimore and Ohio prototype was made from 1900 to 1905. In 1902 he made a steam-type locomotive using electric current from household outlets lowered in voltage through a transformer. This model was manufactured until 1923. He made a locomotive with a body of brass from 1912 to 1923. In the 1930's depression and competition forced Cowen to sell the firm to A.C. Gilbert of New Haven, Conn.

In 1903 J. Chein, then of N.Y.C., was a well known toy manufacturer of tin toys. In 1907 he moved from New York to Harrison, New Jersey where he surprised the toy world by printing pictures and colors on sheet metal before forming and shaping the printed metal into toys. He also made inexpensive novelty items such as the small metal toys given away in Cracker Jack boxes. His greatest contribution to the toy world from his Harrison factory was a complete lithographing department and a paper box factory with which he made the boxes for his beautiful lithograph toys. He also progressed his toy line from strictly Christmas toys to spring and summer toys as well. Mr. Chein passed away in 1924 but his brother-in-law continued the business under the Chein name up until the present time. The toys were sold primarily to Woolworths, Ben Franklin stores and Sears Roebuck. It is sad to learn that the famous line of Chein toys which has moved its operation to Burlington, New Jersey has since discontinued toy making because the more competitive and larger companies are cornering the toy market through expensive television advertising. The Chein Toy business now puts out a line of houseware products.

Though I have only touched briefly on the dolls and toys of New Jersey, it should be enough to give an idea of what beautiful and lasting toys have been created here during the past 100 years.   —JEAN BACH

Bibliography

SPECIAL BIBLIOGRAPHICAL NOTE

ALTHOUGH most dealers', auction, and exhibition catalogs offer fragmented information if they mention New Jersey craftsmen at all, The Newark Museum published a checklist of furniture-makers in their 1958 catalog, *Early Made in New Jersey, 1690-1870*. Although in need of updating, this is still the most comprehensive checklist of New Jersey craftsmen in print. As clockmakers are included in the reprinted articles, two books that offer considerable information on this subject should be noted: William E. Drost, *Clocks and Watches of New Jersey*, Elizabeth, N.J., 1966, and Carl M. Williams, *Silversmiths of New Jersey, 1700-1825*, Philadelphia, 1949.

At the time that Mr. Horner wrote his articles on the Egertons, faking of labels was not as remunerative as it has since become and there was no need to warn a reader of possible pitfalls. This warning should not go unmentioned today, however; original labels have been removed from fragments of Egerton pieces, original unused labels have been found, and out-and-out forged labels have been used, on pieces of furniture that the Egertons never touched. —SUZANNE CORLETTE

Albert, Alphaeus H. *Record of American Uniform & Historical Buttons.* Boyertown Publishing Company, 1973.

Albert, Lillian Smith and Adams, Jane Ford. *The Button Sampler.* M. Barrows Company, 1967.

Albert, Lillian Smith and Kent, Kathryn. *The Complete Button Book.* Doubleday & Company, 1949.

Aronson, Joseph. *The Encyclopedia of Furniture.* Crown Publishers, 1965.

Atwater, Mary Meigs. *The Shuttle-Craft Book of American Hand Weaving.* The Macmillan Company, 1951.

Barber, Joel. *Wild Fowl Decoys.* Dover Publications, 1954.

Barker, John and Howe, Ward H. *Historical Collections of the State of New Jersey.* S. Tuttle, 1844.

Bjerkoe, E. H. *The Cabinetmakers of America.* Doubleday & Company, 1957.

Boyer, Charles S. *Early Forges and Furnaces of New Jersey.* Oxford University Press, 1931.

Cunningham, John T. *Made in New Jersey: The Industrial Story of a State.* Rutgers University Press, 1954.

Daniel, Dorothy. *Cut and Engraved Glass, 1771-1905.* William Morrow & Company, 1952.

Dewitt, J. Doyle. *A Century of Campaign Buttons, 1789-1889.* The Travelers Press, 1959.

Drepperd, Carl W. *Primer of American Antiques.* Garden City Publishing Company, 1944.

Ellis, E. S. *A Brief History of New Jersey.* American Book Company, 1910.

Flockhart, L. W. *Arts and Artists in New Jersey.* Hoagland Company, 1938.

Friedberg, Robert. *Paper Money of the United States.* Coin & Currency Institute, 1975.

Honeyman, A. V. D. *Northwestern New Jersey.* Lewis Historical Publishing Company, 1927.

Hopkins, T. S. and Cox, W. S. *Colonial Furniture of West New Jersey.* Engle Press, 1936.

Johnson, David F. *Uniform Buttons.* Century House, 1948.

Kobbé, Gustave. *New Jersey Coast and Pines,* Kobbé Company, 1891.

Kull, Irving S. *New Jersey, A History.* American Historical Society, 1930-32.

Lewis Historical Society. *South Jersey: A History.* Lewis Historical Publishing Company, 1924.

Mackey, Jr. William F. *American Bird Decoys.* Bonanza Books, 1965.

McKearin, Helen and George S. *American Glass.* Crown Publishers, 1941.

McKearin, Helen and George S. *Two Hundred Years of American Blown Glass.* Doubleday & Company, 1950.

Miller, Jr. E. G. *American Antique Furniture.* Dover Publications, 1937.

Morris, Edward. *A Historical Sketch of the Coins of New Jersey.* Quarterman Publications, 1974.

Nagel, Charles. *American Furniture, 1650-1850.* Chanticleer Press, 1949.

Nutting, Wallace. *The Clock Book.* Garden City Publishing Company, 1924.

Ormsbee, Thomas. *The Story of American Furniture.* The Macmillan Company, 1937.

Palmer, Brooks. *The Book of American Clocks.* The Macmillan Company, 1950.

Parsons, Floyd W. *New Jersey.* New Jersey State Chamber of Commerce, 1928.

Peto, Florence. *Historic Quilts.* The American Historical Company, 1939.

Phillips, J. M. *American Silver.* Chanticleer Press, 1949.

Pierce, Arthur D. *Family Empire in Jersey Iron.* Rutgers University Press, 1964.

Ramsay, John. *American Potters and Potteries.* Hale, Cushman, and Flint, 1939.

Ransom, James M. *Vanishing Ironworks of the Ramapos.*

Rutgers University Press, 1966.

Sickler, Joseph S. *The History of Salem County, New Jersey.* Salem County Historical Society, 1937.

Sloane, Eric. *A Museum of Early American Tools.* Wilfred Funk Company, 1973.

Starr, Jr., George Ross. *Decoys of the Atlantic.* Winchester Press, 1974.

Stockton, Frank R. *Stories of New Jersey.* American Book Company, 1896.

Tunis, Edwin. *Colonial Craftsmen.* Thomas Y. Crowell Company, 1976.

Van Hoesen, Walter Hamilton. *Crafts and Craftsmen of New Jersey.* Fairleigh Dickinson University Press, 1973.

Watkins, L. W. *American Glass and Glassmaking.* Chanticleer Press, 1950.

Watson, Aldren A. *The Village Blacksmith.* Thomas Y. Crowell Company, 1968.

Weygandt, Cornelius. *Down Jersey.* D. Appleton-Century Company, 1940.

White, Margaret E. *The Decorative Arts of Early New Jersey.* D. Van Nostrand Company, 1964.

Williams, Carl M. *Silversmiths of New Jersey, 1700-1825.* George MacManus Company, 1949.

Williamson, Scott Graham. *The American Craftsman.* Bramhall House, 1932.

Wyler, Seymour B. *Old Silver.* Crown Publishers, 1937.

Index

THE following is an index of those individuals and institutions given treatment in the articles collected in this book. Page references which appear in italics indicate illustrations relevant to the particular entry.